Human Sexuality

A BRIEF EDITION

James Leslie McCary
University of Houston

D. Van Nostrand Company
New York   Cincinnati   Toronto   London   Melbourne

Dedicated to my mother, father, sister, and brother, without whose help the road would have been impassable

D. Van Nostrand Company Regional Offices:
New York   Cincinnati   Milbrae

D. Van Nostrand Company International Offices:
London   Toronto   Melbourne

Library of Congress Catalog Card Number 72-7808

ISBN 0-442-25236-6

Published by D. Van Nostrand Company
450 West 33rd Street, New York, N.Y. 10001

Published simultaneously in Canada by
Van Nostrand Reinhold Ltd.

10 9 8 7 6 5 4

Cover photo by Erich Hartmann, Magnum Photos

All illustrations except figures 1.1, 3.5, 5.1, 5.4., and
11.1 by Vantage Art, Inc.

PREFACE

This brief text has been designed for college courses in which human sexuality is a major topic within the framework of a larger discipline. Some study of sexuality is frequently included in courses concerned with the total health of the individual or with personal or societal relationships (introductory courses in health, human biology, marriage and the family, psychology, and sociology, for example). But the regular text in such courses often includes only a superficial overview of sexuality.

Again and again I have heard professors say that their students want more information. My intent has been to present a concise, topical discussion of the many facets of human sexuality that are of deep concern to today's college student. These issues are dealt with in a straightforward manner, with as little technical and/or anatomical terminology as possible. This shorter version of the Second Edition of my *Human Sexuality* has been written especially as a supplementary text that will serve where neither a surface treatment nor an extensive coverage is wanted.

Many of the footnotes and other scholarly apparatus of the larger edition have been omitted as unnecessary for the student in a course for which that edition would be too detailed and too expensive to be used as a supplement. Because of the frequent practice of assigning research papers on this topic, a number of references selected for their balance and timeliness have been appended at the end of each chapter.

The present text differs from other supplementary books in

that it is interdisciplinary—integrating the physiology, psychology, and sociology as well as the myths and fallacies surrounding human sexuality. Whereas most supplements cover only one or two aspects (human orgasm or birth control, for example), the student will find here fundamental, up-to-date information on topics ranging from venereal disease, birth and population control, sexual dysfunction, and the biochemical bases of sexual pleasure to natural childbirth and breast-feeding.

I have tried to avoid advocating a particular set of moral values but at the same time have asked the reader to consider questions about his own sexuality from an ethical as well as simply a biological or societal perspective. In previous years, much of our society has regarded sex and reproduction as synonymous. That misconception and its attendant ill effects should be examined. I do not agree, however, with those who have gone too far in the opposite direction and consider sex as nothing more than eroticism. What I have hoped to do is construct a balanced examination of sexuality, discussing many aspects and attitudes—not as a means of avoiding a point of view (for I have attempted to set out my own personal feeling clearly), but as a means of introducing the reader to the often conflicting assumptions and conclusions of our pluralistic society concerning the whole subject of human sexuality.

My greatest hope is that this book will develop in the reader the objectivity necessary for an understanding and acceptance of the many facets of mature, healthy sexuality. Research findings and my own clinical experience have convinced me that a sound understanding and acceptance of sexuality is necessary if we are to begin to ameliorate our nation's deplorable rate of venereal disease, sexual inadequacies, illegitimate births, unhappy marriages, divorce, and widespread emotional difficulties. It is only from such an understanding and acceptance that an individual can responsibly and creatively direct his sexuality in his various roles as lover, spouse, parent, community member, and world citizen.

I wish to recognize the many contributions—writing, compiling, and editing—made to this book by my friend and colleague, Betty Stewart. The manuscript would have been much delayed and of lesser quality without her efforts.

James Leslie McCary

CONTENTS

1 SEX AND
TODAY'S SOCIETY

Interest in sex and a desire for sex information are not unique to this generation. Every generation of young people has a natural curiosity about sex. When their questions are evaded or ignored by those who should provide answers, they turn to unreliable sources—usually their poorly informed peers. As a result, their confusion and disillusionment increase. The difference between today's youth and the youth of yesterday is that now, for the first time, there is available—in some institutions, at least—accurate information which is presented with honesty and directness. A sizable number of prestigious organizations are making worthwhile information about human sexuality available to professionals and private citizens alike. Medical schools, seminaries, universities, and colleges are taking advantage of these sources and are making what is, at last, more than a token effort to meet their responsibilities to educate young people in sexual matters.

Within the last few years, there have been noticeable changes in the sexual climate of our society. The attitudes and behavior of Americans in general, and young people in particular, have undergone certain significant shifts.

A reflection of these changes is the new wholesome attitude toward sex education in many schools, colleges, and universities throughout the country. Educators are finally beginning to deal with realities and to acknowledge that their students are vitally interested in sex, that they are going to engage in some form of sexual activity, and that they need and deserve as much accurate sex information as possible.

While significant advances are being made in sex education

for young people, the fact remains that the vast majority of the American public is lamentably ignorant about all aspects of human sexuality. Since our scientific expeditions to the moon, in fact, it is not too great an exaggeration to say that the average layman knows just slightly less about the topography of the moon than he knows about his own sexuality.

The extent of sexual ignorance in our society is reflected by the fact that the word "sex" is used by the average person as a synonym for sexual intercourse, as if that were all that sex means. Human sexuality encompasses a broad spectrum of human behavior and includes the biological systems that determine patterns of sexual responsiveness and sexual functioning, the psychological factors that are of vital importance to adequate sexual adjustment, and the sociological implications of individual sexual behavior. Unless one has an understanding of these factors and of their interrelationships, he is likely to perpetuate the warped and guilt-ridden sexual attitudes that presently prevail.

A HERITAGE OF CONFUSION

One of the major reasons why inadequate sex information has been disseminated in the past is that there have been too few sources of accurate information. Unlike other areas of research, sex has not been considered an appropriate topic for investigation, until quite recently, because of the sensitivity of the public toward sexual questions. In the 1940s and 1950s, however, Dr. Alfred Kinsey and his co-workers conducted monumental studies into the sexual habits of American men and women and proved that people would cooperate in sex research if they were treated with anonymity and with dignity. The results of the Kinsey studies both enlightened and surprised many people. Many of the sexual practices traditionally considered taboo were discovered to be common among a large number of Americans, and laymen and scientists were forced to reevaluate their concept of "normal" behavior. Since a number of the sexual activities which had previously been judged to be "abnormal" were found to be practiced by the majority of the population, that judgment was obviously less than sensible or scientific.

In recent years, highly informative studies by many scientists, most notably William H. Masters and Virginia E. Johnson, have added much to our knowledge of human sexual attitudes and behavior. Masters and Johnson, for example, have provided invaluable data on the physiological responses of normal men and women to sexual stimuli. They have also studied the causes and nature of certain human sexual dysfunctions as well as methods of treating these dysfunctions.

In spite of the carefully controlled conditions of the research methodology in studies like those of Kinsey and of Masters and Johnson, laymen and fellow scientists alike have been too often reluctant to accept scientific findings unless new investigations appeared to lend support to time-honored prejudices. One major difficulty with any social research—especially sexual research—is that no single study is equally applicable to all subgroups. We know, for example, that the sexual attitudes and behavior of Americans are greatly influenced by their sex, age, race, geographic area, educational level, socioeconomic level, religious affiliation and degree of devoutness, intelligence, and many other factors. Even when these variables are carefully controlled, however, sexual research is too often discounted because the findings are threatening. Many people are simply unable to change their old notions about this very sensitive and morally loaded subject.

The consequences of our society's tenacious clinging to traditional myths and prejudices about human sexuality are apparent in our divorce rate, our number of illegitimate births, and our soaring incidence of venereal disease. One has only to examine the advertisements, books, magazines, newspapers, movies, and other mass communication media of our culture to see how American attitudes on sex, love, marriage, and family relations have been distorted by our woefully inadequate knowledge of sex.

The neurotic repression and inhibition of normal sexual expression have led to the vicarious release afforded by explicit sexual material portrayed in print and on the stage and screen. Obscenity and pornography have become synonymous with sexual freedom. Sexuality, a natural, healthy part of every human being, has become sadly confused with a variety of lewd, rapacious distortions.

The mass communication media do not control our sexual behavior; they merely mirror our sexual anxieties. Confusion begets confusion, and there is a disturbing conflict in our social order. Our culture condemns illicit sexual relationships, but it also depicts them as desirable and exciting.

"Protecting" Children from Sex

Parents too often suppose that ignorance about sex will keep their children from becoming involved in sexual activity. Nothing could be further from the truth. A recent study compared the sexual habits of women students at a large state university with the accuracy of their knowledge about sexual matters. The study revealed that of the sexually active women, over 25% failed to answer *any* question about sex correctly; only 59% answered half the questions correctly, and none answered all of them correctly. Of the less sexually active women, 80% correctly answered half the questions and 9% correctly answered all of them. This study suggests that the more a woman knows about sexual matters, the more discriminating she is in her sexual behavior.

Other studies have found that unmarried pregnant girls usually have received little or no sex education either at home or school. Their mothers, furthermore, frequently lack adequate sex knowledge themselves, or are unable or unwilling to give appropriate instruction to their daughters.

Similar studies into the relationship between venereal disease and sexual knowledge have found that the incidence of VD is drastically reduced by adequate sex knowledge. In a public school in which a course including factual knowledge about venereal disease was introduced, for example, the cases of gonorrhea, one of the most common venereal diseases, decreased by 50% in two school years. In another school in the same area which did not include such a course, the number of gonorrhea cases increased during the same time period; when a similar course was offered there, the incidence of gonorrhea also decreased by approximately 50%.

Some parents try to keep their children from engaging in premarital sexual activity by instilling fear of illegitimate pregnancy or VD in them. This approach to sex education has been found to be quite ineffective. Studies have shown clearly that neither fear of pregnancy nor fear of VD is an effective deterrent to premarital sexual intercourse.

Before the modern effective cures for venereal disease or reliable birth control methods were available, people blithely had sexual relations with little regard to the possibility of either becoming pregnant or contracting a venereal disease. Even today, an incredible 75% of sexually active single women do not take *contraceptive* (birth control) precautions themselves, and usually they do not insist that their partners do so. This foolhardiness prevails despite the fact that half the men and almost three-fourths of the women involved in sexual relations outside of marriage fear the female partner's becoming pregnant.

Some women with a strong religious background think that premarital *coitus* (sexual intercourse) in which contraceptives are used is more "sinful" than intercourse without birth control protection. This attitude appears to arise from the feeling that pregnancy resulting from premarital intercourse offers some punishment and atonement for their moral transgression. Not surprisingly, then, many unwanted pregnancies occur among the religiously devout who, despite their determination to "refrain from sin," somehow lose control of their emotions and get swept into the act of sexual intercourse. Fewer than 25% of the unwed mothers surveyed in one study thought that it was acceptable to use contraceptives before marriage!

Men also are victims of shame and confusion concerning birth control. In one study, the majority of men questioned expressed reluctance to use what little knowledge of contraception they possessed because they were either too embarrassed to purchase the necessary devices, or they believed that such a purchase made their future sexual relationships "planned sin," which is apparently more damnable than "unplanned sin."

Results of investigations around the world have demonstrated that it is ignorance, not knowledge, of sexual matters that is the cause of sexual misadventure. This fact has been confirmed by psychotherapists and marriage counselors who deal with the subsequent strife and heartbreak experienced by parents and their children who become the victims of such misadventure.

Until fairly recently, parents who did not have adequate sex information themselves, or who were afraid or ashamed to talk with their children about sex, had very few sources to turn to for factual knowledge. Furthermore, medical training traditionally has included little about human sexuality other than its reproductive aspects, leaving physicians as a whole largely ignorant and somewhat prudish about human sexuality. The training of ministers and marriage counselors in this regard has often been poor, so that individuals in search of information about sex have often been in danger of unwittingly selecting an emotionally oriented counselor whose factual knowledge was limited. In recent years, however, medical schools, seminaries, and universities have fortunately begun to reconstruct their coursework and training sessions in this area, significantly raising the level of professional competence.

Adequate sex information has a significant impact not only on the general mental health of an individual but also on his marital adjustment. Surveys indicate that of the leading 10 factors found essential to a successful marriage, an adequate sex education in childhood is ranked third. (The happiness of the parents' marriages and an adequate length of acquaintanceship, courtship, and engagement rank first and second.)

Sex and the Concept of Sin

Ancient man's need for religion probably developed from his inability to cope with various uncontrollable elements of the world such as severe weather and famine. In his feeling of inadequacy, man created a supreme being who had the power to solve the problems that he could not solve for himself. Man believed that he had to pay a price for the privilege of calling on his deity in time of danger. Recognizing the surpassing pleasure of sexual activity, man quite naturally made his sexuality a focal point in his efforts to please or appease the deity. In effect, man tried to save himself from danger by saying to his god, "Protect and help me, and I shall sacrifice my sexuality for your protection." When danger struck, he responded by saying, "I have sinned, I have been evil, and I offer the sacrifice of my sexuality to pay for my sinfulness."

Few people in a position to judge would deny that certain rigid, puritanical, guilt-instilling religions are probably the greatest detriment to the psychosexual health of mankind. Leaders of such religions have succeeded remarkably well in indoctrinating their followers in the belief that sex is dirty and animalistic, and is to be looked upon only as a necessary evil—with emphasis on the word "evil." This attitude is best exemplified in the prudery of the Victorian era, when "decent" women, not daring to expect pleasure from the sexual act, endured it only because of their "duty" to their husbands.

Changes in attitudes toward sex and marriage, which reflect changing needs but often lag behind them, have occurred throughout history. Early Israelite tribes permitted *polygynous* marriage (marriage with more than one wife at a time), for example, and women were regarded as little more than property; marriages were primarily of legal rather than of religious concern. Some men were left without female partners as a result of polygyny, and a more equitable distribution of women became necessary. Thus was *monogamy* (marriage with only one person at a time) evolved.

Much of the ancient interpretation of Mosaic laws—upon which our prevailing Judeo-Christian morality is founded—was based on the need for larger and stronger tribes. From these laws evolved a single justification for sexual expression—*procreation* (the production of offspring). By extension, sexual activity for any other purpose became an act of perversion, a "wasting of seed." The ancient Hebrew man was forbidden to waste his *sperm* (the male seed which is expelled during sexual intercourse) lest he be punished by God for not attempting to add to the strength of his tribe.

Sperm were believed to be miniature human beings who grew in the woman's body after being deposited there by the man. To allow these potential Israelites to be expelled from the man in any way that could not lead to the birth of another member of the tribe was considered disloyal mass murder. Homosexuality, *coitus interruptus* (withdrawal of the penis before ejaculation during sexual intercourse), masturbation, and sexual relationships with women of other nations were all declared unlawful for the Hebrew male because none of these acts could lead to the creation of another Hebrew male. It was for this reason that female homosexuality (lesbianism) was not judged with the same harshness as male homosexuality. The female had no seed to waste, and she was therefore allowed more sexual latitude. Our society still retains vestiges of the old taboos against many sexual practices which were unlawful for the Hebrews, in spite of the fact that the bases for these taboos no longer exist.

While there were definite laws written pertaining to the sexual practices of the Israelites, Jesus spoke surprisingly little about sex. The Bible indicates that he accepted sexual behavior with calm understanding and without moral preachments. It was not Jesus, but later followers of Jesus who placed sex in a grey world of half duty, half sin. The Apostle Paul was probably the first to speak out specifically on sexual morality. Paul himself never married, and he believed that every man would be better off unmarried and *celibate* (completely refraining from sexual intercourse) although he grudgingly admitted that marriage was better than *fornication* (sexual intercourse outside of marriage).

The early Christian church had few definite proscriptions in the matter of sex. It remained for St. Augustine in the fourth century A.D. to give the church the attitudes which have since permeated most of the Western world. His writings severely condemned *premarital* (before marriage) and *extramarital* (outside of marriage) sexual outlets, with masturbation being particularly censured. In time, the Roman Catholic Church elevated celibacy for men and permanent virginity for women into means by which they could expect to reach their greatest glory.

Our culture has derived its sexual mores not only from Judeo-Christian teaching but also from the early Greeks. With the Spartan overthrow of Athens in the fifth century B.C. came a change in the sexual practices of the Greeks. From a philosophy which had accepted sex as a pleasurable and natural function, the Greeks turned to the Spartan philosophy which emphasized denial of pleasure and a rigorous self-control in all matters. Celibacy and other denials of sexual pleasure thus became exercises in self-discipline. Alexander the Great, in his phenomenal swath of world conquest during the fourth century B.C., opened up many new avenues of cultural exchange. Eastern spiritualistic attitudes thus filtered into the Western world; sexual desire was deemed an evil to be overcome by self-denial in order to attain salvation of the soul. In glorifying celibacy, Eastern spiritualism placed sex under the pall of guilt and condemnation long before the advent of Christianity, but the New Testament, written during the latter part of this period, was strongly influenced by the spiritualistic movement.

Virginity has long been associated with purity in religious teachings. The myths of the virgin birth of Jesus and the springing of Athena full grown from Zeus's forehead show that the

Christians and Greeks were in accord with other religions of the world whose teaching also includes the nonsexual origin of their deities. It is therefore not difficult to understand why sex and the concept of sin (impurity) are so closely associated, or how sexual experiences and thoughts, in marriage or out, can easily produce feelings of guilt and emotional stress.

With the development of Judaic and Christian theology came the evolution of an ethical code governing marriage. Morally acceptable sexual activity was henceforth limited to the marriage bed, and any deviation was considered sinful. Fortunately for the mental health of our society, outmoded religious dictates are increasingly being submitted to objective analysis, and their validity is being assessed according to their relevance to present-day circumstances.

When young people are given rigid proscriptions in sexual matters that are not counterbalanced with a rationale for sexual morality, then guilt must be used to control their sexual behavior. Young people incorporate these rules into their emotional makeup, so that if and when the rules are broken, emotional stress often results.

An individual should examine unemotionally the many ramifications of any moral code which includes rules about sexual expression. He can thus arrive at his own conclusions regarding the probable effects of various sexual behavior on himself, his partner, and society. He will then be much more likely to manage his sexuality in a manner that is normal, healthy, and anxiety-free. When we as a society mature to the point that we no longer feel compelled to impose our personal biases on others, we will encounter and engender fewer emotional difficulties, including sexual ones. This tolerance of others is embodied in the Golden Rule, that farsighted and sensible guide to all human behavior in its unequivocal emphasis on the equal rights of all men—"Therefore all things whatsoever you would that men should do to you, do you even so to them . . ."

BREAKING THE BONDS OF SEXUAL FASCISM

An extension of the Golden Rule is the granting of relative freedom of behavior in sexual matters—because there *are* individual differences in sexual drives and preferences. Any sexual behavior between consenting adults and out of the sight and sound of unwilling observers cannot be prohibited or judged by those who wish to be genuinely tolerant. Too often, individuals become "sexual fascists" who arbitrarily evaluate certain sexual behavior—their own, of course—as being right and superior to other sexual behavior. These people will go to great lengths to impose their viewpoints on others, and any individual who fails to comply with their arbitrary standards is labeled a pervert, a sexual inferior, a Communist, or some such similar term.

The sexual fascist neither understands nor cares that women respond to sexual relations differently than men do; he simply expects women to employ and respond to the same sexual techniques that are successful with men. Such bigots live by the traditional *double standard* of morality for men and women. For example, women must be virgins until marriage, while men are allowed, even expected, to have many premarital experiences. Women are much more condemned for having children out of wedlock than the men who father the babies. One standard of acceptable behavior is applied to women and another standard to men.

A reasonable degree of flexibility in the major aspects of one's life is crucial for emotional health and normal adjustment. We do not expect all people to eat or even like asparagus; and indeed we do not expect those who do eat asparagus to want to eat it all the time. When it comes to sex, however, the bigot's philosophy does not allow for any behavioral flexibility. Nor does it condone the experimentation that adds so much pleasure to the sex life of the normal, sexually mature person.

Those who adhere to the tenets and demands of sexual fascism are quick to condemn as deviant any sexual behavior that is not identical to their own. Since sexual practices are largely culturally determined, such attitudes reveal the worst kind of chauvinism. The uninformed in Western cultures, for example, often condemn sexual intercourse in any position other than the man above the woman. These people may also view such noncoital sexual activities as masturbation, petting, and oral-genital contact as perversions. Research findings, however, indicate that masturbation is commonly practiced by most men and women, both single and married; that oral-genital contact occurs in most marriages in the upper socioeconomic-educational stratum of society; and that approximately 50% of women prefer noncoital methods of stimulation to sexual intercourse, and respond more intensely to them.

Significant differences in acceptable norms of sexual behavior are found in various cultures. For example, the man-above coital position is not the most popular position anywhere except in the United States and a few other countries, and masturbation is less acceptable than homosexuality among boys of Arab countries.

No one is justified in saying that the sexual practices of any one culture are more proper and normal than a different set of practices in another culture. It cannot be overemphasized that there are individual and cultural differences that extend into every aspect of human life, including expression of sexuality. Sexually informed people must take these differences into account. The rights of others must be respected, and we must accept the existence of tastes and pleasures quite different from our own. No one has the moral (nor should he have the legal) right to force on others his ethical views, any more than he should hope to impose his esthetic or political convictions on them.

The Sexually Mature Individual

Professionals who have the most intimate knowledge of troubled people—psychologists, psychiatrists, marriage counselors, and ministers—have long realized that guilt feelings aroused by inadequate sex knowledge interefere with happy, effective living. Scientific investigations have confirmed that people who receive an appropriate sex education are less anxious and more able to adjust well to life stresses than those without one, since the latter tend to repress their anxiety by avoidance and denial.

People who are highly knowledgeable in sexual matters are more capable of enjoying their sexual feelings and of deriving pleasure from all forms of sexual activity than are the less knowledgeable. Anxiety has been found to lead to restraint of normal sexual impulses, and the greater the amount of accurate sex information an individual has, the less his anxiety.

The sexually immature individual whose sexual ignorance has resulted in various kinds of physical and psychological maladjustment could have had a different life with early, adequate sex information. Women who suffer from difficult menstruation, for example, typically received their sex education from their mothers, who presented the information in a deprecating way, while women who have relatively comfortable menstruation often received less biased information about sex.

The sexually mature individual is one who can cope effectively with his own sexual feelings and needs. Sexual maturity is fostered when a person is able to learn the basic facts about sex as a child in a manner which helps him to feel natural and comfortable. The child needs to be able to hear the subject of sex presented without embarrassment by at least one trustworthy adult, and to be able to participate in sexual discussions with other children in a healthy and wholesome manner. Parents who wish to help their children grow up to be sexually mature individuals with adequate general psychological adjustment, therefore, should not make the common error of feeling that they should "protect" their children from sexuality. Research and clinical findings have clearly shown that such an idea is a dangerous myth.

The only way our society is going to achieve proper sexual stability and mental health, which are undisputed requirements for maturity, is to provide a sound sex education for everyone. Working toward this goal means that those who are in a position to instruct must freely admit to what they do not know, at the same time teaching that which they know to be the truth. They must educate, not indoctrinate; teach facts, not fallacies; encourage the formulation of a code of ethics, not preach asceticism; and seek objective knowledge, not emotionally biased ideas. This goal is difficult because most people have grown up in a culture which encourages sexual ignorance and maladjustment.

SEX EDUCATION

Those individuals who are aware of the benefits to individuals and to society of an adequate sex education are faced with the problem of how best to provide it. In spite of the fact that a very vocal minority has labeled sex education a "filthy Communist plot," surveys indicate that the majority of American parents and young people are in favor of including sex education in the public schools.

Those who insist that providing the young with sex education is tantamount to giving license to sexual promiscuity frequently cite distorted statistics as proof of their position. However, most studies clearly show, as we have seen, that adequate information about sex encourages sexually responsible behavior.

While it is easy to dismiss the hysterical rantings of certain anti-sex-education groups, one cannot dismiss the genuine concern that responsible parents have with regard to the quality of the instruction that their children receive in this sensitive area. Some are concerned that sex education will be presented in such a sterile, clinical manner that the human element is removed. Others are concerned that sexually irresponsible persons will be given the task of teaching sex education and that they will teach "too much, too soon" or that they will fail to provide their young charges with the proper attitude of sexual responsibility. Both of these parent groups feel that sex education should be provided by the home and not by public educators.

Their objections have merit, and no thoughtful educator would disagree that sex education should ideally be presented in the home *if* the parents are comfortable in their role as teacher. The fact remains, however, that most youngsters are obtaining their sex education from their peers, from books and magazines, and from pornographic material. A small minority receive their sex instruction from parents, the church, or professionals. Studies have indicated that those with the most positive attitudes and the most factual knowledge learned about sex in formal classroom instruction. The same studies found little difference in the accuracy of sex information received from peers and that received from clergy and parents, all these sources providing inaccurate and insufficient information. When parents do provide sex instruction to their children, it is usually limited to the facts of menstruation and pregnancy. Details (usually distorted) about other aspects of sex are typically acquired from peers.

FIGURE 1.1 Sex Education. Copyright 1971, G.B. Trudeau. Distributed by Universal Press Syndicate.

Information about sex must be integrated into the personal ethical code of the individual, and it is clear that the moral climate in which a child lives is the greatest determinant of his ethical values. His personal philosophies are largely molded by his home and by the attitudes of his parents. It is within the context of the morality which comes from the family and society, then, that the schools can impart the factual and objective knowledge which the child needs if he is to develop a mature sexual ethic.

Of all the arguments against school sex education, perhaps the most valid concerns the qualifications of those who teach it. There are far too few institutions that train people specifically to teach this most sensitive subject. Indeed, many of those selected to teach sex-education courses receive no special training beforehand. Because of personal embarrassment, some teachers conduct their course in a strained, mechanical manner, or perhaps avoid material that might be really meaningful to their students. There is considerable evidence, in fact, that many teen-agers are less sensitive and embarrassed about sex-related topics than their teachers are. Still other teachers mingle religious prejudice and personal guilt with their sex instruction, which probably does the student more harm than good.

As every educator and expert in child development knows, children are acquiring a sex education in the public schools in the form of misinformation and frightening half-truths from their peers. The issue, then, is not *whether* sex education should be carried out in the public schools, but *where* and *how* it should be carried out—on the school grounds or in the classroom.

There are several approaches to sex education. Opinions range from the ostrichlike position that there should be no sex education whatsoever to the position which openly approves complete sexual freedom. Most advocates of the first position hope that the "problem" will quietly disappear. Sexual conflicts, unhappy marriages, premarital pregnancies, abortions, and our general anxiety about sexual matters are all sad testimonials to the fallacy of this premise. People who believe that sexual behavior should be something that one does "naturally," and that factual information destroys the enjoyment of it, may also object to any sex education. Behavioral scientists are aware, however, that sexual behavior is not a "natural" phenomenon even in the animal world. Adequate sexual behavior is a learned process and is not simply a matter of "doing what comes naturally."

Next on the continuum of sex-education theories is the "thou shalt not" approach which views as immoral all forms of sexual expression for any other purpose than that of procreation. Such an unrealistic approach probably produces more conflict than the total ignorance imposed by the first theory. It is not an exaggeration to suggest that the guilt-ridden, moralistic patients crowding the offices of marriage counselors, ministers, and psychotherapists have largely been molded by the "thou shalt not" philosophy of sex education.

The next approach is the one which treats sex as a purely physical drive which should be explained to youngsters in purely physiological terms. This approach eliminates the emotional content of sexual behavior and ignores the fact that sexual activity is far more meaningful when it is an expression of affection than when it is merely a release of sexual tension.

At the far end of the continuum is the "sexual anarchy" viewpoint which would grant unrestrained license to any sexual act that individual sexual needs and desires might dictate so long as no injury befalls others. This approach views sex as a pleasurable activity which should not be inhibited by shame, guilt, tradition, or any code of morality. Such a position fails to take into account the fact that man must conform to some extent to the mores of the society in which he lives if he is to have a relatively smooth social interchange with his fellowman. To behave without discretion and in violation of the patterns of behavior which are expected of us by society (at least insofar as others know) is to run the risk of being reprimanded, rejected, or even jailed.

The safest and most effective solution to the various approaches to sex education is obviously a course of compromise. Certain sexual needs should be permitted expression; unadorned information about the physiological and psychological aspects of sex should be presented to all; and the Judeo-Christian traditions within which we live must be understood and dealt with sensibly in the framework of present-day society. Each individual must evolve his own code of sexual morality; only bigots attempt to establish an inflexible code for all.

The Parent's Role in Sex Education

After an individual has developed his own code of acceptable sexual behavior, he must then decide how he is to present that ethic in the sex education of his children—an instructional process that begins at a far earlier age than many suspect. The evidence is clear that sex education begins long before nursery school. It begins, in fact, with the first intimate mother-infant contact after birth.

Experiments have been conducted in which infant monkeys were raised in isolation except for "mother substitutes" made of wire. In the absence of physical contact with their mother or with peers, the monkeys grew up to be disorganized and confused as to what was expected of them in sexual activity. When placed with monkeys who had been normally raised and who were sexually experienced, the deprived monkeys did not know how to assume coital positions and reacted with fear and anxiety.

Another group of baby monkeys were raised in isolation with the wire mother substitutes, but terrycloth coverings were placed over the "mothers." When the infant monkeys had a softer "mother" to which they could cling and cuddle up, they did not become so sexually disorganized. A third group of baby monkeys who were maternally deprived but allowed to play with and cuddle one another eventually learned normal coital and maternal behavior. It is evident from these studies that the sexual training of these primates commenced at birth.

Many factors significantly affect a child's emerging sexual attitudes and conduct: the way in which his mother and father love, fondle, and hold him (as well as each other); the soothing or harsh sound of their voices, which comes to be associated with love or with rejection and hostility; the feel of their skin; the smell of their bodies. Whether they realize it or intend to do so, parents begin a child's sexual training in the earliest days of his life. Even when parents avoid discussing sex altogether, the child nevertheless detects their attitudes—stressful or happy —through nonverbal communications. Some of the most crucial aspects of sex education are thus taught unconsciously.

Hopefully, the material in this book will assist the reader toward a better understanding of himself and his sexuality, and will encourage him to work toward changes in society that will better prepare his children for a healthy, well-adjusted sex life.

What I Would Tell My Daughter and Son about Premarital Sex

Psychologists who deal with problems of sexuality are often asked what they would tell their own children about premarital sex. Most often the question is meant to embarrass the psychologist, the questioner assuming that the psychologist will talk out of both sides of his mouth. That is, he might make certain liberal statements about sexual matters to the public, but when it comes to his own offspring, he will forget his academic views and become as rigid an adherent of a "double standard" as the next parent.

Traditionally, the double standard of sexual ethics, long rampant in our society, has meant that people have not applied the same rules of human behavior and human decency equally to both sexes. Young adult males are expected to try every maneuver, trick, and "line" at their disposal to seduce girls. Girls, on the other hand, must use every method and technique known in order to sexually attract boys, yet they are expected to stop short of sexual intercourse. Such games are obviously immature and foolish. Equally unwise and illogical is a tendency on the part of parents to apply one standard to their own children but another to other people's children.

The question of what I would tell my children about sex is one which cannot be answered in one short statement because a whole lifetime sets the stage for the answer. Basically, there must be a healthy attitude toward sex in the home. If the parents are well adjusted in the area of sex, if they have a healthy attitude toward sex, then the children, also, are likely to have healthy sexual attitudes. Since sexual attitudes are formed in the home, I would want consistency in sexual matters in the home, both within each parent and between the parents. Each parent should feel at ease with his own ideas in order to present the same ideas day in and day out, and one parent should not make certain demands and present one set of ideas while the other makes different demands and presents a different set of ideas. Inconsistency can only produce confusion and insecurity within the children.

In addition to internal consistency within each parent and within the marriage, I would want my children to understand what is expected and demanded of them by society, and I would want our home to be somewhat consistent with the outside world. My children should know, however, that there will be some inconsistencies between society's expectations and what they are taught in our home. They must understand the attitudes of bigots, the sexual fascists who are ready to condemn and even persecute anyone who does not conform to their way of thinking.

I'd want my son and daughter to understand the views of various religions and to know that unwise adherence to some religious ideas and ideals can produce guilt and repression. I'd also want them to understand guilt and repression; if they avoid any aspect of sex, I'd want them to do so because of rational factors and not because of guilt. For guilt in this area, as in others, leads to many problems, and sexual conflicts resulting from guilt can be devastating.

I would want my children to know the physiological and psychological makeup of both sexes, and to understand the differences between men and women. I'd want my daughter to know, for example, that men become sexually excited more easily than women do and that they are excited by different stimuli and different techniques than women are. I'd want her to know what these techniques are, so that she might avoid their use in many situations but also so that she could make use of them in appropriate situations.

By the same token, I would want my son to be well versed in all aspects of sex, especially techniques, in order for him to give the young woman he loves as much pleasure and satisfaction as possible in whatever form of sexual relationship they might enter into. He should place her needs and satisfaction on a plane at least equal to his own. My daughter should have the same knowledge in order for her both to give and to receive the maximum pleasure and fulfillment in sexual exchange.

I'd also want my children to know that young men between the ages of 17 and 21 have reached the height of their sex drive and that there is a sound biological basis for their great interest in sex at this time. Women, however, do not have such a strong physical drive until they are about 30 years old. If a young girl *does* become sexually involved with a boy, therefore, she usually does so because of emotional rather than sexual needs. I would want my son to realize that the responsibility in these matters is largely his and that he should take into careful consideration possible outcomes of premarital sex, including feelings of guilt, and pregnancy.

I would want both of my children to have a kind and fair attitude toward their fellowman. I'd want them to be ethical in all relationships, including sexual ones. There should be no cheating, no lying, no taking advantage of others. I'd want each of them to understand that when their behavior in any way harms other persons or themselves, that behavior should be reconsidered.

Each of my children should understand that the seductive behavior of others may be motivated by feelings other than affection. Boys and men who feel sexually inferior, for instance, find an ego boost in seduction. When my daughter finds men behaving in such a manner, she must understand that it is their problem and not a personal thing directed toward her, and she must deal with it accordingly. Similarly, my son should realize that an immature and maladjusted woman may try to "prove" her desirability and worth as a person through sex; or she may use sex to snare some man who appeals to her; or she may attempt to shore up a faltering relationship through sex. He should be aware of these possibilities and avoid entering into sexual relationships that he thinks are motivated by emotional disturbances.

I'd want both my daughter and my son to know methods and techniques of sexual outlet other than sexual intercourse, and I'd want them to know the values of these methods. I would want them to know that masturbation and petting are perfectly normal modes of behavior—that they can and will satisfy sexual urges, yet do not cause some of the problems that can result from premarital sexual intercourse.

The elements basic to all successful human relationships, and perhaps most especially to sexual relationships, are honesty, fairness, decency, kindness, respect, understanding, and love. If these qualities are present and maintained, no relationship is likely to be harmful to the people involved. Neither party, in my opinion, is likely to be damaged by premarital sexual intercourse—*if* they are believers in decency and fair play; *if* they have a mature, guilt-free attitude toward sex; *if* they have decided that they wish to go ahead only after a rational discussion, and not when they are caught up in the passion of sex play; and *if* they are mature enough to accept the responsibilities that go along with intercourse.

If, with all this information, together with the attitudes and background of our home, my son or daughter still decided to engage in premarital sexual intercourse, then I would certainly want them to know about and have access to contraceptive devices. I'd also want them both to be informed about pregnancy and venereal diseases.

If either of them decided to have sexual intercourse before marriage, furthermore, I would want them to know that so long as they hurt neither themselves or others, my respect and love for them would not change. And I would hope—and I believe it would follow—that if either of them ever needed a friend, they would turn first to their parents and know that we would support them. These are the principles in which my wife and I believe and the ones by which we have reared our daughter and son, both of whom are now happily married. I do not know whether or not either of them had premarital sexual intercourse—and frankly, I couldn't care less. I respect and love both of them too much to pry, although I could ask and they could answer without embarrassment to any of us.

Neither my son nor my daughter has the guilt, shame, or fear that causes sexual repression. Their attitudes and behavior toward their fellowman are honorable and decent. Because of their ethical and sexual philosophies, among other things, both of them are likely to remain emotionally stable and healthy.

FURTHER READING

Oh! Sex Education! by M. Breasted. New York: Praeger, 1970.

This book is the best available survey of the current controversy over whether or not sex education should be taught formally in the schools.

Toward a Psychology of Being, by A. H. Maslow. New York: D. Van Nostrand, 1968.

Written by the father of humanistic psychology, this book presents the positive and optimistic view that the natural instincts of man are healthy. Maslow discusses the conditions which he believes are necessary for individual happiness and fulfillment. He also explores the relationships between sickness in the individual and sickness in the society.

Sexuality and Man, by SIECUS. New York: Charles Scribner's Sons, 1970.

Compiled and edited by the Sex Information and Education Council of the United States, this book gives much information concerning the interrelationships between sex and society. Chapters 9, 10, and 11 are particularly relevant.

A Report of the Commission on Obscenity and Pornography, by the Commission on Obscenity and Pornography. New York: Bantam Books, 1970.

A paperback book containing the complete report of both the majority and the minority conclusions of the President's Commission, this volume includes data which expose many popularly held misconceptions about obscenity and pornography.

Human Sexuality, 2d ed., by J. L. McCary. New York: D. Van Nostrand, 1973.

This book is the "mother" of the present volume and includes a more detailed and technical discussion of all of the topics in the brief edition. Chapter 1 is especially pertinent to sex and today's society.

2 THE BIOCHEMISTRY OF SEX

Sexual maturation and a good deal of sexual functioning are controlled primarily by sex hormones. These substances, produced by the *endocrine glands* under the direction of the central nervous system, are secreted directly into the bloodstream and distributed throughout the body. Because hormones are secreted into the bloodsteam without passing through any duct or canal, endocrine glands are also referred to as ductless glands or glands of internal secretion.

While sex hormones are essential for the development of physiological sexual characteristics, human sexual motivation and activation also depend on the *cerebral cortex* (the surface of the human brain) and the *hypothalamus* (that part of the brain lying nearest to the "master gland," the pituitary gland). The hypothalamus appears to function as a biological timing device. Interacting with the endocrine glands, it monitors and controls the onset of puberty, the fertility cycles, and sexual arousal. Stimulation of the hypothalamus dramatically influences emotional reaction, including that of sexual response. In addition to hormonal influence, then, a normal sexual life is also dependent on the interplay between the emotional impulses generated in the hypothalamus and the behavioral impulses generated by the cerebral cortex.

THE PHYSICAL CHANGES OF PUBERTY

Adolescence is the period of life between childhood and adulthood. It begins with the onset of *puberty*, the time when the sexual organs become capable of reproduction and the influence of the sex hormones first becomes prominent, and ends with the cessation of major body growth. Just before puberty, there is a preadolescent period of rapid change and growth known as *pubescence* or the pubic growth cycle. During this time, the sexual glands mature and physiological differences between the sexes become more marked. Attitudes, emotions, and interests change, and experimentation such as masturbation either first occurs or begins to increase in frequency.

Sexual Development in Girls

The pubescent period begins about two years earlier in girls than it does in boys, giving girls a temporary superiority—physically, sexually, and socially—over boys. Most girls reach their full stature by their sixteenth year, for example, while boys do not reach theirs until the eighteenth year or later.

As pubescence begins in the girl, her small, conical breasts begin to increase in size, and the nipples begin to project forward. As the size and sensitivity of breast tissue continue to grow, the body contour begins to round out and the pelvic area broadens. The bony structure of the pelvis widens, and a growth of fatty pads develops on the hips. The vaginal lining also begins to thicken. At about age 13, soft, downy, rather colorless pubic hair appears, together with some axillary (underarm) hair growth. Gradually, the pubic hair thickens and coarsens, becoming curly and dark in color as it grows downward to the pubic area in the inverted triangular shape peculiar to women. With these bodily changes and the unfolding of the classic feminine form, *menstruation* (the monthly discharge of blood and other material from the uterus through the vagina) is imminent.

Menstruation (also called the *menarche*) begins about two years after the breasts begin budding, about one year after pubic hair appears. However, *ovulation* (the release of a mature egg) usually does not begin until a year or so after menstruation first occurs. Puberty has been reached at the time that a girl's ovaries produce their first mature eggs, at about the age of 14.

There is considerable variation in the age of puberty because of individual differences in general health, developmental maturation, and heredity. Evidence that puberty occasionally occurs at a very early age was provided in 1939 in the incredible birth of a normal, healthy son to a Peruvian girl of 5 years of age. The baby had been fathered by a mentally retarded teenage stepbrother and was delivered by caesarean section. The 5-year-old mother was sexually mature, and physicians confirmed that she had menstruated, atypically, since approximately the age of one month. Although menstruation ordinarily precedes ovulation, there are exceptional cases on record of pregnancy and childbirth having occurred before the onset of menstruation. The apparent explanation is that the girl released a mature ovum just before she would have begun menstruating, so that the resulting pregnancy delayed menstruation until after delivery.

In the last few centuries, girls have begun to menstruate at a younger age, with the average age dropping about four months per decade. The age of puberty seems now to be leveling off. Approximately one-half of American girls are believed to begin ovulation between the ages of 12.5 and 14.5 years.

One of the factors which seems to affect both physical growth and date of menarche is altitude. One study found that girls from Denver, Colorado, at 5300 feet above sea level, for example, weighed less at birth and reached menarche later than girls from Berkeley, California, at sea level. The oxygen-rare atmosphere of Denver's high altitude apparently caused an early lag in development, although the weight difference disappeared when both groups reached menarche.

Both the prepubertal growth spurt and the menarche appear to be determined by body weight, regardless of age or height. The growth spurt tends to begin when a girl's weight reaches about 68 pounds, and the menarche when she weighs about 106 pounds.

As a girl grows into adolescence, genital changes continue. It is during this time that the *mons pubis* (or *mons veneris,* a fleshy mound situated over the pubic bone) becomes prominent and the *labia majora* (major lips) develop and become more fleshy, hiding the rest of the external genitalia, which are ordinarily visible during childhood. The *labia minora* (inner lips) also develop and grow, and the *Bartholin's glands* on each side of the vaginal opening become capable of secreting fluid, especially during sexual excitement.

At this time, the *clitoris* rapidly develops its extensive system of blood vessels and the *vagina* turns a deeper red color. The mucous lining of the vagina becomes thicker, remaining so until the *menopause* (the cessation of menstruation), when it reverts to the thinness of childhood. Vaginal secretions now become acid.

The female *uterus* is unique in its pattern of response to hormonal secretions. At birth, the uterus of a female infant is larger that it will be again until hormonal production commences. The abrupt withdrawal of the maternal hormones at birth causes the infant's uterus to shrink within a few days after birth. Occasionally this shrinking is significant enough to result in vaginal spotting or staining. From that time until the ovaries begin hormone production, the size of the uterus remains constant. At about age 10, 11, or 12, the uterus begins to grow rapidly and doubles in size by age 18. In 60% of 15-year-old girls, the uterus has already reached adult size.

Sexual Development in Boys

Generally speaking, a boy's physiological maturation occurs later, progresses more slowly, and continues longer than a girl's. While there is great variation in the date and progress of puberty in boys, the average boy first begins to manifest changes in physiological characteristics around age 12 or 13. The transformation continues to or beyond the age of 17, with pubic growth lasting from 4 to 7 years.

A frequent precursor of male pubescence is a "fat period," which may occur around age 11. At this age, penile *erection* (the stiffening and enlargement of the penis) occurs spontaneously, due to various sources of sexual and nonsexual stimulation. The boy's *penis* and *scrotum* begin to increase in size around age 12, and erections occur more often, although the average 12-year-old has not yet experienced *ejaculation* (the expulsion of semen, containing male reproductive cells, from the urethra).

At 13 or 14, the average boy's pubic hair appears, and ejaculation is now possible. At about this time, too, secretion of *sperm* (the male reproductive cell) begins, although the sperm may not be mature. Growth of axillary and facial hair follows that of the pubic hair, and *nocturnal emissions* ("wet dreams") are now possible.

Around the fourteenth or fifteenth year, the average boy's voice drops about an octave. It is interesting to note not only that boys are reaching their prepubertal growth period sooner today than they did in the past, but that the average age at which their voices change occurs earlier. In the eighteenth century, for example, the average age of voice change in the Bach Boys' Choir in Leipzig was 18; in 1959 the average age of voice change among boys in London was 13.3 years.

SEX GLANDS AND HORMONES

The growth, development, and sexual activity of both males and females is greatly influenced by the *pituitary gland,* which can have a harmonizing or disturbing effect on the other endocrine glands. Lying at the base of the brain, the pituitary is divided into an anterior (front) lobe, an intermediary lobe, and a posterior (back) lobe.

The anterior pituitary lobe serves as the coordinator of the functions of all other endocrine glands. At least six hormones are secreted by the anterior lobe, three of which are *gonadotropic,* that is, directly related to ovary and testis function. These three hormones are concerned with the production of sperm and ova and with the secretion of milk by the mammary glands following childbirth.

The sex glands or *gonads* (ovaries and testes) produce three groups of sex hormones. Two of these hormone groups are female and one is male. Each is a natural substance that is a basic component of living cells. Once used by the body, the sex hormones are broken down and eliminated, usually in the urine.

Estrogen, one of the two female hormones, is highly important in controlling body structure and in the development and functioning of genital organs. The menstrual cycle is influenced by estrogen, as are the development and maintenance of secondary sexual characteristics. Estrogen also aids in maintaining the normal condition and function of nasal and oral mucous membranes, in influencing normal uterine contractions, in controlling the growth of breast-duct tissue, and in developing and maintaining physical and mental health in the mature female.

Unlike the hormones of subhuman females, such as the dog, the hormones produced by the ovaries of a woman do not play a major role in regulating her sex drive. In fact, a study of women who had experienced bilateral *ovariectomies* (surgical removal of the ovaries) showed that 90% of such women experienced no change in sexual desire or in functioning. In contrast, 84% of women whose pituitary and *adrenal glands* (a pair of endocrine glands located near the kidneys) had been removed reported a complete loss of sex drive. The hormones produced by the pituitary and the adrenal glands therefore appear to be vastly more important in determining the level of a woman's sex drive than are the estrogenic hormones. It should be noted, however, that the woman's sexual responsiveness, assuming her glands are intact and functioning normally, is more influenced by emotional and physical factors than by hormonal conditions.

Certain neural centers of the brain are also directly affected by sex hormones. Women have greater smell acuity than men, for example, and their olfactory sensitivity is greatest midway between menstrual periods, when the estrogen levels are highest. Smell acuity decreases after an ovariectomy but can be restored through administration of estrogen.

Progesterone is the second female hormone. It is of primary importance in preparing the lining of the uterus for implantation of fertilized ova and in maintaining pregnancy. As we shall discuss in some detail in the section of Chapter 4 which deals with menstruation, progesterone is gradually withdrawn if impregnation does not occur, resulting in a breakdown of the uterine lining and the onset of the monthly menstrual flow. If an ovum is fertilized, on the other hand, progesterone is produced for the duration of the pregnancy.

Progesterone stimulates the secretion capacity of a pregnant woman's mammary glands, causing her breasts to enlarge. It also acts to inhibit premature uterine contractions. For this reason, physicians often prescribe progesterone when there is danger of a spontaneous abortion, especially during the tenth to sixteenth week of pregnancy when the threat of miscarriage is greatest.

Testosterone, the male sex hormone, is produced in a young boy's body as part of a larger process in which various hormones manufactured by the pituitary gland affect the maturing of sperm as well as the stimulation and maintenance of cells in the male reproductive glands, the *testes*. Produced in the testes, testosterone is responsible for the development and preservation of masculine secondary sexual characteristics, including facial and body hair, change of voice, muscular and skeletal development, attraction to the opposite sex, and mental attitudes. In addition, testosterone is responsible for the development, size, and function of accessory male sex organs (seminal vesicles, prostate, penis, and scrotum).

Healthy males produce more than an ample supply of sex hormones for adequate sexual functioning. Men who have only one testicle, for example, show no evidence of hormonal deficiency. Even men whose ejaculate contains as little as 60% of the usual hormonal content lead normal, satisfactory sex lives.

Although testosterone was unknown to primitive man, the testes themselves have long been associated with male virility. Early historical records tell of men attempting to increase their sexual prowess by eating the testicles of defeated enemies, for example. And 4000 years ago tiger testicles were being eaten by decrepit or impotent Chinese ancients.

As late as 1889, the renowned French physiologist Charles E. Brown-Sequard attempted, at the age of 72, to revive his failing sexual vigor by injecting himself with extracts of dog's testicles. Although this famous scientist reported spectacular sexual rejuvenation, modern science indicates that approximately 500 pounds of bull testicles would be necessary to furnish an average dose of male sex hormones. Brown-Sequard's happy results were apparently the result of autosuggestion. Although he was barking up the wrong tree, Brown-Sequard stimulated considerable research in this area. Well-controlled experiments have since shown that we are physically, mentally, and emotionally dependent upon the action of our endocrine glands.

A phenomenon that is not altogether understood is the fact that each sex possesses small amounts of the hormones of the opposite sex. The source of these "opposite" hormones is not definitely known, although it is thought that the gonads and the adrenals are probably responsible.

An excessive amount of the "opposite" hormones can produce marked changes in secondary sexual characteristics in adults. In an infant or growing child, such an imbalance can produce deviations in primary sexual characteristics as well as changes in the secondary characteristics. Hormonal therapy is often successful in adjusting this rare imbalance and in correcting or preventing associated problems.

The endocrine system is quite complex, and only those hormones which more or less directly affect the sexual systems have been discussed here. As we have seen, sexual development, growth, and functioning depend upon these sex hormones. Released into the bloodstream in small, measured doses, they have a tremendous impact on the physiology and psychology of the individual.

FURTHER READING

The Reproductive System, by F. H. Netter. Summit, N. J.: CIBA Pharmaceutical Products, 1961.

> This outstanding book gives a detailed account of all phases of human reproduction and of all forms of sexual disorders and venereal diseases. Every section of the book is generously illustrated with exceptionally vivid color drawings. Section I is related to the biochemistry of sex.

Sex Research: New Developments, edited by J. Money. New York: Holt, Rinehart and Winston, 1965.

> This compendium of sex research studies includes a chapter on psychosexual differentiation which is especially applicable to the study of hormonal effects on the differentiation and development of the sexes.

Health: Man in a Changing Environment, by B. A. Kogan. New York: Harcourt, Brace Jovanovich, 1970.

> Designed for use in college health courses, this book includes material on the endocrine system and on genetics, as well as several chapters dealing with emotional health in the context of sexuality.

Human Sexuality, 2d ed., by J. L. McCary. New York: D. Van Nostrand, 1973.

> Chapters 4 and 5 are related to the biochemistry of sex.

3 THE SEXUAL SYSTEMS
OF MEN AND WOMEN

While a thorough anatomical knowledge of the male and female sexual systems is not absolutely necessary for an understanding of sexual response, every individual who hopes to understand human sexuality should be familiar with certain of the body's major sexual structures and their development.

Perhaps the most central fact about human sexual systems is that the male and female systems are counterparts of one another. They originate in the same cell mass in the *embryo* (the unborn young in its early stage of development) and gradually differentiate according to the sex of the embryo. Many structures in the male are, in fact, parallel to those in the female. Some of these parallel structures are the testes and the ovaries, the scrotum and the labia majora, the penis and the clitoris, and the skin of the penis and the labia minora.

Although the sex of an embryo is fixed at the time of fertilization, the sex genes do not exert their influence until about the fifth or sixth week of prenatal life. Prior to this time, all embryos appear to be structurally female. Since the male hormone *androgen* is necessary for the differentiation of male sexual organs, and since no such hormonal addition is necessary for the development of female sexual structures, some biologists believe that the female is the primal sex. In those rare cases in which the male embryo is deprived of androgen, the external genitalia cannot differentiate into penis, foreskin, and scrotum (although the testes and the male accessory organs are present internally). Instead they form homologous (parallel) female sex organs: clitoris, clitoral hood, and the labia minora and majora. At birth, these rare males appear to be completely female and are usually reared as such. The error may not be discovered until they reach adolescence, if then.

THE MALE GENITALIA

In the male, the *testicles*, also called the *testes*, are the first sexual structures to develop. They descend shortly before or just after birth into the *scrotum*, a loose pouch of skin that is an out-pocket of the abdominal cavity. The scrotum is supported by muscles and tissues which regulate the gonadal temperature. The temperature of the scrotum is lower than that of the body itself, this lower temperature being necessary for the production of sperm. For this reason the muscles and tissue of the scrotum contract when the outside temperature is low, thus bringing the

---

FIGURE 3.1 Schematic representation of the male pelvic region, showing organs of reproduction.

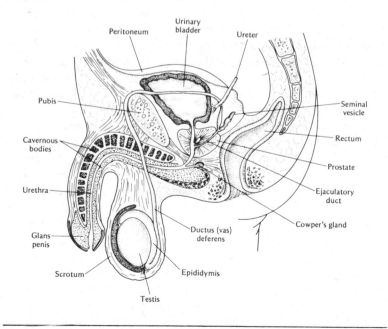

testicles closer to the warm body; they relax when the temperature is high.

There are time-honored arguments that long hot baths, prolonged use of athletic supporters, high fever, and the like can cause infertility. However, although a 2°C to 3°C increase in temperature does in fact occasionally result in temporary sterility, fertility returns in a short time. There is little evidence that taking prolonged hot baths is an effective contraceptive technique, despite the fact that one researcher reported that heat which is tolerable to the hand can, in a 30-minute period, arrest the testicular manufacture of sperm for weeks.

Sperm are produced within each testis in tubules which are lined with germinal tissue. The sperm are emptied into the *epididymis,* a swelling attached to each testicle, where they mature or ripen for as long as six weeks. They are then transported into the *vas deferens,* a small tube about 18 inches in length that serves as a passage to one of the two *seminal vesicles,* pouches near the top of the *prostate gland* behind the bladder. The mature sperm have little motility until they mix with prostatic fluid to form *semen.* That part of the prostatic secretion which constitutes the larger portion of the semen, or ejaculate, is a highly alkaline, thick, milky fluid that contains many substances, including proteins, calcium, citric acid, cholesterol, and various enzymes and acids. The alkalinity of the secretion apparently serves to allow the sperm to move through acid areas at a rapid pace. Acid in the vaginal fluid will easily destroy them if left in contact for even a short time.

The substance of seminal fluid varies from man to man, and variations in the fluid are to be expected in a single individual. Sometimes the fluid is thick and almost gelatinlike, while another time it will be thin and somewhat watery. Frequent ejaculations generally result in a thinner fluid.

The average amount of semen ejaculated at any one time is 4 cc; it weighs about 4 grams. Given the protein and fat contained in semen, the average ejaculate probably represents less than 36 calories. The evidence is therefore convincing that a normal discharge of semen cannot in any way "weaken" a man.

Along with the seminal vesicles and the prostate, the *Cowper's glands* make up a man's accessory reproductive glands. During sexual excitement, the Cowper's glands secrete an alkaline fluid that lubricates and neutralizes the acidity of the *urethra* (the duct through which urine and seminal fluid pass out of the body) for easy and safe passage of the semen. This fluid from the Cowper's glands can be observed at the opening of the head of the penis during sexual excitement and before ejaculation. The fluid does not ordinarily contain sperm, but some sperm occasionally make their way into the fluid. It is therefore possible for a woman to be impregnated by penetration of the penis without ejaculation.

FIGURE 3.2 Schematic representation of the prostate gland, showing ejaculatory duct openings joining the urethra.

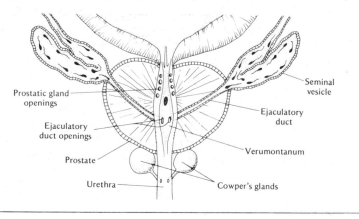

The *penis* is composed mostly of erectile tissue. In the adult male it averages from 2.5 to 4 inches in length when flaccid, is slightly over 1 inch in diameter, and is about 3.5 inches in circumference. Its size varies considerably from man to man. When in a state of tumescence (erection), the average penis extends 5.5 to 6.5 inches in length, and becomes 1.5 inches in diameter and about 4.5 inches in circumference. The size of the erect penis also varies considerably from man to man.

There is little relationship between the size of a flaccid penis and its size when erect, and there is even less relationship between penile and general body size than exists between the dimensions of other organs and body size. The measurement of a perfectly functioning erect penis can vary from 2 inches in one man to 10 inches in another, but one is no less capable of coital performance than the other.

Men are often concerned about the dimensions of their penises because childhood experiences have conditioned them to associate an adult's larger penis with strength and masculinity. When a boy conditioned in this way grows up, he may think that in order to be a man of sexual prowess he must have an inordinately large penis. However, a woman's vagina has few nerve endings. Aside from psychological influences, therefore, the size of a man's penis has nothing to do with the pleasure experienced by either partner, unless there is some physical or hormonal dysfunction.

Recent investigations into the relationship between penile size, male hormone functioning, and potency (the ability to achieve an erection) have indicated that abnormally small adult penises caused by hormone deficiency usually can be increased to normal size within a few months by hormonal treatment.

The penis is composed of three bodies of spongy, erectile tissue which become erect when filled with blood. The erection is lost when blood leaves the penis venously faster than it flows in through the arteries.

The *glans* is the smooth conelike head of the penis, and is by far the most sexually sensitive and excitable part of a man's body.

The *corona*, the ridge at the back edge of the glans at the juncture of the glans and penile shaft, is filled with many sensitive nerve endings. When stimulated, the corona is a primary source of sexual pleasure and excitement. The most highly sensitive area is the *frenulum* (also called the *frenum*), the thin tissue on the underside of the glans which is also attached to the skin at the top of the penile shaft.

The *shaft* of the penis is covered by loose skin which allows free movement and full erection when the penis becomes engorged with blood and elongates and enlarges. Near the tip of the penis, the skin is no longer attached to the organ directly. Encompassing the glans, it usually hangs loosely and the flap of overhanging skin is known as the *prepuce* or *foreskin*. For hygienic or religious reasons, a portion of the prepuce covering the glans is frequently removed surgically in the well-known procedure called *circumcision.*

FIGURE 3.3 Diagram of the penis, showing a collection of smegma.

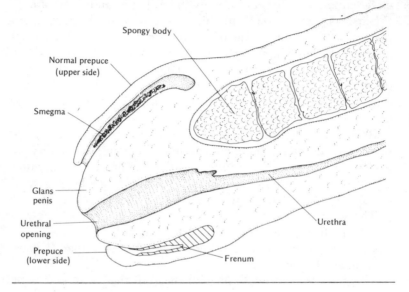

Spongy body

Normal prepuce (upper side)

Smegma

Glans penis

Urethral opening

Prepuce (lower side)

Urethra

Frenum

Just behind the glans are modified *sebaceous glands,* which secrete a fatty lubricant material. These secretions, together with cells shed from the glans and the corona, form a smelly, cheese-like substance known as *smegma.* If the prepuce is tight over the glans, smegma may collect and emit an unpleasant odor. Smegma may also act as a breeding ground for irritants and disease. Prevention of this condition is one of the main purposes of circumcision. Research has also shown that the accumulation of smegma may encourage penile cancer, making circumcision even more important.

Ordinarily, erection sets the stage for *ejaculation,* the spurting discharge of semen through the penis. This physical reaction is accompanied by a distinct and highly pleasurable sensation known as *orgasm,* to which a later chapter of this book is devoted. The strength of the ejaculation varies from man to man.

Some men ejaculate with such force that the discharged semen may go three feet or more beyond the penis, while the semen of others may travel only a few inches or simply ooze out the urethra. The extent of the force usually depends upon such factors as general health, age, degree of sexual stimulation, and the condition of the prostate. Most men report that semen is ejaculated with little force, although they sometimes tend to correlate the subjective pleasures of orgasm with the force of ejaculation.

It is perhaps coincidental that ejaculation and orgasm occur together. Ejaculation can occur in paraplegics and quadriplegics, for example, if the spinal injury is high enough not to have damaged the nerve area directly responsible for the emission of the semen. But ejaculation in men who have had spinal cord transections is not accompanied by the usual subjective sensation of orgasm unless the transection is incomplete. Paraplegic men may, however, have dreams of vivid orgasmic imagery despite their inability to experience the sensation of orgasm while awake.

It should be mentioned at this point that the loss of erection and impotence are usually due to emotional, not physical, difficulties. A man who fails to have a satisfying erection will tend to worry about his "failure" the next time he attempts intercourse. He may thus establish a vicious cycle of failure in his sexual behavior.

Both erection and ejaculation may occur without any physical stimulation. The best example is nocturnal emission, which is primarily the result of an erotic dream. In many instances nocturnal emissions occur to sexually active people who, despite a recent orgasm, may become so sexually aroused by some new erotic stimuli that they experience another orgasm during sleep. These nocturnal responses can occur quite frequently—especially among better educated young men, who appear more responsive than others to erotic stimuli of a psychological nature. Furthermore, both men and women have been known to have orgasms from erotic thoughts alone or from stimulation of nongenital areas, such as the lips and breasts.

Ordinarily each ejaculation contains millions of sperm, although the sperm count per ejaculate tends to diminish as frequency of intercourse increases. The higher the sperm count is, the greater the proportion of male-producing sperm; conversely, the lower the sperm count, the greater the proportion of female-producing sperm. (See Chapter 5 for a discussion of the role of sperm in sex determination.)

One of the persistent myths in human sexuality is that humans can get "hung up" in sexual intercourse. Most people have heard stories of couples who became locked together while copulating, the services of a physician being required before the penis could be released. The story is characteristically told as the truth and as having happened to a friend (or to a friend of a friend), although no one has ever witnessed the phenomenon or experienced it. This notion perhaps results from man's observation of dogs becoming "hung up" because of the peculiar anatomical structure of the male dog's sexual organs. The dog's penis contains a bone which allows for penetration of the bitch's vagina before complete penile erection. With ensuing tumescence, a knot forms on the base of the dog's penis as it fills the vaginal barrel. At the same time the walls of the bitch's vagina swell, all of which serve to "trap" the penis and prevent its withdrawal before ejaculation.

There are no scientifically verified cases of *penis captivus* among humans in modern medical literature. It is theoretically possible for a woman to experience sudden strong muscle spasms of the vagina (*vaginismus*) during sexual intercourse, and the vagina may momentarily tighten around her partner's penis. But even in these circumstances, the pain or fear that the man would experience would cause loss of erection, permitting easy withdrawal of the penis.

THE FEMALE GENITALIA

The internal female genital organs consist of two ovaries, two uterine or fallopian tubes, the uterus (or womb), and the inner four-fifths of the vagina.

The *ovaries* produce *ova*, or eggs, and are homologous to the testes of the male. In addition, they manufacture hormones (estrogen and progesterone) that prepare and maintain the uterus for implantation of the fertilized ovum.

In the physically mature female, ovulation is generally assumed to occur alternately in each ovary, but one ovary may in fact discharge several times in succession. A single egg is usually released at the time of ovulation, but two or more ova may be discharged. Although women are generally assumed to ovulate once a month, an additional egg may be discharged during the month, especially during a peak of sexual excitement. This eventuality may contribute to the high incidence of impregnation occurring during the so-called "safe" period—the time of the menstrual month at which conception is considered least likely to occur.

Fertilization usually occurs in the *ampulla* portion of the *fallopian tube* which cups over the ovary and picks up each ovum as it is discharged. The *conceptus* (fertilized ovum) is then swept by tiny, hairlike projections called cilia toward the *uterus*, a hollow, thick-walled muscular organ shaped somewhat like a pear. The fallopian tubes enter the uterus at the upper, larger portion of the organ, known as the *corpus* or body. The cavity of the uterus is a flattened space that is little more than a slit, its total length being about 2.5 inches. The flattened cavity narrows to a tiny opening near the center of the organ, then continues through the *cervix* (the lower end of the uterus) as an opening smaller than a soda straw.

The cervix is smaller than the body of the uterus, the size ratio in mature women being about one to two. In the newborn female, this ratio is reversed, the cervix being about twice as large as the corpus. In young children, the ratio is about one to one. Physicians describe women as having an "infantile uterus" when the corpus and the cervix are nearly the same size; such women are usually incapable of bearing children. The body of the normal uterus grows proportionately larger because of hormonal secretions that commence at puberty, while the growth of the cervix merely keeps pace with the growth rate of the rest of the body.

The *vagina* is a muscular tube, capable of considerable dilation, which extends from just behind the cervix to an external opening in the vestibule of the vulva. About 3 inches long on the front wall, and about 3.5 inches on the back wall, the vagina extends upwards in an approximately vertical manner in a standing woman, roughly at right angles to her uterus. It is the organ

FIGURE 3.4 Schematic representation of the female pelvic region, showing organs of reproduction.

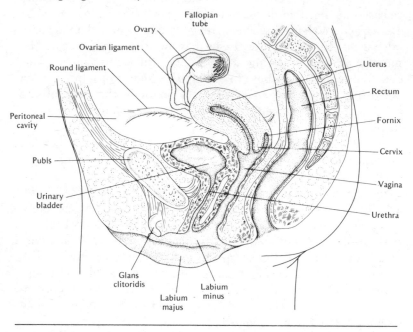

that receives the penis during the act of sexual intercourse. The vaginal tube elongates somewhat during sexual excitation.

About a third to a half inch of the cervix extends into the vagina, providing a path for the sperm's passage into the fallopian tubes where they usually meet the ovum if fertilization takes place. During pregnancy, the cervix is often closed by a mucous plug which separates the uterus from the vagina and keeps bacteria and other undesirable matter from entering the uterus. This plug reduces the possibility of infection in the uterus.

The walls of the vagina are in contact with each other under ordinary conditions. They have a wrinkled appearance and contain an intricate network of erectile tissue which helps to dilate and close the vaginal channel.

As sexual excitement builds and continues, small beads of "sweat" appear on the vaginal surface. Occasionally, the vaginal muscles contract suddenly, bringing the walls of the vagina together in a manner that forces secretions out in a spurting fashion. These secretions, along with the contractions which accompany orgasm, are probably the cause of the mistaken notion that women ejaculate as men do. Actually, the "sweat" merely serves as a lubricant to aid in penile penetration, making sexual intercourse easier to perform.

Although many women claim that the sex act is incomplete and unsatisfying to them without penetration, the vagina contains very few nerve endings that give sexual pleasure. Penetration would appear to afford more psychological than physiological pleasure. Empirical findings indicate that, physically speaking, an orgasm is an orgasm, whether it is attained by penetration, manual manipulation of the genital area, or some other technique.

The *hymen,* or maidenhead, is the fold of connective tissue that partially closes the external opening of the vagina. This tissue may prevent full penetration of the penis and, if intact, is usually ruptured by the first act of sexual intercourse. More often, however, the tissue is broken during the young girl's masturbation or other sexual experimentation, or the tissue is naturally structured in such a way that it does not obstruct the vagina. A ruptured hymen is certainly not categorical evidence that a girl is not a virgin. In fact, rare cases exist in which the hymen is so flexible or pliable that repeated coitus—or, more rarely, childbirth—can take place without rupturing the tissue.

If a woman approaches marriage with her hymen still intact, it is common practice for her physician to cut the tissue after applying a mild anesthetic to the area. In the case of a ring-shaped hymen, the doctor may suggest inserting and rotating the fingertips or using a small dilator (an instrument for stretching tissues), either of which will enlarge the opening in the hymen and permit penile penetration without pain or difficulty. Obviously, the hymenal tissue usually does not seal or close off the vagina completely, since the menstrual flow is discharged as easily from virgins as from nonvirgins. The tissue is usually annular or perforated, or in some other way only partially obstructs the opening.

Pain accompanying first sexual intercourse—frequently assumed to be one cause of *frigidity* (the inability to experience sexual pleasure)—is usually the result of the hymen's being ruptured at that time. If the hymen has not been previously ruptured, it is foolish to allow the tissue to be torn by forceful penile penetration when a physician can easily cut or remove it beforehand.

In addition to the pain of tearing the hymenal tissue, there is sometimes pain during early, and especially first, sexual inter-course because of powerful contractions of the vaginal muscles—usually the result of fear and ignorance of the facts of coitus. If the woman is relaxed and unafraid, there is little reason why she cannot comfortably and pleasurably accommodate a very large penis, even though she has not had sexual intercourse before. Women under emotional stress, however, even though they might be highly experienced sexually, can experience these vaginal muscle spasms (vaginismus), making forced penetration ex-tremely painful or even impossible.

The external genitalia of a female are collectively called the *vulva* and consist of the mons veneris (or mons pubis), the labia majora, the labia minora, the clitoris, the vestibule, and the outer one-fifth of the vagina.

The *mons veneris* is made up of pads of fatty tissue lying below the skin over the pubic bone and covered with springy, curly hair. Certain nerve endings concentrated in this area can produce sexual excitement when stimulated by weight, pressure, or similar conditions.

The *labia majora* are composed of two longitudinal folds of skin which arise from the mound of the mons veneris. These folds bear pubic hair on their outer sides and contain sebaceous follicles and sweat glands on their inner sides.

The *labia minora* are also two longitudinal folds and are lo-cated within the major lips. Rich in blood vessels, nerve endings, and small sebaceous glands, they contain no hair or fat cells. These small lips form the lateral and lower borders of the vestibule; they fuse at the top to form the prepuce that encloses the clitoris.

The labia minora are highly *erogenous* (sexually sensitive), even though they actually contain no erectile tissue of the usual type. The area does change its structure somewhat during sexual excitement, however, apparently through some manner of trapping blood. Under the influence of stimulation they flare

FIGURE 3.5 External female genitalia with four types of hymens. © Copyright 1954 and 1965 Ciba Pharmaceutical Co., Division of CIBA–GEIGY CORP. Reproduced with permission from THE CIBA COLLECTION OF MEDICAL ILLUSTRATIONS by Frank H. Netter, M.D. All rights reserved.

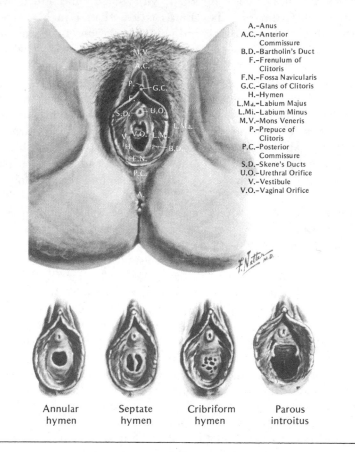

A.-Anus
A.C.-Anterior
        Commissure
B.D.-Bartholin's Duct
F.-Frenulum of
        Clitoris
F.N.-Fossa Navicularis
G.C.-Glans of Clitoris
H.-Hymen
L.M$_4$.-Labium Majus
L.Mi.-Labium Minus
M.V.-Mons Veneris
P.-Prepuce of
        Clitoris
P.C.-Posterior
        Commissure
S.D.-Skene's Ducts
U.O.-Urethral Orifice
V.-Vestibule
V.O.-Vaginal Orifice

| Annular hymen | Septate hymen | Cribriform hymen | Parous introitus |

out, exposing the vestibule, whereas under ordinary circumstances the lips are together, more or less sealing off the inner region.

The *clitoris* is a small cylindrical erectile structure which terminates in the *glans*, or head, and is situated at the top of the vestibule. The entire clitoris, except the glans, is underneath the upper part of the labia minora where its two lips join to form the clitoral prepuce. Unlike the penis, the clitoris does not hang free; only its glans is exposed.

Like the penis, the clitoris is composed of spongy erectile bodies which become engorged with blood, and erect, when stimulated. Ordinarily, the clitoris is less than 1 inch in length, although there are striking individual variations in its measurements. When sexually stimulated, it may enlarge to twice its flaccid size or more. The diameter of the clitoral shaft becomes especially enlarged.

The glans of the clitoris has a diameter of about 4 to 5 mm. Like the glans of the penis, it contains an abundance of nerve endings and is the most sexually excitable area of a woman's body. Coital methods of clitoral stimulation involve both direct contact with the glans—such as the man's pubic bone rubbing against it—and indirect stimulation through the pulling and tugging of the minor lips as the penis moves in and out of the vagina. Masters and Johnson, whose research in human sexual response has greatly increased our understanding of sexual behavior, have pointed out that, in self-manipulation of the clitoris, women stimulate to the side of it—usually the right side if they are right-handed—rather than stimulating it directly.

Although clitoral stimulation is most conducive to a woman's sexual pleasure, it is possible to remove the clitoris completely without destroying a woman's erotic sensations or her orgasmic capability. The nerve supply to the vulval area is so great that large amounts of erogenous tissue may actually be surgically removed without significantly decreasing sexual gratification. Indeed, some women who have had their entire vulval region surgically removed for one reason or another have reported that they remain orgasmically responsive.

Smegma, an accumulation of genital secretions, can collect under the prepuce covering the clitoris, resulting in abrasions and adhesions between it and the glans. This can cause pain when the clitoris enlarges during sexual excitement. The present-day medical practice is to rid the area of the smelly ragged lumps by means of a probe.

The *vestibule* is the region enclosed by the labia minora. It houses the openings of the vagina and the urethra. This area is rich in nerve endings and blood vessels, and is highly responsive to stimulation. The *Bartholin's glands* are situated on each side of the vaginal orifice. Each gland secretes a drop or so of lubricating fluid during sexual excitement. Although this fluid was once thought to aid in penile penetration, recent research has shown that the secretion is too slight to be of significant benefit in vaginal lubrication.

The individual who hopes to express his or her own sexuality wholesomely and with confidence will find support in a basic understanding of the anatomy of the sexual systems. This understanding can encourage a comfortable familiarity with one's own body as well as helping to dispel false notions about the sexual functioning of the opposite sex.

FURTHER READING

Human Sexual Response, by W. H. Masters and V. E. Johnson. Boston: Little, Brown, 1966.

> This book contains highly meaningful material related to the physiological and psychological reactions during the four phases of the human sexual response cycle. It is written for professionals and the language is likely to appear pedantic and unreasonably complex to the undergraduate student. Nonetheless, it should be studied carefully by every serious student of human sexuality.

Our Bodies, Our Selves: A Course by and for Women, by the Boston Women's Health Course Collective. Boston: New England Free Press, 1971.

> Originally developed from the experiences of a group of women in a college course on Women and Their Bodies, this group of papers deals with women's sexuality from the point of view of the radical feminist. The book advocates familiarity with and acceptance of one's own body and is

critical of the medical profession and of American culture in general for perpetuating a number of myths about women.

Anatomy and Physiology, Vol. 2, by E. B. Steen and A. Montague. New York: Barnes and Noble, 1959.

This paperback book gives a brief but accurate summary of fertilization, the development and formation of the anatomical structures of the human sexual systems, and the birth process. Chapter 7 is related to the male and female sexual systems.

The Reproductive System, by F. H. Netter. Summit, N. J.: CIBA Pharmaceutical Products, 1961.

Sections II (male) and IV (female) are related to this chapter.

Human Sexuality, 2d ed., by J. L. McCary. New York: D. Van Nostrand, 1973.

Chapters 6 and 7 are specifically related to the male and female sexual systems.

Sexual Myths and Fallacies, by J. L. McCary. New York: D. Van Nostrand, 1971.

Sexual myths and fallacies in all areas of human sexuality that plague the average person are exploded and the misinformation replaced by accurate facts. The section on Sexual Physiology and Functioning is related to this chapter.

4 SEXUAL MATURITY

The beginning and the end of a woman's reproductive capacity are marked by two major events within her body. The first of these is the *menarche,* or onset of menstruation, during puberty. The second is the *climacteric,* or *menopause,* which signals the end of menstruation later in life. In men, sexual maturity is not accompanied by such dramatic bodily occurrences. Once the changes of puberty have taken place, men do not experience "milestones" comparable to the menarche or menopause in women, although some men undergo a psychological climacteric in their mid-50s.

MENSTRUATION

Menstruation, a monthly discharge of blood and other fluids and debris from the uterine wall, begins between age 11 and 15 in most girls, and accompanies the development of their breasts and other secondary sexual characteristics. Between the menarche and the climacteric, the average woman menstruates from 300 to 500 times.

The menstrual "cycle" is measured from the onset of one menstrual flow to the day before the next flow, and varies considerably in women. While the average length is from 28 to 30 days, young women tend to have longer cycles than do older women, and young women also tend to have greater variation in the length of their cycles. Actually, the menstrual cycle can vary from 21 to 90 days and still be considered physiologically normal.

In each cycle, the menstrual flow commences when progesterone, the hormone which has prepared and maintained the
walls of the uterus for the implantation of a fertilized ovum, is
withdrawn because no egg has been fertilized. Withdrawal of
the hormone causes the lining of the uterus to break down and
slough off, as it is not needed for nourishment of a fertilized egg.

The time required for the discharge of the uterine fluids and
debris is from 3 to 7 days, and at the end of that time the uterine
wall is very thin. The amount of fluid discharged varies from
woman to woman, and sometimes from cycle to cycle in the same
woman, but the average amount is approximately one cupful.
However, the amount of actual blood loss on even the heaviest
day of menstruation is rarely more than one tablespoon.

There are a few physical and psychological signals of the beginning of the menstrual flow. Some are due to the toxic condition of the body at this time as well as to an imbalance between
progesterone and estrogen. Others are due to negative attitudes
toward sex in general and menstruation in particular. Immediately before and during her menstrual flow, the woman may
experience an increase in the size and firmness of her breasts
and in the frequency of her urination. She may also be annoyed
by abdominal distension or by skin eruptions. Fatigue, headaches, and irritability are sometimes involved. In some cases,
premenstrual congestion and swelling of certain mucous membranes cause fluid retention, which can result in a consequent
weight gain of as much as 5 pounds.

Women seem to be able to withstand and recover from
premenstrual stress according to their ability to deal with stress
in general. In this country, the majority of women report some
premenstrual changes in mood and body. There is research
evidence, in fact, indicating that women's intellectual functioning is affected by menstrual or premenstrual malaise, and that
they may score 3% to 5% lower on high school or college examinations at this time.

Because of ectopic (misplaced) endometrium tissue, there
are rare instances in which extragenital bleeding occurs just
before or during the menstrual flow in a phenomenon known as
"vicarious menstruation." Bleeding is usually from the nose
although it has also been known to occur from the lungs, the
retina of the eye, etc. This phenomenon supports scientific

observation that an indirect relationship exists between nasal functions and sexual activity. For example, the mucous membrane of the nose frequently swells during sexual excitation and may secrete more than its usual amount of mucus. In addition, oral or nasal decongestants have been found to reduce the discomfort as well as the flow of the menstrual period, and there is an interesting similarity between a sneeze and an orgasm in the physiologic buildup and explosive discharge of tensons.

Regardless of old wives' tales of the harmful effects of physical activity during menstruation, physicians agree that women

---

FIGURE 4.1 The Menstrual Cycle: (1) During the early part of the cycle, an egg matures in the ovary; the endometrium begins to thicken. (2) About 14 days after the onset of the last menstruation, a mature ovum is released; the endometrium is thick and spongy. (3) The ovum travels through the fallopian tube; the ruptured follicle becomes the corpus luteum; fluids and blood engorge the uterine lining. (4) If the ovum is not fertilized, the endometrium breaks down and sloughs off in the form of bleeding (menstruation).

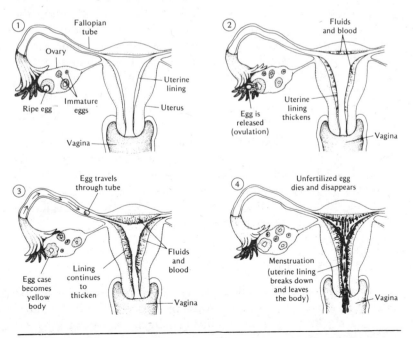

should carry on their activities as usual. Certainly, bathing and participation in sports will cause neither undue stress nor harm to the reproductive organs.

Another myth is that sexual intercourse during the menstrual flow will cause physical distress. To the contrary, research has clearly indicated that sexual activity may provide relief from pain or discomfort connected with menstruation. Women who have experienced orgasm shortly after the onset of menstruation have reported reduced pelvic cramping and backache, possibly due to the sudden expulsion of menstrual fluid by orgasmic contractions of the uterine muscles.

Studies indicate wide variations in the effect of the menstrual cycle on women's sex drive. Some women experience the peak of their sexual desire just before menstruation. Others experience it just after the flow begins or midway in the menstrual cycle.

Ovulation

After the menstrual flow stops, the secretion of estrogen gradually increases, and a new *follicle* (the sac containing the developing egg) in the ovary begins to mature. (Although many follicles contain developing ova, usually only one ovum reaches maturity during a single menstrual cycle.) The follicle ruptures, discharging the mature ovum on about the fourteenth day of the cycle. This discharge of the ovum, known as *ovulation,* occurs when the concentration of estrogen in the blood is greatest.

Following ovulation, the hormone progesterone is secreted, and the preparation of the uterus for a fertilized egg begins again. If fertilization does not occur, the concentration of both estrogen and progesterone decreases sharply, leading to the breaking down of the tissue lining the uterus and the beginning of another menstrual cycle.

THE CLIMACTERIC

When the woman is about 45 or 50 years of age, ovulation begins to taper off, usually stopping altogether within about two years. The time interval during which the woman's ovulation and menstrual cycles gradually cease to exist is known as the *climacteric* or *menopause*. Ovulation and the menstrual flow are erratic at this time, sometimes causing the woman to believe that there is no longer a possibility of pregnancy. So long as any menstrual periods occur at all, however, the possibility of pregnancy remains. The woman cannot be reasonably sure that ovulation has ceased completely until she has gone a year without a menstrual period.

While reports of childbirth by women over age 50 are publicized occasionally by the news media, there have been in the last 100 years fewer than 30 authenticated cases of women past the age of 50 giving birth.

Although the menopause is surrounded by myths and fears of distressing side effects, hormonal therapy and other medication can prevent or alleviate most if not all of the unpleasant reactions that sometimes accompany this "change of life." Only about 25% of all menopausal women experience any sort of distressing symptoms. On the whole, the better the emotional health of the woman before her climacteric, the fewer unpleasant symptoms she will have when it occurs.

Probably the most well known symptom of the menopause is the "hot flashes" that occur because of a fluctuation in the diameter of the blood vessels. The fluctuation is due to a glandular imbalance that accompanies the climacteric, causing more blood to flow at one time than at another. It is when the greater amount of blood flows that the flashes occur, lasting from a second to several minutes. Interestingly enough, the more hot flashes a woman experiences during menopause, the less likely she is to have other annoying symptoms.

The median age for the onset of menopause has advanced in the last hundred years from 46.6 to 50.1 years. Those who start menstruating earlier in life tend to continue to menstruate longer. Similar patterns occur in other spheres of sexual life: people who begin erotic activity at an earlier age tend to maintain their sexual vigor longer, for example, and those who engage in frequent sexual activity tend to continue sexual activity later in life than those whose activity is less frequent.

The Climacteric in Men

Though sperm production does not cease in men as ovulation does in women, men do undergo certain physical changes as they age. Some men undergo a psychological climacteric at about age 55 which results in a reduction of sexual vigor and interest. This reduction is usually due to the man's negative reactions to observed changes in his orgasmic responses or his general physical endurance. Physical changes that occur with aging include a slackening of sperm production and a slight shriveling of the testes, which become less firm. The prostate gland enlarges, and the ejaculatory fluid becomes thinner and less copious. Orgasmic capacity decreases, and some men feel that a loss of their ability to have several orgasms in a short time period means that they are "over the hill" sexually. As a result, they may begin to take less interest in sexual activity.

THE SEX DRIVE IN MEN AND WOMEN

Although a man's sex drive peaks in young manhood and steadily (though only gradually) declines thereafter, sexual activity need not cease during the later years. In fact, in studies of sexually active men over 75, most reported that they engaged in sexual intercourse on an average of four times a month.

A woman's sex drive, on the other hand, is slower to peak but remains at peak level for a longer period than a man's. A woman's sex drive peaks in her 30s and remains at that level until she is in her 60s or even older. The disparity between the peak levels of sex drive in men and women may account for some of the frustration that a couple may encounter as they grow older. The fact that in our culture it is often assumed that the woman of a couple should be younger than the man may further complicate the search of both men and women for sexual realization.

It is difficult to determine how much of the reported variation in the sex drives of men and women is the result of physiological differences and how much is due to cultural conditioning. Clearly, the expectation in some parts of our society that men are more sexually active than women influences both sexes. As we have seen, a woman's physiological reactions to menstruation or to the climacteric may be influenced by her psychological expectations about these changes in her body. In the same way, the strength of a man's sex drive in later life may be related to his feelings about what is appropriate or possible sexual expression for an older man. A more complete consideration of the relationships between cultural attitudes and individual sexual behavior will be found in Chapters 7 and 13.

FURTHER READING

Sexual Behavior in the Human Female, by A. C. Kinsey, W. B. Pomeroy, C. E. Martin, and P. H. Gebhard. Philadelphia: W. B. Saunders, 1953.

> This book is the summary of the Kinsey research into the sexual behavior of the American human female. Chapters 4, 15, and 18 are particularly related to sexual maturation.

The Reproductive System, by F. H. Netter. Summit, N. J.: CIBA Pharmaceutical Products, 1961.

> Section VI contains material on the process of sexual maturation.

Human Sexuality, 2d ed., by J. L. McCary, New York: D. Van Nostrand, 1973.

> Chapter 8 discusses the menarche, menstruation, and the climacteric.

Sexual Myths and Fallacies, by J. L. McCary. New York: D. Van Nostrand, 1971.

> The section on Sexual Physiology and Function is meaningful in the context of this chapter.

5 THE CREATION
OF NEW LIFE

At the moment of *conception*, when a sperm penetrates an ovum, one of the oldest and most profound of all miracles occurs—the beginning of a new human life. These two microscopic cells carry the basic units of heredity, the *genes*, which hold a complex and detailed design for building all of the parts of the human body. An equal number of genes from the father and the mother are combined in the union of the sperm and the ovum, so that the new person is a unique combination of his parents. Thus is the fundamental material of life passed on from one generation to the next.

THE GENETICS OF CONCEPTION

The *cell* is the basic unit of all life. Within the nucleus of the human cell are 46 *chromosomes*, arranged in 23 pairs, which contain the genes. (The word "chromosome" comes from the Latin words "chromo," meaning color, and "soma," meaning body. The structures are so named because they become visible if put in special dyes.) The human body has millions of different kinds of cells, all of which develop from a single cell (the combined sperm and ovum) by a process of cell division called *mitosis* in which a single cell divides into two new cells, each with a full set of 46 chromosomes. These two cells divide into four, and so on. This same cell division process is also responsible for body growth and repair.

There are two kinds of cells in the human body: germ cells

(*gametes*) and somatic cells. The gametes function to reproduce the organism; all other body cells are somatic.

The gametes begin their development with a full component of 46 chromosomes. However, when they are fully developed, each gamete (either a mature ovum or a mature sperm) contains only 23 chromosomes. Of these, 22 are single, nonsex chromosomes (*autosomes*). Each autosome has a different genetic content and is usually different in appearance from the others. The twenty-third chromosome is either an X or a Y *sex chromosome*, and is the one which determines the sex of the new individual.

When a mature sperm fertilizes a mature ovum, each parent contributes 23 chromosomes to the genetic makeup of the new individual: 22 autosomes and 1 sex chromosome. All normal, mature ova contain one X chromosome. Normal, mature sperm cointain either an X (female-producing) or a Y (male-producing)

FIGURE 5.1 Microscopic view of sperm, showing the difference between X–bearing sperm (with larger, oval–shaped head) and Y–bearing sperm (with smaller head, longer tail). Photograph courtesy of Dr. Landrum B. Shettles.

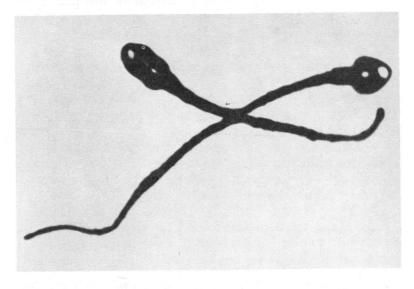

chromosome, and sperm containing X-bearing and Y-bearing chromosomes are produced in precisely equal numbers. Should the ovum be fertilized by an X-bearing sperm, an XX (female) child is conceived. Should the ovum be fertilized by a Y-bearing sperm, an XY (male) child is conceived. Thus it is that the genetic characteristics of the newly conceived individual are equally given by his two parents, and the sex of the individual is determined by the kind of sperm which fertilizes the egg.

When an ovum is penetrated by a sperm, an immediate change occurs in the egg which prevents other sperm from penetrating it. The gene-carrying portions of the nuclei of the sperm and ovum join, resulting in a fertilized egg that contains the full component of 46 chromosomes common to all human cells.

FIGURE 5.2 Ovulation, fertilization, and implantation.

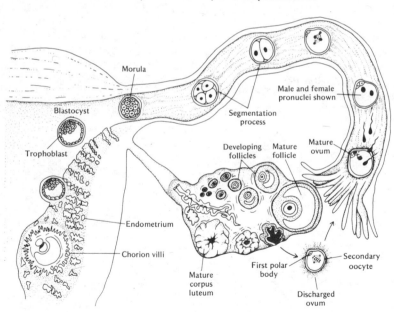

Factors That Affect Fertility

The age of the woman has a significant bearing on her ability to conceive. Generally speaking, the younger the mature woman, the higher her rate of fertility, with fertility progressively decreasing from the early 20s onward. No such age differences appear to exist in the fertility rates of men.

There are many reasons why a couple are, or seem to be, unable to conceive a child. The cause lies with the husband in more cases than are usually acknowledged, perhaps because many men find the fact that they might be responsible for the couple's barrenness to be a reflection on their manhood. In studies of married couples who are unable to conceive, the responsibility lies solely with the husband in 30% of the cases, and he is an important contributor to the problem in another 20%.

Often the difficulty is caused by a low sperm count. A sperm count of less than 200 million per ejaculate is considered to be too small for impregnation. A man's sperm count, however, in no way affects his erectile or ejaculatory capacities or his ability to have frequent and pleasurable sexual intercourse. Either too much or too little sexual activity can lower a man's sperm count. Generally speaking, the optimum sperm count is achieved when there is an interval of about 48 hours between ejaculations.

PRENATAL DEVELOPMENT

The fertilized ovum is called a *conceptus* from the moment of fertilization (conception) until its delivery as the infant we know at birth. In addition to this generic term, three general stages of conceptus development are differentiated: it is first a zygote, then an embryo, and finally a fetus.

From the time of fertilization until the second week, the developing cell mass is referred to as a *zygote*. The zygote undergoes mitotic cell division, forming a spherical cell mass, which moves through the uterine tubes into the uterus. This cell mass forms three internal cellular layers: the *ectoderm*, or outermost layer; the *mesoderm*, or middle layer; and the *endoderm*, or innermost layer. These three layers constitute the *embryonic disc*, from which the embryo develops.

From the second to the eighth week, the developing conceptus is referred to as an *embryo*. It implants itself in the wall of the uterus; and the ectoderm, mesoderm, and endoderm become differentiated. The nervous system, sense organs, mouth cavity, and skin eventually come from the ectoderm; the muscular, skeletal, circulatory, excretory, and sexual systems develop from the mesoderm; and the digestive and respiratory systems come from the endoderm.

After the eighth week, the developing conceptus is referred to as a *fetus*. At this time, the rudimentary systems of the body have all appeared and initial development has begun. The fetal stage consists of further growth and elaboration of the existing rudimentary systems. From approximately one inch in length and one-thirtieth of an ounce in weight, the fetus develops until birth, when the average infant is 20 inches in length and 7 pounds in weight.

Before the body of the embryo has taken a definite shape, the *amnion,* a thin, transparent, tough membrane, forms. Within its hollow cavity is a clear watery fluid called the *amniotic fluid.* The amniotic fluid equalizes the pressure around the embryo, preventing jolts and injuries, and also prevents the embryo from

FIGURE 5.3 Schematic representation of an implanted embryo.

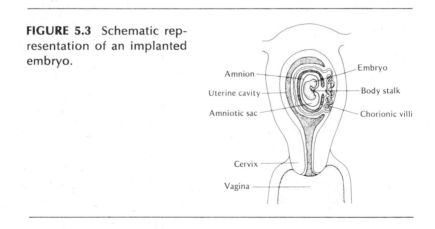

Amnion

Uterine cavity

Amniotic sac

Embryo

Body stalk

Chorionic villi

Cervix

Vagina

forming adhesions to the amnion. In addition, it allows for changes in position of the developing conceptus and facilitates childbirth by helping to dilate the neck of the uterus. The fetus usually begins to swallow some of the amniotic fluid at about the fifth month of pregnancy, and his first bowel movements are a discharge of this liquid. At birth, the baby's respiratory passages may have to be cleared of some of the fluid in order for normal respiration to begin.

An organ of interchange between the conceptus and the mother is the *placenta,* comprised of uterine tissue and interwoven villi. The *villi* (fingerlike protrusions that enter the maternal tissue) of the placenta are kept steeped in fresh maternal blood, which enters the placental spaces about the villi by means of small blood vessels. As the blood drains back into the veins of the uterus, it is replaced by fresh blood from the uterine arteries.

At no time during any stage of normal pregnancy do maternal and fetal blood intermingle. Both the maternal and fetal blood circulate within the placenta, but they are kept separated by the walls of the umbilical blood vessels. The interchange between the two systems, which is by diffusion and absorption, provides for the nourishment of the fetus and for elimination of fetal waste products.

The fetal blood absorbs food and oxygen and eliminates carbon dioxide and other metabolic waste products. These are taken into the mother's blood and expelled along with her own waste. Although the cellular barrier between the two blood systems generally prevents the passage of bacteria and other disease germs, some substances, such as antibiotics and certain viruses and disease germs, are capable of crossing the barrier. During the fifth week of pregnancy, the *umbilical cord* is formed, by which the embryo is suspended in the amniotic fluid. The fully developed cord is about 20 inches long.

The expected birth date of a child can be estimated by adding 280 days to the date on which the mother's last menstruation started. To be more precise, one would have to know the exact date of conception. The period of *gestation* (pregnancy) varies among women and according to the sex of the child. Women who engage in strenuous physical exercise usually have their babies 20 days earlier than less athletic women, and brunette women deliver slightly sooner than blondes. Furthermore, girls are often born from 5 to 9 days earlier than boys. Although about 3% of pregnancies last 300 days or more, placental withering may occur after an overlong gestation, increasing the possibility of infant death. Most obstetricians induce labor if they suspect placental shrinkage when the pregnancy is prolonged.

FIGURE 5.4 Human embryos aged 25 days to 4 months. Actual size. From Arey. *Developmental Anatomy*, 3rd ed. Philadelphia: W.B. Saunders Co., 1934.

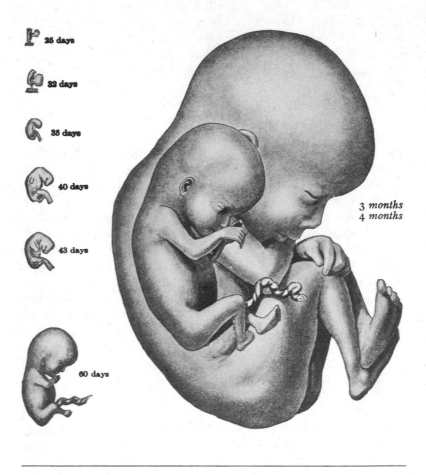

25 days

32 days

35 days

40 days

43 days

3 *months*
4 *months*

60 days

There is an old wives' tale that a 7-month fetus has a better chance of survival than an 8-month fetus does. The myth is untrue and probably stems from the fact that most allegedly 7-month infants are in reality full-term. ("7-month babies" are frequently born in marriages which have been arranged after the woman learns that she is pregnant. The time necessary to discover the pregnancy and to arrange for a wedding is usually about 2 months.) The truth is that the closer the birth of the fetus is to the normal 9-month delivery date, the better its chance of survival.

Pregnancy: The Expectant Parents' Point of View

Surely one of the most dramatic and important changes in the relationship of any couple occurs when their first child is born. Yet the child's conception cannot be perceived when it occurs, and pregnancy may not be suspected for several weeks—or even months—after conception.

When a woman becomes pregnant, the first signs she notices are a cessation of menstruation; nausea, which often occurs on rising in the morning and is called "morning sickness"; changes in the size and fullness of the breasts; dark coloration of the areolae (the brown pigmented area) around the nipples; fatigue; and frequency of urination.

More objective indications of pregnancy are discernible by pelvic examination by a physician and include an increase in the size of the uterus and a considerable softening of the cervix. By the third month, the distended uterus can be felt through the abdominal wall and the abdomen is enlarged. By this time, too, there are slight, intermittent contractions of the uterus.

Signs which positively confirm pregnancy are fetal heartbeats, active fetal movements, and X-ray detection of the fetal skeleton.

Most women are not willing to wait for confirming signs of pregnancy and depend instead on their physician or a laboratory technician to determine their pregnancy. Endocrine tests can give accurate proof of pregnancy approximately 3 weeks after implantation of the fertilized ovum, which is about 6 weeks after the last menstrual period. In the *agglutination test,* a sample of the woman's urine is mixed with certain chemicals. A hormone found in the urine of pregnant women will prevent agglutination or clotting; if agglutination occurs, she is not pregnant. Depending on the pharmaceutical house that prepared the testing apparatus, test results can be determined in from 3 minutes to 2 hours. When performed at least 2 weeks after a menstrual period is missed, the test has about 97% accuracy and has become the most popular pregnancy test used by laboratory technicians.

Another test for pregnancy is the oral administration of the hormone progesterone. The heightened progesterone level will cause menstruation to begin within 4 or 5 days if the woman is not pregnant. If menstruation does not begin, she is assumed to be pregnant.

Despite the myths about the dangers of physical activity during pregnancy, moderate and sensible exercise is not dangerous for the healthy woman, and is often beneficial. Women are frequently warned against traveling while pregnant. During recent wars, however, pregnant women traveled for hundreds of

---

FIGURE 5.5   Lateral representation of the fetus in the mother's pelvis.

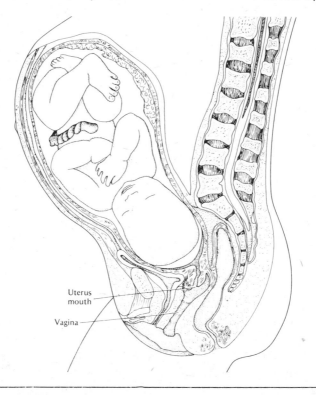

Uterus mouth

Vagina

miles by all modes of transportation, much of it uncomfortable, in order to be with their husbands. Interestingly enough, they had a lower miscarriage rate than those women who stayed home.

Sexual intercourse is also encouraged during pregnancy until the final few weeks. After this time, sexual relief through non-coital means such as mutual masturbation is now recognized as valuable to both the husband and wife as well as to the marriage itself.

BIRTH

The process of childbirth, or *parturition,* takes place in three stages. The first stage begins when contractions of the uterus commence, usually at 15- to 20-minute intervals. Initially, each contraction lasts about 30 seconds, and they increase steadily in frequency, intensity, and duration until they finally occur every 3 to 4 minutes, at which time the fetus is well on its way. Toward the end of labor, each contraction lasts a minute or more. During the first stage, the cervix dilates from its normal size of about one-eighth inch to approximately 4 inches. Full dilation of the cervix marks the beginning of the second stage of parturition.

Two other events that occur during the first stage are the expulsion of the mucous plug from the base of the uterus, and the rupture of the amniotic membrane with a resulting flow of clear, waterlike fluid from the vagina. Both of these signs of imminent delivery, together with the increased strength and duration of uterine contractions, are indications that the time to notify the obstetrician has arrived.

The second phase of parturition extends from the time the cervix is completely dilated until the fetus is expelled. When the infant's head emerges from the vagina, it turns spontaneously either to the right or left, depending upon the way the shoulders are turned. After expulsion of the head and shoulders, delivery of the rest of the infant is a simple matter because the trunk and limbs are quite small in comparison with the head and shoulders.

Over 99% of all infants are born in a *longitudinal* position (with the body trunk presented vertically), usually with their

FIGURE 5.6 Principal movements in the procedure of labor and delivery.

1. Head floating, before engagement

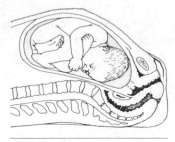

2. Engagement, flexion, descent

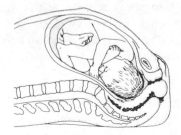

3. Further descent, internal rotation

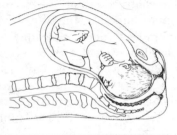

4. Complete rotation, beginning extension

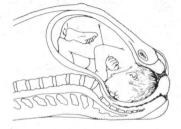

5. Complete extension

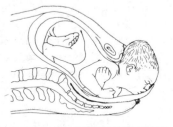

6. Restitution, (external rotation)

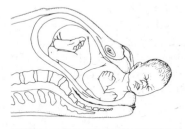

7. Delivery of anterior shoulder

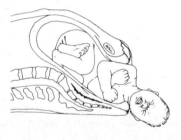

8. Delivery of posterior shoulder

heads first. Because of the great pressure exerted on a baby during delivery, his head may be oddly molded in the birth process, or his facial features may be bruised and swollen. While this may be distressing to the new parents, the irregularities correct themselves within a few days and there is rarely permanent damage.

In 4% of longitudinal births, the buttocks are presented first (the so-called *breech* birth), resulting in temporary swelling and discoloration of the infant's buttocks and genital area. Almost 50% of infants assume the breech presentation prior to the seventh month of fetal life, then make a 180° turn before the ninth month. A fetus that does not make the turn can often by manipulated by the obstetrician into the head-first position during the later stages of pregnancy.

Once in every 200 births, the fetus lies crosswise with a shoulder, arm, or hand entering the birth canal first. In these cases either the fetus must be turned during labor or a *caesarean section*, in which the child is delivered through a surgical incision in the abdominal and uterine walls, must be performed.

About 15 minutes after the baby's birth, the placenta is delivered, marking the third stage of parturition. Muscular contractions shrink the uterus and the area of placental attachment, detaching the placenta from the uterine wall and expelling it into the vagina. The obstetrician sometimes presses the uterus downward to facilitate expulsion.

Now that the infant is breathing oxygen from the outside world, he no longer needs the placenta or the umbilical cord. Once the cord stops pulsating and the baby is breathing regularly, the cord is clamped and cut about three inches from the infant's abdomen. The clamp is left in place until the stub dries up and drops off.

If the birth has been uncomplicated, the new mother and her infant usually leave the hospital within four days after the delivery. The birth of a child is traditionally the cause of celebration for the new parents and their families; however, the first few weeks at home can be difficult for the mother. She must deal simultaneously with the many needs of her infant, who is totally dependent, and also with her own feelings about the changes in her life which the child creates.

Many women experience feelings of sadness and periods of

crying sometime during the first 10 days after delivery. These "postpartum blues" are attributed partly to psychological factors and partly to the drastic hormonal changes which occur at this time.

Lactation

Lactation is the process of milk secretion from the mother's breasts following childbirth. The placenta not only provides for the development of the fetus; but it also produces hormones that prepare the mammary glands in the breasts for secretion of milk. During pregnancy, these same hormones inhibit the pituitary gland from producing the milk-forming chemical until such time as it is needed.

After the placenta has been expelled in the last stages of childbirth, its inhibiting hormones are no longer produced, and the mother's pituitary gland begins to produce *prolactin,* the hormone that induces lactation. The first secretion the baby receives from the breast is *colostrum,* a substance present in the breast immediately after birth. Colostrum is of high protein content and is believed to aid in giving the infant immunity to many infectious diseases during the early months of life. True milk replaces colostrum within two or three days after delivery.

The infant's sucking prompts contractions in the mother's uterus that help reduce it to its normal size. Breast-feeding also provides certain psychological satisfactions to the mother and can lead to a greater feeling of closeness to the baby. Other advantages of breast-feeding are that the milk is free, always at the right temperature, and always immediately available.

The tenderness and discomfort of the nipples that frequently occur in the first few days of breast-feeding can be avoided if the expectant mother will prepare her nipples prior to parturition. At about the seventh month of pregnancy, she should begin toughening her nipples by gently washing them with a very soft-bristled brush and then massaging bath oil or baby oil into them. By the time of her baby's birth, her nipples will be sufficiently pliable so that the sucking motion of the baby will not cause any discomfort. Women who desire information about breast-feeding should contact their local La Leche League. This organization provides both factual information and emotional support.

Although breast-feeding prolongs the absence of menstruation following childbirth, it is possible for a woman to ovulate before her first postpartum (after birth) menstrual flow. About 1 woman in 20 becomes pregnant again without having menstruated after childbirth.

As many as 90% of all babies were breast-fed in the not too distant past, but the practice has declined. There are indications, however, that young mothers of today are turning again to the practice of breast-feeding in larger numbers.

NATURAL CHILDBIRTH

There is a growing trend among expectant parents to want to share the experiences of pregnancy and childbirth more actively. New approaches to childbirth education have been developed in recent years which seek to increase the understanding and involvement of both the husband and the wife. Termed "natural childbirth" by its originator, Dr. Grantly Dick-Read, this training is now also called "prepared," "controlled," or "cooperative" childbirth.

Several methods of preparation for childbirth, ranging from physical training to hypnosis, are now prevalent. The approach most favored in this country is the psychophysical one, typified by the Lamaze method, which originated in Russia and was introduced to the Western world in 1951 by Dr. Fernand Lamaze.

Advocates of natural childbirth feel that childbirth should be a rewarding experience for both parents. Consequently they are critical of the routine use of heavy sedation during labor and delivery, since a heavily sedated woman is hardly aware of what is happening and cannot participate actively. Although none of the approaches insists on a woman's doing without light medication during labor or without some form of anesthesia during the actual birth if she wishes it, these approaches also encourage parents to consider the possible ill effects of anesthetic drugs on the newborn. They criticize depersonalized obstetrical care and the arbitrary separation of mother, father, and baby practiced in many hospitals. Those who believe in natural childbirth also favor the presence of the husband in the labor room and in the delivery room; "rooming-in" privileges, in which the mother and her baby are in the same room during their hospital stay; and breast-feeding.

In the Lamaze method, classes are held in which both the expectant mother and the father are given detailed accounts of what they may expect during pregnancy, labor, and delivery. Training in muscle-control exercises and breathing techniques to be used during labor is provided, and the husband is taught how to assist his wife in her practice sessions at home and during her confinement. The primary goal is to help the woman participate actively in the birth of her baby with the support of her husband and a minimum of fear and pain.

MYTHS ABOUT CONCEPTION AND CHILDBIRTH

Myths and folklore concerning fertility, conception, pregnancy and childbirth abound in every society. In our own, one of the most persistent and somewhat comforting myths is that nature compensates for the men lost during wars by increasing, in some mystical way, the ratio of male to female births. The fact that there was an increase in male births following World Wars I and II has lent surface validity to this myth.

At any time, it is a fact that more males than females are conceived, but the female survival ratio is higher than that of the male. The conception ratio is about 160 males to 100 females; but the birth ratio is 105 males to 100 females. This fact, plus the fact that the health of the mother affects the success of a pregnancy, suggests an explanation for the increase in male births after wars. People tend to marry at younger ages during wartime, and young healthy mothers provide fertilized ova the best chance for survival and implantation. The higher rate of ova survival leads to a higher percentage of males born to these younger mothers. Furthermore, spacing between births is longer than usual during wartime due to the enforced separation that wartime causes. This longer spacing leaves the mothers in stronger physical condition to carry the next child to term, thereby increasing the likelihood of a male birth. By this reasoning, more male zygotes are implanted in the uterus during and immediately after wartime, and fewer male embryos die, producing a greater male to female ratio of births.

Another widespread myth concerning pregnancy is that an unborn fetus can be "marked" by some experience of the mother. This notion, of course, is completely false since there is no direct connection between the nervous systems or blood systems of mother and fetus. What usually happens is that when a child is born with an unusual birthmark, the parents attempt to explain the mark by "remembering" some incident during the mother's pregnancy when she was in some way unsettled by something bearing that general shape.

Unfortunately, some scientists have contributed to the "marking" myth, either out of ignorance or because they enjoyed the public's fascination with this dramatic theory. In 1836, for example, an American medical journal published a report signed by eight physicians who described a man with a face like a snake. The physicians claimed that his condition existed because his mother had been frightened by a rattlesnake during her sixth month of pregnancy. The report even stated that the man had the ability to coil and uncoil his arm in a snakelike fashion!

Even scientists of the stature of the great Charles Darwin have believed and written about *telegony*, which is another myth having to do with conception and pregnancy. According to this theory, children sired by one man may bear characteristics of a man with whom their mother had intercourse at some previous time in her life. Belief in this fallacy sometimes leads to the conclusion that the offspring of a second husband are affected by the wife's first husband. Obviously, it is a genetic impossibility that there could be any relationship between a previous husband and children born to a second marriage.

The theory of telegony is rather widely accepted among animal breeders, probably because of spurious evidence provided by female dogs. Bitches remain in heat for several days, during which time they may mate with several males. It is quite possible for a female dog to have a litter of puppies which have been sired by more than one male and which consequently are not similar in size or markings. There is in this instance no "carry-over" from the bitch's previous matings; it is simply that the puppies of the same litter have been sired by different dogs.

Another myth which has been prevalent for centuries is that human beings and lower animals can interbreed. This myth finds expression in Greek and Roman mythology, where creatures which are part human and part animal (such as centaurs, sphinxes, mermaids, and satyrs) abound. The truth is that it is not only impossible for humans to crossbread with infrahuman (lower than human) animals, but interbreeding among the various genera of lower animals is equally impossible. Two species of the *same* genus, such as two members of different species in the cat family, may crossbreed, however, producing offspring such as the much-publicized and recently defunct "liger," a cross between a lion and a tiger.

There are three interesting phenomena concerning pregnancy that are rare but known to actually occur. One of these is *pseudocyesis*, or false pregnancy. This occurs in both animals and humans, and the symptoms are remarkably similar to those of true pregnancy. In some cases a woman will actually go into labor to deliver only an accumulation of air and fluids. This condition is due to a strong desire on the part of the woman to have a child, and psychotherapy is sometimes required to dispel the notion that she is indeed pregnant.

A second, and somewhat related, phenomenon is the practice in primitive cultures of *couvade*, wherein the husband experiences labor in much the same manner as his wife. In our own society the husband sometimes shows symptoms related to his wife's pregnancy. The expectant father may become nauseated, vomit, and suffer abdominal pains, all such symptoms disappearing after his wife has delivered their infant.

The third phenomenon, *parthenogenesis* or "virgin birth," is known to exist in animals, and is the sole method of reproduction among certain insects. In parthenogenesis, a female egg is "fertilized" without contact with a spermatozoon. Animal experiments have indicated that various stimuli may induce development just as if the egg had been fertilized in the usual manner. For example, cooling the fallopian tubes of rabbits, heating the eggs of certain moths, and even applying saliva of human males to carp eggs have sufficiently stimulated the eggs to prompt their development.

There is considerable disagreement among researchers as to whether the phenomenon of parthenogenesis is possible in human beings. If parthenogenesis were to occur in humans, the offspring would be invariably female because of the way chromosomes are arranged in men and women. Since women have only one type of sex-determining chromosome (X), only the X chromosome could be passed on. Furthermore, a child born of partheongenesis would inevitably be a replication of her mother, since her heredity would be based solely on the mother's genes.

The phrase "virgin birth" usually denotes a human pregnancy and subsequent birth without union of ovum and sperm. In this context, the possibility of a true virgin birth has never been scientifically established. However, "virgin birth" also suggests pregnancy and subsequent birth without sexual intercourse, the connotation being that the woman who delivers as a virgin is more "pure" than ordinary mothers. It is possible for a woman to become pregnant without experiencing sexual intercourse. Sperm make their way toward ova with complete disregard for the manner in which they are deposited in the vagina, and an ovum which is fertilized without intercourse develops in the same manner as an ovum fertilized as a result of coitus.

Presence or absence of a hymen is incidental in such cases, since an intact hymen does not prevent migration of sperm to the uterus any more than it prevents the menstrual flow from the uterus. During sex play, for example, a man may have his penis near or on a woman's vulva. If he ejaculates, semen can enter the vaginal opening and make its way through the vagina into the uterus. Sperm can also be introduced into the vaginal canal by way of manual manipulation of the woman's genitals after a man's hands have come into contact with his ejaculate. This is a particular possibility if he should insert a semen-covered finger into the vagina. If pregnancy were to result in either of these instances, the subsequent childbirth might accurately be called a "virgin birth." It can certainly be recognized that a virgin woman may become pregnant through artificial insemination. Since no penis enters her vagina, the resulting conception and delivery could be classified as a "virgin birth."

FURTHER READING

Childbirth Without Fear: The Principles and Practice of Natural Childbirth, by G. Dick-Read. New York: Harper & Row, 1970.

This paperback book by one of the pioneers in new approaches to childbirth explains both the philosophy and the techniques of natural childbirth.

Our Bodies, Our Selves: A Course by and for Women, by the Boston Women's Health Course Collective. Boston: New England Free Press, 1971.

The sections on pregnancy, delivery, and natural childbirth include personal descriptions of the experiences of women with both positive and negative emotions expressed.

Anatomy and Physiology, Vol. 2, by E. B. Steen and A. Montague. New York: Barnes and Noble, 1959.

Chapter 8 contains material on fertilization, prenatal development, and birth.

Human Sexuality, 2d ed., by J. L. McCary. New York: D. Van Nostrand, 1973.

Chapter 9 contains an abundance of material which is related to the creation of life.

Sexual Myths and Fallacies, by J. L. McCary. New York: D. Van Nostrand, 1971.

The section on Reproduction and Birth Control explodes many myths and fallacies pertaining to conception, pregnancy, and other aspects of new life.

6 BIRTH CONTROL

Today, more than at any previous time in recorded history, people around the world are interested in means of controlling birth. From a global standpoint, birth control is essential in order to keep the world's population at a level which can be sustained by the earth's resources. Some unthinking individuals insist that the world has vast untapped territory and natural resources. However, most experts who have studied the problem extensively maintain that in order to have a population that can be adequately fed and housed and that is psychologically healthy, every couple should limit the number of children they produce to two.

In terms of individual emotional well-being, the matter of population control becomes much more than an academic exercise or public debate over the world's resources; it becomes a personal matter of critical importance. A conservative estimate is that in the United States alone there are over 1 million unwanted children born every year. These children grow up with emotional difficulties which are directly related to the fact of their being unwanted, regardless of how conscientiously the parents may try to disguise their feelings. These difficulties, of course, are then passed to the next generation, and the problem perpetuates itself indefinitely. Many of the emotional ills that plague our population would be eliminated if every child born were truly wanted.

In addition to the need to insure that every child born is a wanted child, there is often a need to postpone a first pregnancy and to control the spacing of subsequent pregnancies. Young married couples need time to adjust to each other and to marriage before they add the complicating presence of a baby. In addition, most young couples require some time before they become completely sexually compatible. The fear of pregnancy can interfere with both sexual and marital adjustment. Adequate birth-control measures are important to a newly married couple's feeling of being in control of their own lives.

Couples who have reached the stage in their marriage when they feel that they are physically, emotionally, and financially capable of providing a loving home for children need to space the births of the children they decide to have. Adequate spacing will insure that the mother does not become physically debilitated from too-frequent pregnancies and also will increase her chances of producing healthy babies.

In some cases, there is a need to prevent the perpetuation of inherited diseases, and a couple may elect to adopt the children they want rather than risk inflicting a natural child with a problem such as Huntington's chorea (a genetically carried disease characterized by irregular movements, disturbance of speech, and gradually increasing loss of intellectual facility). In other cases, a chronic illness, such as heart disease, may make it inadvisable for a woman to become pregnant.

For all these reasons, birth control is of vital importance for married couples. The decision they make regarding the number, spacing, and timing of pregnancies affects not only their immediate family circle but their community and, eventually, the world.

Married couples, however, are not the only people who are concerned with birth control. The increasing number of unwanted illegitimate births in our society indicates that there are large numbers of sexually active women who are not taking measures to prevent unwanted pregnancies. The personal distress and numerous sociological problems created by an unwanted nonmarital pregnancy could be avoided if adequate birth-control measures were taken.

Although birth control and contraception are often discussed as if they were synonymous, they are not. *Contraception* is any means or device that prevents conception when two fertile partners have sexual intercourse. As such, contraception is only one of several means of birth control. Other methods of birth control are abstinence, sterilization, and abortion.

ABSTINENCE

Abstinence—the self-denial of sexual gratification—is still the most socially acceptable form of birth control for the unmarried. Studies into the effect of abstinence on future marital sexual adjustment show conflicting results. Some studies indicate that there are advantages to one or both partners' having had some sexual experience, while other studies show no such advantage.

Within marriage, there are sometimes sensible reasons for temporary abstinence, as during an illness, during late pregnancy, or immediately after childbirth. In these cases, other sexual outlets may be enjoyed, such as mutual oral or manual stimulation.

When abstinence is regularly practiced as a means of birth control and not because of temporary physical conditions, the practice is contrary to normal sexual urges. Any such practice should, of course, be a mutual decision of the partners involved and not merely the decision of one spouse who neglects to take the needs of the other into consideration.

It should be pointed out that while it is possible to abstain from sexual *activity,* it is not possible to abstain from biological sexual *urges.* Whether abstinence is a voluntary or an involuntary condition, normal sexual urges will find outlets in both men and women. Dreaming to orgasm is one example of an involuntary method of obtaining sexual relief.

STERILIZATION

Sterilization is a procedure, usually surgical, that renders a person incapable of reproduction. It may be sought by men and women who wish to end permanently any possibility of their having more children. There are also cases in which other factors are involved.

Eugenic sterilization, for example, is performed as a means of protecting the physical or mental well-being of the next generation. Sterilization in these cases is usually involuntary, and may be performed on the habitual criminal, the moral pervert, or a person with an inheritable mental disease or deficiency. Sterilization is of value in some cases involving inheritable diseases, but forced sterilization of the habitual criminal or so-called moral pervert is virtually uncalled for because there is little scientific evidence that heredity plays any part in criminal or other amoral acts.

Therapeutic sterilization is sometimes performed when either the husband or the wife suffers from certain chronic diseases or disabilities, or when certain irreversible blood incompatibilities exist.

• Methods of Sterilization in Women

Tubal ligation is a major surgical procedure in which the fallopian tubes are cut, a small section of the tube is removed, and the ends are tied to prevent them from meeting. The sperm and the ova are thus kept from coming into contact. The operation takes about 15 minutes to perform but requires a 5-day hospitalization, and it takes about 3 or 4 weeks for the woman to regain preoperative physical strength. Surgeons' fees vary, but they average about $300. Successful reversal of a tubal ligation (in which another surgical procedure rejoins the tubes) is highly questionable.

Laparoscopic sterilization, or *laparascopy,* has recently captured considerable attention in this country. Performed under general anesthesia, this operation involves two small incisions, which are made in a woman's abdomen. The fallopian tubes are severed, and the ends are cauterized (sealed) by an electrical instrument. Only Band-Aids are needed to cover the incisions, causing the procedure to be called the "Band-Aid operation," and the patient need remain in the hospital only until she is fully awake. The procedure is inexpensive and leaves no unsightly scars. Of the operations performed in this country, only 1 fallopian tube in 1000 has spontaneously rejoined.

Oophorectomy, the surgical removal of the ovaries, brings the process of ovulation permanently to a halt. *Hysterectomy,* the surgical removal of the uterus, may or may not include the removal of the uterine tubes and the ovaries. *Salpingectomy* is the surgical removal of the fallopian tubes. While these last three procedures result in permanent sterility, they are usually performed for the purpose of correcting certain abnormalities rather than for sterilization alone.

FIGURE 6.1 Schematic representation of the female reproductive system, showing the effects of a tubal ligation. Note that in sterilization, the surgical procedure is followed on both sides of the body.

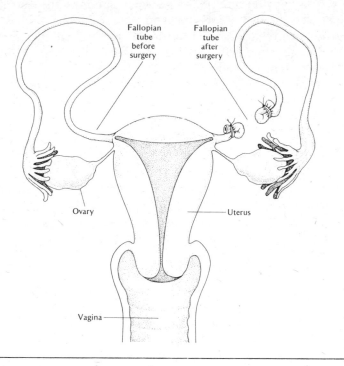

Fallopian tube before surgery

Fallopian tube after surgery

Ovary

Uterus

Vagina

A form of *reversible sterilization* has very recently been developed which appears to be safe and effective, with minimal complications. In a minor surgical procedure, small clips are placed around the fallopian tubes, sealing them closed and blocking the union of sperm and egg. The clips can easily be removed if the woman later wishes to become pregnant. It is expected that the procedure may soon be offered on an outpatient basis.

None of these procedures will impair a woman's sex drive. On the contrary, there may be an increase in drive because of the sense of freedom a woman has when she is no longer threatened by an unwanted pregnancy.

Methods of Sterilization in Men

Vasectomy, by far the most desirable of the two surgical procedures available to men, consists of cutting and tying the vas deferens, thus preventing the passage of sperm to the ejaculatory ducts. The site of the incision is in the scrotum, well above the testicles, and the operation is a simple one that can be performed in a doctor's office with a local anesthetic. The man is usually advised to remain relatively inactive for about 48 hours and to wear a suspensory (a fabric supporter for the scrotum) for a week or two to prevent any pulling of the testicles.

Since sperm will already have been stored in the seminal vesicles and ejaculatory ducts prior to surgery, the man's first few ejaculations after a vasectomy will contain sperm. Although

FIGURE 6.2 Schematic representation of the male reproductive system, showing the effects of a vasectomy. Note that in sterilization, the surgical procedure is followed on both sides of the body.

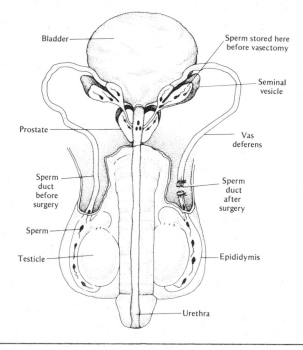

the vasectomized man's seminal fluid will probably be sperm-free after 6 to 10 ejaculations, it is wise to have a laboratory examination of the ejaculate before assuming that it is sperm-free.

Although studies have indicated that very few men ever ask for a reversal of a vasectomy (there have been fewer than 10 requests for reversal surgery out of the 11.5 million vasectomies performed in India), the effects can be undone surgically by rejoining the severed ends of the vas deferens. There is a 30% to 40% chance of impregnation after reversal.

For men who would like to retain the option of fathering a child without undergoing reversal surgery, there are at least four centers in the United States where a man's sperm may be frozen and stored for future insertion into the vagina or uterus of a woman in a process called *artificial insemination.*

Despite the fact that a vasectomy is simple, quick, inexpensive, and safe, many married men steadfastly refuse to have the operation, but willingly agree to a tubal ligation—a major surgical operation—for their wives. Their attitude seems to be that since women are the ones who must suffer any pain or difficulty associated with childbirth, they should be "willing to pay the price" for the operation! Such an attitude is another example of the double standard which prevails in our society.

Another reason that men may avoid vasectomy is that they have an inadequate understanding of male sexual anatomy and fear that any cutting near their testicles will result in loss of sexual functioning. Since the operation only involves severing the tubes leading from the testicles, the capacity of the testicles to produce sperm is not disturbed; the sperm produced after a vasectomy are absorbed by the body. There is no interference with the hormonal production of the testicles, and there is absolutely no effect on sexual functioning or sexual satisfaction. The majority of men report no change in sex drive after a vasectomy. A few report an increase in sexual appetite, and fewer still report a slight decrease in sex drive. Both the increase and decrease are due to psychological factors.

In a very few cases, there is a spontaneous, natural rejoining of the severed vas deferens, or there may be an unsuspected third or even fourth vas which has never been severed. If either of these conditions should exist, the man could impregnate a woman. Pregnancy following a vasectomy can understandably be the source of severe marital misunderstanding if it is not understood by both partners that the procedure is not 100% successful. A laboratory examination of the semen following the operation, and at annual or semiannual intervals, will protect against the possibility of pregnancy resulting from an unlikely rejoining of the vas deferens following vasectomy. Despite the remote possibility of natural reversal or of the presence of an unsuspected extra vas, a vasectomy remains one of the most successful methods of birth control.

Voluntary vasectomy is becoming increasingly common in the United States, particularly among better-educated men. 750,000 operations were performed in 1970 alone, 90% of them in a physician's office. The number of men who seek this operation will undoubtedly rise in the future, and many vasectomy clinics are now being established throughout the country, primarily under the aegis of local Planned Parenthood Centers. Information and counseling are provided at these centers, as well as surgical assistance.

Castration, the second surgical procedure of sterilization available to men, involves the removal of both testicles. This operation does not necessarily mean *impotence* (the inability to achieve an erection sufficient for satisfactory sexual intercourse) if performed on an adult, although there is a gradual loss of sexual desire because of the loss of male hormones produced by the testicles. The hormonal deficiency may also cause the man's voice to become higher, his beard may become sparse, and he may acquire excess fat. Hormone therapy can correct these undesirable changes in secondary sexual characteristics.

ABORTION

Spontaneous abortion is the term applied to an unintentional expulsion of the fetus from the uterus before the third month of pregnancy. It is not a form of purposeful birth control. *Induced abortion,* on the other hand, is the term used to describe the intentional termination of pregnancy.

Historically, attitudes toward abortion have varied. The Chinese are said to possess the oldest method of abortion, a procedure described in a manuscript which is over 4000 years old.

The ancient Jews, although they were desirous of increasing their tribal numbers, had no proscription against abortion in either the Talmud or any related Judaic law. Like Japanese Shintoism, Judaism holds that the fetus becomes human when it is born, and not before.

The Greeks considered abortion an acceptable method of birth control. Aristotle spoke for the majority of Greeks when he wrote that birth control was the best method of population control for the development of an orderly community. Abortion was regarded by Aristotle as an acceptable alternative if other methods of birth control failed. A Greek who reflected the views of the dissenting minority was Hippocrates, author of the Hippocratic Oath for physicians. The oath, which is still taken by physicians today, includes a pledge not to give a woman an abortive remedy. It is interesting to speculate on what present-day attitudes toward abortion would be if someone whose views represented those of the Greek majority had written the physicians' oath.

To the Romans, abortion was simply the removal of a portion of the body. The idea that abortion was akin to murder did not occur to them. Here again, considerations of population control predominated, although abortion came to be practiced so extensively among the ruling classes that the ratio of citizens to slaves became a matter of grave political concern. As a result, efforts were made to outlaw abortion, but they met with only partial success.

Abortion's strongest and most vocal opponent today is the Roman Catholic Church. Yet the Church's position has shifted several times over the centuries. In the twelfth century, abortion was not condemned unless the fetus was over 40 days old if male and over 80 days old if female. (The Church did not explain how one could differentiate between the two.) This position remained unchanged for 4 centuries, until Pope Sixtus V in 1588 declared all abortion a form of murder. Three years later his successor, Pope Gregory XIV, negated that decree and reinstated the earlier law which allowed abortion performed before the fortieth day of pregnancy. This decree held until 1869, when Pope Pius XI condemned all abortion, regardless of circumstances and length of pregnancy. The present attitude of the Roman Catholic Church is thus only 100 years old.

Among certain primitive tribes as well as in some developed

nations, abortion is presently the principal method of population control. Some of the world's most "advanced" nations, however, have come to depend on war and famine to reduce burgeoning populations. Today man possesses awesome control over natural forces, but he still waits passively for a tragic war or for large masses of people to starve in order to remedy the problem of overpopulation. This paradox disturbs many segments of our society. Groups of private citizens together with many physicians, medical societies, government officials, and certain religious groups have demanded that laws forbidding abortion and other methods of population control be restudied and changed in the light of today's conditions. Indeed, as revealed by a June 1972 Gallup poll, 64% of the American public—including a majority of Roman Catholics—favor liberalization of abortion laws. In keeping with these demands and changing attitudes, in 1973 the United States Supreme Court ruled invalid all existing state laws prohibiting abortion. The new ruling permits abortion in the early months of pregnancy at the discretion of the woman and her doctor, making abortion a medical matter rather than a legal one.

The incidence of abortion varies around the world. In Chile, the estimated ratio of illegal abortions to live births is 1 to 2.5. In certain Middle European countries, the incidence of legal abortions appears to be greater than that of live births. Hungary, for example, has a ratio of 150 abortions per 100 births. In Belgrade alone there are 4 abortions for every child born. In Yugoslavia, Czechoslovakia, and Poland, the ratio is about 130 to 100.

In the United States, some authorities estimate that there are as many as 1 million induced abortions annually. The vast majority of these have been criminal abortions since they were performed in areas where almost all abortions were illegal. However, women who could afford to do so often traveled to states where abortion was legal. In the first 6 months following the liberalization of abortion laws in New York State, for example, 75,000 legal abortions were performed in New York City alone. Induced abortions terminate 89% of the pregnancies of single women in the United States and 17% of the pregnancies of married women. As one would expect, there is a considerably greater incidence of abortion in urban areas than in rural areas.

Although maternal deaths resulting from both legal and illegal abortions constitute about one-third of all maternal deaths in the United States, most authorities agree that the death rate from abortions performed under medical supervision in sterile conditions is lower than the death rate in full-term deliveries. Until recently, however, anti-abortion laws have caused most of the abortions in the United States to be performed under non-sterile conditions and by unskilled persons. The death rate in these circumstances is understandably high.

Abortion Techniques

Research has indicated that the optimum time to perform an abortion is between the eighth and tenth week of pregnancy. Abortions taking place after the thirteenth week of pregnancy are 3 to 4 times more risky than those performed earlier. The greatest risk of all is to women who wait until the fifteenth week or later to seek an abortion.

A wide range of techniques is utilized in attempts to induce an abortion. Primitive methods include jumping on the abdomen; probing the uterus with sticks; using potions made from animal secretions, dung, herbs, or seawater; and relying on magic and mystical incantations. In spite of the recent Supreme Court ruling that legalized abortion, many women in this country undoubtedly will continue attempts at self-induced abortion through medications or violent physical exercise.

Strenuous physical exercise is ineffective in inducing an abortion. Similarly ineffective are pills which are advertised to correct menstrual irregularities and are frequently taken in the hope of inducing an abortion. These pills are usually strong laxatives which contain herbs such as tansy, ergot of rye, aloes, or quinine. Strong medication of this type has been known to produce poisoning, leading to blindness or other permanent disabilities.

Abortion may be attempted by persons other than the pregnant woman who are equally untrained, such as her husband or an abortionist who is not a physician. These abortions are, of course, illegal and may involve such methods as spraying the uterus with chemicals or using various drugs. The most common procedure involves inserting some sort of instrument into the uterus and scraping the embryo away, with the attendant dangers of perforating the uterus or causing an infection.

Therapeutic abortions are recommended when certain conditions exist such as serious heart disease, some kidney diseases, or German measles during the first 3 months of pregnancy. Since the recent annulment of laws against abortion, therapeutic abortions may also be performed for nonphysical reasons.

Therapeutic abortions are performed in several ways, one of which is the procedure of *dilation and curettage* ("D and C"). This method is frequently used before the twelfth week of pregnancy, and should be performed only in a hospital with the patient under anesthesia. The cervix is gradually dilated (stretched) and a curette, a spoonlike instrument, is used to scrape the embryo from the uterus.

FIGURE 6.3   Lateral view of the female reproductive system, showing a dilation and curettement. The dilator opens the cervix through which the curette is inserted to scrape the lining of the uterus.

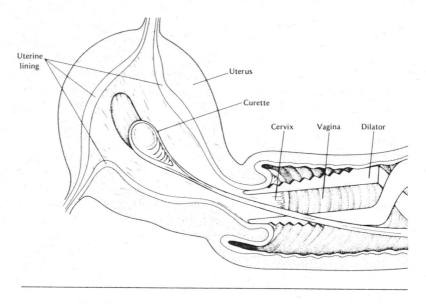

A new method of abortion, *vacuum curettage*, has recently become widely used in the early weeks of pregnancy. In this procedure, a tube is inserted into the uterus and a vacuum pump is used to suck out the embryo and other uterine content. The technique is safe; it is easier and faster to perform than the D and C, and it causes the patient less trauma.

The vacuum (suction) technique is also used to correct delayed menstruation. Called *menstrual regulation,* this process requires no medication, takes about 2 minutes to perform, can be done on an outpatient basis at a relatively low cost, and ends a delayed menstruation without pain or bothersome side effects. The process involves inserting a thin, flexible plastic tube into the uterus without the necessity of cervical dilation; then the month's menstrual lining (including a fertilized egg, if one happens to be present) is sucked out with a specially designed suction syringe.

The procedure is performed within the first 2 weeks of the woman's missed period and since this is too soon after ovulation for existing laboratory tests to make an accurate diagnosis of pregnancy, there is no way for the women to know whether she was pregnant when the procedure was performed. Some women still have serious reservations about abortion, and menstrual regulation permits the woman who might be bothered by having an abortion to free herself of the possibility of the burden of an unwanted pregnancy without having the guilt of a known abortion.

Another method, developed in Sweden for abortion after the third month of pregnancy, is used with some frequency in this country. A needle is used to withdraw about 200 cc of amniotic fluid through the wall of the woman's abdomen. The fluid is then replaced with an equal amount of salt solution of a specified strength. Abortion occurs spontaneously, usually within 24 hours.

Hysterotomy is a method used after pregnancy has reached 12 weeks. One technique, actually a minor caesarean section, is resorted to because the fetus is too large for the usual vaginal methods of removal. Another technique entails a vaginal incision near the cervix; a slit is then made in the lower part of the uterus through which the fetus is removed.

Attitudes toward Abortion

Generally speaking, the higher a woman's educational level, the more receptive she is to the idea of abortion. More white women tend to favor abortion than black women at all levels of education. White Catholic college graduates are least favorable to abortion for any reason, while white non-Catholics with the same level of education are the most favorable to abortion.

Better mental adjustment is reported in women who have sought and been granted therapeutic abortions than in women whose requests for therapeutic abortions were denied. Furthermore, the children born to those mothers who had requested and been denied therapeutic abortions have greater social and emotional handicaps than do their peers.

Most physicians, psychiatrists, and psychologists agree that abortion in itself is a safe, simple procedure which does not result in emotional problems. The obstacles erected by laws against the procedure, however, caused it to become an emotionally traumatic experience. The Supreme Court's decision to remove early abortion from the jurisdiction of the law and make it a medical matter should help to end the needless suffering which women who were denied the right to legal abortions have endured.

In New York, 80% to 90% of the legal abortions now performed are done on an outpatient basis, under local anesthetic, and through the vacuum-suction technique. The Blue Cross Insurance Company of New York will cover abortions for single women and dependent children, and Medicaid covers abortion for both single and married women. City hospitals perform the operation on minors without parental consent if the patient is at least 17 years old and is married, or is self-supporting and living away from home. Fees for abortion at city hospitals in a pregnancy of less than 12 weeks begin at about $200 for an abortion performed on an outpatient basis.

Before abortion was made legal by the 1973 ruling, referral services operated around the country to provide information to pregnant women who sought legal abortions. Group flights were made from cities within states where abortion was illegal to states such as New York, California, and Alaska, where abortion was legally performed. Abortions were performed in hospitals or clinics under antiseptic conditions, and the woman was usually home within 24 hours. The fee, including plane fare, was often considerably less than she would have paid a local illegal abortionist.

Illegal abortionists' fees varied according to the socioeconomic status of the patient and, supposedly, of the abortionist as well: the higher the status, the higher the cost. Single women paid a higher fee than married women, but the highest price of all was paid by widows and divorcees. Age and race were additional factors in abortion cost: women under 31 paid about 20% more than older women; white women paid more than black women. Abortionists' fees ranged from $150 to $1000 or more, with a stagering $350 million being spent annually in the United States on abortions.

Prior to 1973, those states with stringent laws against abortion placed the affluent woman in a favored position. Women in this financial bracket could go to a local hospital and have a "perfectly legal" curettment performed by a physician. The woman from the slums, on the other hand, was more likely to turn to a poorly trained abortionist who might use a knitting needle or coat hanger in an attempt to induce an abortion. Undoubtedly, these inequities in the law influenced the Supreme Court's recent ruling.

CONTRACEPTION

Since the beginning of recorded history, man has employed contraceptive techniques—some of them effective, most of them ineffective, and many of them dangerous. Religious beliefs, superstitions, and magic were frequently involved in man's early efforts to control fertility. The ancient Chinese, for example, believed that a woman would not become pregnant if she remained completely passive during coitus. The philosophy underlying this belief was that a woman's enjoyment of intercourse was evil and merited punishment, of which pregnancy apparently was one form.

The oldest medical prescription for a contraceptive, dating back to about 1850 B.C., is found in the Egyptian Petri Papyrus. Women were advised to use a vaginal suppository concocted of crocodile dung and honey. The pastelike substance was apparently expected to prevent the sperm from entering the cervix. (One would think that it might have prevented the possibility of intercourse at all!)

Other incredible birth-preventive substances and techniques have been tried over the centuries—mouse dung, amulets, and induced sneezing, for example. Some methods were partially

effective and a refinement of these occasionally led to a reasonably efficient contraceptive. The ancient Greeks, for example,
wrote that certain materials permeated with oil might constitute
a workable contraceptive because oil impedes the movement of
sperm. Thereafter, oil-saturated papers were inserted in the
vagina to cover the cervix—a crude forerunner of today's diaphragm.

Casanova, the eighteenth-century Italian adventurer, is alleged to have used a gold ball as a contraceptive by placing it
in the woman's vagina to block the passage of his sperm. He is
also credited with using a hollowed-out lemon as a diaphragm
to cover the woman's cervix. Perhaps the lemon shell did serve
as an effective contraceptive, for citric acid can immobilize
sperm. However, if Casanova deserved his reputation for prodi-
gious sexual activity and if his claims of never impregnating any
of his lovers were true, the logical explanation is that frequent
ejaculations kept his sperm count so low that he was sterile in
effect if not in actuality.

The *condom* or penile sheath has been used for many centuries. Some say that it originated with the ancient Romans and
that the word comes from the Latin "condus," meaning a collector. Others maintain that it was invented by the sixteenth-century
anatomist Fallopius, who identified the female uterine tubes bearing his name. Dr. Canton or Condom, a physician in the court
of England's Charles II (1660-1685), is also credited with origi-
nating the sheath. Whatever its early history, the condom was
originally used more as protection against venereal disease than
as a contraceptive.

The German scientist Graefenburg in 1920 used a coiled silver
ring as an *intrauterine contraceptive device* (IUD), one of the
most popular methods of present-day birth control. Unlike the
plastic coil used today, however, the metal in Graefenburg's IUD
often caused an infection. Although he is credited with having
introduced the use of foreign objects in the uterus to prevent
pregnancy, he was actually not the first to use this technique.
Centuries ago the Arabs put pebbles into the vagina or the uterus
of their female camels to keep them from becoming pregnant
on long caravan treks across the desert!

It should perhaps be mentioned here that ancient people were
not unique in having superstitious and irrational beliefs about

contraceptive techniques. Even today there are people who believe that having sexual intercourse while standing will prevent pregnancy or that urinating immediately after intercourse will have a contraceptive effect. Neither of these beliefs, of course, is true.

Modern contraceptive methods are evaluated according to their effectiveness in preventing pregnancy. A formula is used to compare the number of pregnancies which occur when a given contraceptive method is used with the number of pregnancies which occur when no contraceptive is used. Applying this formula produces a rating number which shows the relative effectiveness of various methods. When the pregnancy rating of a contraceptive method is below 10, its effectiveness is rated as high; if the rating is between 10 and 20, the effectiveness is considered to be medium, and if the rating is above 20, the effectiveness is ranked as low.

As in other forms of birth control, the higher the level of education, the higher the likelihood that an individual will use some form of contraception.

Contraceptives Available Only with a Doctor's Prescription

A *diaphragm* is a thin rubber dome-shaped cup stretched over a collapsible metal ring, designed to cover the mouth of the uterus (the cervix). The diaphragm must be fitted by a physician because of individual physiological differences in women. Having the correct size and shape in a diaphragm is important for both the wearer's comfort and for its effectiveness as a contraceptive. A virgin cannot be fitted with one until her hymen has been broken or incised by the physician. The device in no way interferes with the conduct or pleasure of intercourse for either partner.

Used with contraceptive cream or jelly, the diaphragm seals off the cervix and prevents sperm from entering the uterus. The cream or jelly is toxic to sperm and provides lubrication as well. The diaphragm may be inserted several hours before coitus or immediately before. It must not be removed until 4 to 6 hours after intercourse, and it may be left in place for as long as 24 hours. Although it is unnecessary, the woman using a diaphragm may *douche* (cleanse the vagina with a jet or current of water) if she waits at least 6 hours after coitus in order for the cream or jelly, or the naturally acid condition of the vagina, to destroy the sperm.

When the diaphragm is used with contraceptive foam, its effectiveness improves significantly, making it one of the safest of all birth-control techniques. Used together, the two have a pregnancy rate of 4 to 10.

Oral contraceptives in the form of a pill were first used in 1956 in Puerto Rico and Haiti in well-controlled studies of their safety and effectiveness. The experiments were tremendously successful. Since that time, pharmaceutical houses have been working overtime to supply the public with oral contraceptives and to produce even better ones.

The birth-control pill, popularly called "the Pill," is a combination of synthetic progesterone (progestin) and estrogen that prevents ovulation by mimicking the hormonal state of the body during pregnancy. Since no ovum is released, pregnancy cannot occur.

Most of the approximately 30 different brands of oral contraceptives are taken for 20 days, beginning on the fifth day after the beginning of a menstrual period. The pills are preferably taken at the same hour each day. Menstruation will commence within 2 to 5 days after the last pill is taken, although in about 3% of the cases it may fail to occur altogether. In the latter event, a physician usually advises his patient to take another round of 20 pills, beginning 7 days after the last pill was taken.

If one pill is missed, there is a remote chance of pregnancy, and a woman is usually advised to take the missed pill as soon as she realizes she has omitted it. If taken as prescribed, oral contraceptives are virtually 100% effective—a success that is unequalled by any other means of contraception.

Both men and women are relieved of considerable anxiety when they know that there is no danger of an unwanted pregnancy; thus, effective contraception may increase sexual desire in both partners. Women who use the Pill are reported to engage in coitus with an 18% to 45% higher frequency than nonusers of similar ages, education, and religious background. Even when frequency of intercourse is unchanged, women taking the Pill report that they derive greater satisfaction in sexual relations than they did when using other forms of birth control or none at all.

Authorities warn women, however, to expect a reduction in sex drive after taking the Pill for 18 to 36 months, and women are advised to substitute other methods of contraception after about 18 months of continual use in order to restore the original hormonal balance of the body. After the woman uses other contraceptive methods for about 3 months, the physician will usually again prescribe the Pill for her. In addition to its contraceptive effect, the Pill is also used to treat certain discomforts and disorders of the menstrual cycle, such as irregularity, an excessive flow of blood, and discomfort before or during menstruation.

Although most of the negative side effects of the Pill have been eliminated, occasional discomfort or unpleasantness, such as nausea, weight gain, headaches, and irregular bleeding may still be experienced by some women, especially in the first few months. These symptoms usually are temporary, however, and disappear as the cycles of pills are repeated. In cases where the discomfort persists, a change in strength or brand of pills usually eliminates the problem.

The most serious side effect associated with the Pill is that its estrogen content increases the coagulatory action of the blood, thereby increasing the risk of thromboembolic (clotting) disorders. Many women have been alarmed by reports that 3 out of every 100,000 women taking the Pill are expected to die of thromboembolism caused by the Pill. What the reports neglect to explain, however, is that women using birth-control methods other than the Pill have 3.5 times greater risk of dying from complications of pregnancy, childbirth, and the postpartum period than do women who use the Pill, simply because there are so many more unwanted pregnancies among women using the less reliable methods of control. Among women who use *no* method of birth control, the risk of maternal death is 7.5 times greater than among women taking the Pill. Furthermore, there is no evidence of cancer being caused by the Pill, even in women who have taken it for as long as 10 years.

Many women stopped taking the Pill—and the birth rate rose accordingly—following the alarmist U.S. Senate hearings in 1970 concerning the contraceptive. Since that time, however, endocrinologists and gynecologists alike have proclaimed the Pill eminently safe for most women, especially when its advantages are weighed against its risks. The Pill has the excellent pregnancy rate of 0 to 3.

The Pill is not recommended during the period when a mother is nursing her baby since it suppresses milk production. There is also evidence that if a mother takes the Pill while she is nursing a male infant, the unusual combination of hormones present in her body can work their way into the baby's bloodstream via her milk and have a feminizing effect on him.

Intrauterine contraceptive devices (IUDs) are small plastic devices of various sizes and shapes that are designed to fit into the womb. Plastic is preferred over metal because of its flexibility and because of the greater chance of its not being rejected by the body. It is thought that the IUD in some way acts as an irritant to prevent the implantation of the fertilized ovum in the uterine wall. Technically, therefore, this method is more correctly called *contraimplantation* than contraception.

The device must be placed in the uterus by a physician, who can remove it at any time that the woman wishes to become pregnant. After the birth of a child, it may be repositioned in the uterus until another pregnancy is desired. The device in no way affects the fertility of the woman or the health of children who are born after the removal of the IUD.

Of the variety of shapes which have been available, the loop has generally proven most comfortable and effective. But a new T-shaped or 7-shaped IUD has recently been developed that is much smaller and easier to insert than the more conventional IUD. The incidence of spontaneous ejection, bleeding, and cramping, the most common unpleasant side effects of use of the device, is considerably less than with the loop. Wrapped with copper—which appears to be an additional deterrent to embryo implantation—the polyethylene T has proved, in the initial stages of its use, to be virtually 100% effective. Its cost is minimal, and its effectiveness lasts several years.

The IUDs are gaining in popularity and in 1970 were being used by an estimated 2 million women. Unlike the Pill, the IUD's effectiveness does not depend on the memory of the user, and the most successful of the IUDs have a pregnancy rating of about 2 to 3. There is no evidence that the IUD increases the chance of cervical cancer, nor is there evidence of any other adverse physical effects from its use.

Contraceptives Available without a Doctor's Prescription

The *condom*, one of the most popular contraceptives in the United States, is cheap, easy to use and to obtain, and easily disposable. Designed to fit the erect penis, the condom is made of thin rubber or of sheep's intestine and measures about 7½ inches in length.

Unless the condom breaks during intercourse or slips off after ejaculation, it offers almost total effectiveness. To lessen the possibility of accidental pregnancies while using the condom, the man should blow air into it before usage to make sure there are no tears or breaks. After intercourse, he should carefully hold

FIGURE 6.4   The major contraceptive measures in use today.

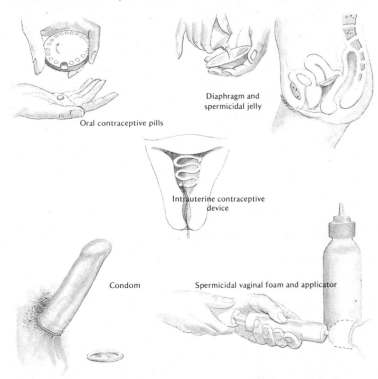

Oral contraceptive pills

Diaphragm and spermicidal jelly

Intrauterine contraceptive device

Condom

Spermicidal vaginal foam and applicator

it while he withdraws his penis from his partner's vagina in order to prevent semen from spilling into the vaginal opening. He can then fill the used condom with water in another test to make sure that no breakage has occurred. If a condom should prove to be broken, the woman should immediately insert a contraceptive cream or jelly into her vagina. If neither of these is available, a douche, even if with plain water, is the next best course of action.

About 750 million condoms are produced each year in the United States, and their pregnancy rate is about 10 or 11. In addition to its use as a contraceptive, the condom is the best method of preventing the spread of venereal disease.

Chemical methods include *creams, jellies,* and *vaginal foams* which block the entrance to the uterus and which are toxic to sperm. They must be inserted into the vagina at least 5 to 15 minutes before ejaculation occurs, and they must be reapplied if intercourse is repeated. Pregnancy rating for the foam (3 to 10) is somewhat better than for creams and jellies.

Another chemical method is the *vaginal suppository,* a small solid cone that melts at about 95°F. Suppositories must be inserted at least 15 minutes before ejaculation, and the pregnancy rates vary from 5 to 27. *Vaginal tablets* need more moisture to dissolve than may be present in the vagina, and the tablets are very unstable in damp climates. They have a pregnancy rate of 8 to 27.

Douching, while it cleans the vagina and offers a feeling of security to many women, has a very unsatisfactory pregnancy rate of 36. Sperm move so quickly that a douche fails to reach them in time.

Other Methods of Birth Prevention

Coitus interruptus or *withdrawal,* the oldest known form of contraception, requires that the male withdraw his penis from the vagina of the female before he ejaculates. Many couples use this method exclusively and find it satisfactory, while other couples find the technique highly undesirable, both because of its effect on the enjoyment of intercourse and because of its undependability. The man must withdraw just at the crucial moment and must wait a considerable period of time before having intercourse again because of the possibility of sperm remaining in his urethra. The technique has a pregnancy rate of from 8 to 40. Its effectiveness is based solely on the man's timing and his sincerity in wanting to withdraw at the most crucial time of the coital act.

The *rhythm method* requires that a couple abstain from sexual intercourse during the period of a woman's menstrual cycle when she is capable of conception—just before, during, and just after ovulation. The major problem with the rhythm method is that only about 30% of women have sufficiently regular menstrual cycles that they can correctly pinpoint their "safe" period. The *temperature method* is a variation of the rhythm method and is based on the belief that a woman's temperature changes according to the changes in her menstrual cycle. One problem with this method is that many women have no marked or consistent temperature changes. Another difficulty is that many women ovulate more than one time during a menstrual cycle, with the possibility existing that sexual excitement itself can trigger ovulation. Both the rhythm and temperature methods have a medium pregnancy rate of 14.

Regardless of the contraceptive technique used, its effectiveness depends on how well the user follows prescribed directions and how consistently the method is used. Carelessness in the use of even the most effective contraceptive increases the chances of pregnancy.

BIRTH CONTROL IN THE FUTURE

Scientists are now experimenting with new methods of birth control. The *mini-pill,* for example, contains no estrogen and little progestin. Unlike the Pill, the mini-pill does not interfere with the woman's ovulatory process. Instead, it makes the cervical mucosa thick and sticky, thus preventing sperm from passing through to the uterus. It must be taken every day of the month, but the dangers of thrombogenic complications and other unpleasant side effects are virtually eliminated.

Another technique being developed which involves a low dosage of progestin is an inch-long spaghettilike capsule that can be inserted into a woman's leg, arm, or groin by means of a hypodermic needle. The capsule, containing enough progestin to last from a year to a lifetime, releases just enough progestin at a constant rate to prevent pregnancy. The capsule can easily be removed whenever the woman wants to become pregnant. Safe and convenient, the cost of this contraceptive technique will probably be less than a dollar, plus the doctor's fee for injecting it.

Another device is the *vaginal ring*, made of progestin and plastic. It is inserted into the vagina, where it releases enough progestin to keep a woman infertile for 1 month, after which it must be replaced.

A new and unique form of contraception is the *ovariotexy*, which requires an incision in the lower abdomen of the woman and the placement around each ovary of a silastic bag which traps discharged ova. If pregnancy is desired, another incision is made and the bags are removed.

Although the idea of a *"morning-after" pill* is alluring, the presently developed one contains such a large amount of estrogen that it usually makes the woman quite ill. It does prevent implantation of the fertilized ovum in the uterine wall, however, and is effective even if taken as long as 3 to 5 days after coitus. Its primary value therefore lies in its use as an emergency procedure in, for example, cases of rape.

A birth-control method with great promise is the insertion into the vagina of tablets containing *prostaglandins*, fatty-acid derivatives produced by the body which act on the uterus to cause contractions. The tablets are inserted every 2.5 hours until menstrual bleeding begins. Complete abortions, requiring no curettage, result in almost every case, even for those women who are as much as 22 weeks pregnant. To date, no serious side effects have been encountered.

The tablets offer a happy solution for the woman who accepts other birth-control methods but rejects the idea of abortion. She can simply insert a tablet into her vagina a day or so before her menstrual period is due, and she will never know whether the resulting flow is a normal menstrual period or the result of an abortion.

Other futuristic contraceptive methods include vaccines to immunize a woman against her husband's sperm, or to immunize a man with substances inhibitory to sperm production. Also, scientists are working on a way to prevent the removal of a substance in the protective fluid which surrounds human sperm. If this substance is not removed, the sperm is incapable of penetrating ova.

Birth-control methods designed for men have been less successful than those for women. A pill to induce temporary sterility, for example, causes a reduction in sex drive and abnormal reactions when alcohol is consumed. Another possibility, a hormonal implant similar to the one devised for women, also is viewed with caution. While a capsule containing testosterone would act to block sperm production, the procedure would increase the possibility of prostatic cancer. More probable is the development of a pill that will prevent sperm from maturing. Another probable male contraceptive device of the future is a plastic plug which will be inserted in the vas deferens, blocking the passage of sperm. The plug would have the same effect as a vasectomy, but could be removed with comparative ease if the man later wished to father a child.

For the first time in recorded history, the technology necessary to control the world's population is available. Adequate birth control, however, depends upon more than technology; it also requires persons who are willing to accept the responsibility for using contraceptives and a society in which the decision to have children is no more honored than the decision to remain childless. In the United States, television commercials depict the "ideal family" as one with four children, and college alumna magazines list new babies as the chief accomplishment of married women graduates. Clearly our cultural values lag behind our cultural needs.

The individual's decision to use a contraceptive is complicated and personal, but it is upon this decision that the control of the world's population ultimately depends.

FURTHER READING

From Now to Zero: Fertility, Contraception, and Abortion in America, by L. A. Westoff and C. F. Westoff. Boston: Little, Brown, 1971.

This paperback book gives the best available current information on methods of birth control. Discussion includes which segments of the population use which methods, and why. Also presented is information on the progress being made in new methods of birth control. Efforts to maintain population growth at zero are discussed.

Birth Control Handbook, edited by D. Cherniak and A. Feingold. Montreal: Handbook Collective, 1970.

Old, new, and experimental birth control methods are described in this booklet. The discussion includes sections on the significance of contraception in women's liberation and the influence of sexism in contraception research.

Pregnancy, Birth and Abortion, by P. H. Gebhard, W. B. Pomeroy, C. E. Martin, and C. V. Christenson. New York: Harper & Row, 1958.

Demographic data regarding pregnancy, birth, and abortion gathered by the researchers of the Kinsey group are detailed in this book.

Human Sexuality, 2d ed., by J. L. McCary. New York: D. Van Nostrand, 1973.

Chapter 14 gives detailed information on all forms of birth control, past, present, and future, including abortion, sterilization, and contraception.

Sexual Myths and Fallacies, by J. L. McCary. New York: D. Van Nostrand, 1971.

Myths and fallacies pertaining to birth control techniques and methods are corrected in the section on Reproduction and Birth Control.

7 SEXUAL ATTITUDES

Sexual behavior is essentially determined by an individual's attitudes toward sex; these attitudes, in turn, are the result of one's upbringing. Sex education begins with the first intimate mother-infant contacts, but it involves infinitely more than the interrelations between parents and child; significant roles are played by many other influences. The demands and expectations of the culture in which one lives as well as the special differences in sexual ethics within that culture work to shape sexual attitudes—and, in consequence, sexual behavior.

Cultural differences produce a wide variety of attitudes toward sex, just as they do in other areas of human interaction. It comes as a surprise to many Americans to learn, for instance, that their condemnatory views on premarital and postmarital sexual activity are not shared by the majority of the world's cultures.

Anthropological investigations have consistently found that cultures which encourage women to be completely free in their sexual expression produce women who are as uninhibited as men. Cultures in which there is approval of women having orgasms produce women who have orgasms. Cultures withholding such approval produce women who are incapable of orgasm.

Regrettably, sexual attitudes are easily influenced by the misinformation and prudery within a culture. For example, women of modern societies are frequently troubled with menstrual difficulties of one sort or another. Yet Margaret Mead's studies of the women of Samoa uncovered only one woman in the entire population who even understood what was meant by pain or emotional upset during menstruation. That particular girl was employed by the island's white missionary family!

People in every culture are inclined to cling to their traditional ways of thinking and behaving, whether in political, religious, or sexual matters. Reluctance to accept change or to be swayed by outside influences, however rational or beneficial, is found not only within cultures but within subcultures as well.

Every culture attempts to control the sexual expression of its members to some extent. Restrictions vary widely from culture to culture, but most cultures recognize the fact that a sexual need not expressed in one manner *will* be expressed in another. When healthy sexual outlets are denied an individual, sexual feelings are expressed vicariously through neuroses, personality maladjustments, guilt, inadequacy feelings, or sexual perversion. Certainly no sensible person suggests that standards for appropriate expression and control of sexual needs are unnecessary. But unrealistic and unreasonable restrictions, whether set up directly or through the mechanism of guilt, invite trouble.

A CLIMATE OF CONFLICT AND CHANGE

Much has been said and written in recent years about the sexual revolution that is supposedly taking place. A true sexual revolution involves a dramatic change in the attitudes and ethics governing sexual behavior as well as in the behavior itself. Conclusive evidence of such a change does not as yet exist, but there are signs that the trend is in that direction.

Recent research indicates that the incidence of sexual *activity* among young adults has increased, primarily in heavy petting and sexual intercourse within relationships of deep emotional involvement. The most significant change by far, however, has been a growing liberalization of sexual *attitudes*.

Changes in premarital sexual behavior and sexual attitudes are particularly pronounced among young adult women. Their liberalized approaches to sex are becoming close to those of young adult men, though they lag somewhat behind. Women are becoming clearly conscious of their sexual urges, and a majority of college women engage in heavy petting and approve of premarital coitus when love or a meaningful relationship exists between partners. A substantial minority (perhaps a majority by the senior year) engage in premarital intercourse. Today's college woman is having more sexual experiences, earlier and probably with more partners, than was true of the woman student before 1960.

A change in sexual attitudes within the general populace has been apparent in the last few years. There is a growing freedom, for example, with which sexual topics are discussed in the various communication media, schools, churches, and governmental circles—as well as by the man on the street.

Many persons who are unaccustomed to casual conversation on sexual topics fail to understand that talk and action are not necessarily the same. Attitudes—and ease in discussing them—are not to be confused with behavior. Rather, inconsistency between sexual attitudes and sexual behavior is still very much a part of the American culture. Young people, among whom the change in behavior is reputed to be the greatest, are themselves confused about the distance between talk and behavior. The majority of college women in one study, for example, stated that their female classmates "slept around." In actual fact, only 20% of all college women at that time were experiencing premarital intercourse.

Among the various conflicting American premarital sexual standards are *abstinence* (premarital intercourse is wrong for both men and women, regardless of circumstances); the *double standard* (premarital intercourse is acceptable for men, but unacceptable for women); *sexual permissiveness when affection exists* (premarital intercourse is right for both men and women under certain conditions—in a stable relationship involving engagement, love, or strong affection); and *permissiveness without affection* (physical attraction alone justifies premarital intercourse for both men and women). When the sexual attitudes of students in high school and college were compared with those of older adults, the results indicated that both students and adults approved of petting and coitus more for men than for women. Apparently vestiges of the traditional double standard persist.

In Kinsey's study of American sexual behavior in the early 1950s, women were found to be less likely than men to demand virginity of their mates at the time of marriage. Today, the double standard seems to be collapsing insofar as virginity is concerned. A recent Gallup poll, conducted on 55 separate college campuses, revealed that men and women now think very much alike on the subject; 75% of these students expressed the view that virginity is unimportant in the person whom they marry.

The double standard continues to influence the views of some American college students, however. One study that seems to be fairly typical of men's attitudes found that more than 50% of the college men sampled expressed approval of premarital coitus, but 75% of them nevertheless stated that they would prefer to marry a virgin. Many college women continue to believe that a man's sexual conquests indicate his masculinity, and they prefer that their husbands be sexually experienced at the time of marriage.

One authority in the field of sexology has developed an ethical approach to premarital intercourse which goes beyond blanket acceptance or rejection. This ethic is based on the premise that premarital sex is acceptable *if* it increases the capacity of the couple to trust, brings greater integrity to their personal relationships, dissolves the barriers separating them from other people, enhances their self-respect, fulfills their individual potentials, and fosters in them a zest for living.

Generally speaking, the sexual attitudes and behavior of men and those of women seem to be converging. Women are coming to expect the same sexual freedom that has traditionally been accorded men. Men, on the other hand, are slowly drifting toward the traditional female norms.

Several studies made in the late 1960s and early 1970s revealed that from 50% to 85% of college males considered premarital coitus acceptable although only about 65% actually had experienced premarital intercourse. Factors affecting the permissive attitude were race, age, semester in college, strength of religious belief, and region of the country. Older students who had little religious conviction and who were attending eastern, western, or southern colleges were more permissive than younger, religiously inclined midwesterners.

As many as 70% of the college women sampled in these same studies approved of premarital coitus for themselves if they were "in love," although only about 35% to 50% actually engaged in coitus before marriage. Less than half found it acceptable in a relationship in which only "strong affection" existed. College women who had permissive sexual attitudes were likely to feel that they had been in love two or more times and were going steady or engaged at the time of the study. A woman's view of herself as a sexual being appears still to be strongly related to feelings of romance, affection, and love.

In recent years, sexual attitudes have become much more predictive of sexual behavior. Men and women with premarital sexual experience in 1958, for example, were far less likely to hold permissive sexual attitudes than were individuals with similar experience in 1968.

One of the most significant social changes in recent years has been the movement to provide equal opportunities for women in American society. The freedom and equality that women are demanding—and, to some extent, receiving—have had a profound effect upon prevailing sexual attitudes. Most women today are unwilling to accept the notion that they are subject to different sexual standards than men are. They view the pleasures and responsibilities of sex as being equally applicable to both sexes. Despite this recent liberalizing of attitudes toward equality for women, however, certain sexual differences in attitudes continue to be imposed by childhood rearing, societal expectations, and physiological forces.

One interesting side effect of the struggle for sexual equality is that the sexual attitudes of present-day American women are considerably healthier than those of American men. Researchers and clinicians have found that women are far more open and honest in supplying personal sexual data than men are. Men frequently become entrapped in questions of self-esteem and may attempt to compensate through boasting for what they feel is a threat to their self-image. As a consequence, the data they provide are often unreliable.

Is There Growing Moral Decadence Among Today's Youth?

Since the beginning of recorded history, older generations have been in a state of shock over the supposed immorality of the younger generation. It is not surprising, then, that newspaper and magazine articles, organized groups, and individual citizens are crying out that America is on the brink of ruin because of the sexual misconduct of its young people. Isolated incidents that incite public outrage become the "evidence" of a general moral degeneration among the young. There have always been such occurrences, and there are no more now—if as many—than there have been in the past. There is considerable evidence, in fact, that young people today are behaving responsibly and that they demonstrate moral strength in their active concern for the welfare and rights of others. Young men of today, furthermore, do not seem to lie, cheat, or otherwise trick young women into bed as their fathers might have done. And women who enter into sexual relationships with men before marriage are more likely to do so because they want to, and because they enjoy the experience. Women today are likely to enjoy sexual expression more than ever before because of the gradual decline of Victorian and puritanical inhibitions that have traditionally hampered their sexual enjoyment.

The new sexual climate has many advantages. The sex-related guilt, hypocrisy, dehumanization, secrecy, and morbid fascination which so long clouded physical relationships are greatly reduced, leading to a much more healthy attitude toward sex.

It might be mentioned that young people who use drugs are apparently more likely to have premarital coitus than nonusers. Using drugs does not lead to sexual activity, however; it appears that if a youth engages in one socially unacceptable activity, such as drug usage, he is more likely to engage in other socially unacceptable activities, such as premarital sex.

Religious, Racial, and Cultural Influences on Sexual Attitudes

The intensity of an individual's religious beliefs greatly influences his attitude toward and involvement in sexual behavior. When background variables such as age, marital status, size of hometown, fraternity membership, father's political preference, and religious affiliation are held constant, the relationship between sex attitudes and religiosity remains significant. There seems to be a direct relationship between the degree of an individual's religious devoutness and his attitude toward premarital sexual relations.

Among whites, the more devout and frequent a churchgoer an individual is, the more conservative his sexual attitudes and behavior are likely to be. This tendency has not been found to a significant degree among blacks.

According to recent studies, three to four times more black girls than white girls experience premarital coitus in their teens. Furthermore, more grammar-school- and high-school-educated black girls have experienced coitus than have white boys of the same educational level. This higher frequency in sexual activity among blacks is a reflection of the fact that premarital intercourse is more likely to be viewed as acceptable behavior by black males and females than it is by white males and females. This finding holds even when socioeconomic and education factors are matched between the two racial groups, as well as the incomes and occupations of the fathers.

ATTITUDE FORMATION IN YOUNG PEOPLE

Many of the changes in sexual attitudes are due to the protracted period of adolescence imposed on today's youth. Our society requires longer periods of scholastic and vocational training than ever before, while today's youth become physically mature at an earlier age. Thus the period of social adolescence is now approximately twice as long at it was 100 years ago.

During this prolonged period of social adolescence, the two sexes begin to develop divergent attitudes toward premarital sexual activity. Sex appeal is extolled by the various mass communication media as a means to instant popularity, success, admiration, and security. Young men, whose heightened sex drives are equaled only by their feelings of adolescent insecurity, are particularly susceptible to the idea that their masculinity is measured by the number of women they have seduced. To retain his masculine image in the eyes of his peers, a young man may boast about sexual exploits which have occurred mainly in his imagination. His listeners, however, accept these exaggerations as truth, and each dejectedly concludes that *he* is the only young man in the world who does not have erotic escapades with voluptuous females.

Believing that he must prove his masculinity to young women by attempting to seduce them, a young man may make untimely advances and insult the women, who believe in their insecurity that the advances are made out of disrespect for them. Finding himself rebuffed, he may morosely conclude that all women "put out" for every other man except him, and that there must be something especially repulsive about him. The truth is, of course, that his peers are equally confused and unhappy because of their failure to live up to some imaginary norm.

Young women, on the other hand, become indoctrinated by the communication media with the importance of being "sexy." They are lured to purchase an often ludicrous conglomeration of products that are guaranteed to increase their sexual attractiveness.

To a maturing young woman, the push to be "sexy" and at the same time to be "good" causes considerable confusion and conflict. Like her male counterpart, the adolescent female is unsure of herself and of her sex role. She wants to be admired and respected, but she also wants to be "popular," and the road to popularity appears to be paved with panting young men. All too often, the adolescent girl is rated by her peer group in terms of her ability to maintain her popularity with boys while remaining a virgin.

One logical outcome of such attitudes is for the young woman to become a female sexual tease. Like the legendary Don Juan, she may become a "Donna Juanita," satisfied only when she knows she has captured a man's attention and has made him desire her sexually. If she can accomplish this goal without coitus, so much the better. Underlying this behavior are pervading doubts about her sexual desirability and capability. She frequently sees herself as being in competition with all women, so that the only man who can fulfill her needs is one already committed to another woman.

It is easy to understand how a woman can come to have an exaggerated need to be appreciated for her physical beauty. As a young child, she gained considerable attention simply by wearing a pretty dress and smiling sweetly. By contrast, a small boy must "do something" to prove his worth—flex his muscles or show how fast he can run. Youngsters thus become conditioned to feel that their worth is determined by their ability to perform well in certain narrowly-defined sex roles. A woman's recognition becomes dependent upon her beauty, while a man's desirability is equated with his physical power or success. These attitudes become firmly entrenched; over 80% of men report that sexual attraction is a distinct factor in their selection of a partner, while only 50% of women look for sexual attractiveness in their prospective mate.

Parents, Children, and Sexuality

Young teen-agers tend to accept the traditional sexual standards of their parents uncritically. But as they grow older and begin to evaluate those standards, they become influenced by outside values, particularly those of their peer group. They may reject the preachments of their parents and adopt a more permissive code of sexual behavior. Teen-agers also learn from their peers how to keep from being "found out" and thus to avoid parental or societal wrath.

More and more young people today are openly challenging the theological doctrines and traditional codes of ethics that have formerly served as guidelines for sexual behavior. Unfortunately, many parents try to control their children with fear of punishment; the sexual expression of these young people is limited only because they fear the consequences of doing otherwise. When they reject their old patterns of behavior, they are left with no standards by which to conduct their lives; then they are controlled by their impulses and their strong sexual feelings. Sensible parents should anticipate these possibilities and take steps to instill in their children a realistic code of ethical behavior, a code that will retain its validity after the children have left the home and its direct influence. The edict "don't do it because you will be punished" simply will not hold over the years.

A close, accepting, and loving family relationship is far more effective in controlling the sexual behavior of teen-agers than are threats of dire punishment. Studies have indicated that girls who get along well with their fathers and mothers, and boys who get along well with their mothers, are far less likely to become sexually involved than those who do not.

There is frequently a marked discrepancy between the past (or present) sexual behavior of parents and the code of sexual ethics which they profess to their children. Interestingly, a young person's sexual permissiveness is not related to his parents' *actual* attitude toward sexual permissiveness but to his *perception* or *interpretation* of his parents' attitude.

Psychotherapists have long observed more regret among women who remained virgins till marriage than among those who did not. Several investigations have shown that those women who have had premarital coition are not sorry, and they maintain that they would repeat their behavior if they had it to do over again. They expect their daughters, however, to conform to a more conservative ethic.

The question naturally arises: why do mothers who feel no regret about their own premarital experiences expect their daughters to behave differently? This apparent contradiction can be understood by examining the differences with which men and women perceive the relationship between sexual attraction and emotional commitment.

A man usually is sexually attracted to a woman before he falls in love with her; a woman, on the other hand, often must have a strong emotional attachment to a man before she allows herself to become sexually involved. She must be convinced that it is she, the person, who is important to the relationship and not simply her sexual potential. A woman's attitudes toward sexual involvement often become liberalized as an outgrowth of her emotional commitment.

The mother who believes strongly that emotional involvement should precede sexual expression and who experienced such involvement before her own premarital sexual relationships may not be able to accept the fact that her daughter can also experience intense feeling for a young man. She may not be able to identify sufficiently with her daughter to appreciate the strength of her feelings. Furthermore, because the mother defied the sexual prohibitions of her own parents by engaging in premarital coitus, she may now carry residual guilt. This guilt can break through and be projected onto her maturing daughter in the form of disapproval of any premarital sexual expression. The mother may also be unable to accept the fact that her daughter has, after careful thought, evolved a liberal sexual ethic of her own which includes the requirement that emotional commitment precede sexual involvement.

The admonishments through which a mother attempts to sexually inhibit her daughter quite likely will be no more effective than they were in the mother's generation. But the unfortunate consequence will be the same—generation after generation of women who tend to follow their emotional and sexual inclinations but who also feel guilt and shame because they have violated the sexual ethic of their upbringing.

Parents stress to their daughters (and, to a lesser extent, to their sons) that love is a goal in any happy man-woman relationship. They thereby increase the likelihood that their children will engage in premarital sexual intercourse, for research clearly indicates that love is a key motivation for young women who experience premarital coitus.

The indications are that those girls who start dating, kissing, and other sexual behavior at an early age are the ones most likely to have early sexual intercourse.

Although it appears that there is a wide disparity between the attitudes of older and young people regarding premarital intercourse, a national survey found only an 8 or 9 percentage-point difference in attitudes between them (the older group being the more conservative, needless to say). When the older group was divided into subgroups according to their marital status, whether or not they had children, and the ages of their children, however, some radical differences emerged. Acceptance of premarital intercourse spiralled significantly downward within the same age group from the single person to the married, to the married person with young children, to the parent with teen-age children. The author of the study concluded that these differences in attitude were based not upon age, but upon the individual's feelings of responsibility for the behavior of others, especially his dependents.

THE PROBLEM OF GUILT

The more guilt a young person feels about his sexual behavior, the more restricted is his level of intimacy in premarital sexual experiences. However, guilt itself does not necessarily inhibit sexual behavior. Interestingly enough, most young people gradually increase their sexual involvement in order to minimize whatever guilt they feel about their premarital sexual activity.

For example, a couple might begin with kissing only and feel some guilt about it. On a subsequent date, they involve themselves in the kissing behavior again, but this time they do not feel the same degree of guilt. They continue the kissing episodes until the guilt disappears altogether. Next they move to a level of greater sexual intimacy—say, to petting. Again they feel guilty, but they overcome it by repeating the same behavior over and over again until the guilt disappears. They then move to another level of intimacy, and so on.

Ten levels of intimacy may be involved in the progress from kissing to coitus. Although there is considerable distance between levels 1 and 10, there is likely to be no more distance between levels 9 and 10 than there is between levels 1 and 2. In new dating situations with different partners, furthermore, both will quickly progress to the level of sexual activity that they had reached in earlier relationships.

Patterns of guilt feelings appear to undergo a change over a period of time, especially among older unmarried men and women. Many men suffer more guilt feelings over sexual matters than women do. Women, in nonmarital sexual relationships especially, want assurance that they are desired and respected for more than their sexual performance. They also want reassurance that their sexual partners will not "kiss and tell," and that the men will retain the same level of regard for them after intercourse as before.

Because society assigns the more active role in a sexual relationship to the man, he may feel that he is the "seducer," placing the responsibility for the woman's participation squarely on his shoulders. In order to reduce his feelings of guilt or anxiety, he must feel either that there is love in the relationship or that the woman is "bad." Since he feels guilty about his "seduction" of her, he comes to regard her as the cause of his guilt. He is then impelled to express his hostility and anger by quarreling or fighting with her, speaking to her in a degrading manner, or otherwise indicating his rejection of her—the very woman who thought enough of him to share with him the most intimate of human experiences.

SEXUAL ATTITUDES AND MARITAL ADJUSTMENT

In addition to the external influences exerted by culture, race, religion, upbringing, and other factors, there are also internal influences exerted on the individual in the formation of his sexual attitudes. The importance of emotions and of personality factors in sexual adjustment and marital happiness has been clearly indicated in research findings.

Self-esteem, for example, has been related to sexual feelings and behavior in women. Women who rate high in self-esteem, or dominance feelings, are self-confident, self-assured, and display feelings of superiority. Women who rate low in dominance feelings, or who have low self-esteem, show the opposite personality characteristics, while middle-dominance women fall about midway between the two extremes.

Dominance traits affect sexual behavior as well as feelings. High-dominance women are much more likely than low-dominance women to masturbate and to have premarital sexual intercourse. An exception to this finding is in Jewish women, who are generally found to be higher in dominance feelings and behavior than Catholic or Protestant women; they are nonetheless more apt to remain virgins until marriage than women of the other two religious groups. Women of low dominance feelings avoid the woman-above positions during sexual intercourse while those with very high dominance feelings frequently prefer those positions. The low-dominance man or woman often dislikes or is afraid of sex.

The most satisfactory marriages are those in which the husband equals or is somewhat (but not markedly) superior to his wife in dominance feelings. On the other hand, if the wife has higher dominance feelings than her husband or if the husband is markedly more dominant than his wife, social and sexual maladjustments are likely to be found, unless both are very secure persons.

A high-dominance woman is usually attracted to a high-dominance man and wants him to be straightforward, passionate, and somewhat violent in their lovemaking. She wishes him to proceed quickly without prolonged wooing. The middle-dominance woman prefers slower, gentler wooing in which sex is woven into a pattern of loving words, tenderness, soft music, and low lights. It has been said that the high-dominance woman unconsciously wants to be raped; the middle-dominance woman wants to be seduced; and the low-dominance woman wants to be left alone.

People who rate high in "sex attitude" appreciate sex for its own sake and wholeheartedly approve of it; people who rate very low are highly puritanical and inhibited in their sexual attitudes, and reject sex as something disgusting. A large portion of high-dominance individuals like and engage in oral-genital activity. Generally speaking, the higher the dominance rating, the more attractive they find the external genitalia of the sexual partner. In marriages of high-dominance people, the couples very frequently have experimented with almost every form of sexual activity known to sexologists. While these sexual acts would likely be considered pathological by low-dominance subjects, they contain no pathological connotation for high-dominance subjects. These findings lead to the conclusion that no one can judge a sexual act as intrinsically abnormal or perverted. Only abnormal or perverted individuals can commit abnormal or perverted acts. That is, the motivation behind the act is far more important than the act itself.

Although marital happiness depends to an important degree upon sexual adjustment, the consistent observation of clinicians is that sexual adjustment in marriage is possible even when sexual responsiveness is quite limited. Furthermore, if most other areas of the marital interrelationship are satisfactory, a woman may consider herself happy in marriage even though she is unresponsive sexually. Conversely, when any significant non-sexual aspect of the marriage is unsatisfactory, a woman may be unhappy in marriage even though she may be highly responsive sexually.

Interestingly enough, the strongest relationships between marital happiness and female orgasm seem to be in marriages at the extremes of the continuum—"very happy" and "very unhappy" ones. Research has shown that wives who always or almost always reach orgasm are more often "very happy" in their marriages. Only 4% of women in reportedly "very happy" marriages fail to reach orgasm in intercourse, while 19% of women in "very unhappy" marriages fail to reach orgasm.

The relationships between sexual satisfaction and marital satisfaction are complex and intertwined. A wife's sexual re-

sponsiveness is directly related to her husband's sexual satisfaction, which in turn contributes to his marital satisfaction,
which contributes to his wife's marital satisfaction, which increases her sex interest and responsiveness . . . *ad infinitum.*

A word about affection. Many people in our culture, especially
men, have difficulty entering into a warm, close, loving interchange with others. Little boys are often taught that tenderness
and compassion are "sissy" characteristics; little girls are ad-
monished that being warmly responsive is "forward." Growing
up in an environment that restricts positive emotional responses,
the individual may learn to express only negative emotions, such
as anger and hostility. Nonetheless these people grow into
adulthood with the abstract knowledge that some warm emotional exchanges are vital and expected in successful sexual
interaction. But because they learned in their formative years
to express only negative emotional responses, such people will
actually instigate quarrels or fights with their sexual partner in
order to express the only type of emotionality they understand.
Men who have never learned how to express tenderness, or who
are afraid to do so, will often ignore the woman with whom
they are sexually involved, or make belittling remarks to her.
These men *want* to demonstrate their commitment but do not
know how to use the appropriate positive emotions. Instead,
they use the only emotional expressions that they are familiar
with—the negative ones.

Women often accuse men of showing affection toward them
only when they have intercourse in mind; men deny this. What
often happens is that the man begins simply with the intention of
expressing affection. If the woman responds warmly, he becomes sexually excited. The woman then judges only in terms
of the final outcome and not the initial intent of the man.

Fortunately, both men and women can be taught the joy of
experiencing close, warm, loving relationships. If they have not
acquired this knowledge through normal maturational processes
or through experience and observation, psychotherapy can help
them gain insight into the immense value of expressing and
receiving affection. When men and women recognize that free
expression of affection is neither to be feared nor to be used as a
barometer of weakness, all their human relationships, including
the sexual one, will be much fuller and happier.

Much is heard today about the role of love in all aspects of human behavior, especially sexual behavior. The arguments range from "sex is empty and animalistic without love" to "sex can be fun and enjoyable without love, and those who insist upon imposing love into a sexual relation are simply guilty about sex and trying to convince themselves that the act can somehow be made acceptable."

Distinctions are drawn between "loving" someone and "being in love" with someone. "Love" is interpreted to mean a deep concern over the welfare of another person, and "being in love" as a romantic or sexual feeling for another person. The two types of love are not, of course, necessarily exclusive. Indeed, the two coexist in courtship days, in the early part of most marriages, and in those fortunate marriages of long and happy duration. It is when the romance, excitement, and "magic" in a marriage disappear or significantly decrease that the marriage counselor most often hears "I still love my husband (or wife) but I am just not 'in love' with him anymore." Such a state can be dangerous in any marriage; it can be disasterous when either or both spouses are immature or hold unreasonable expectations for their marriage. Married partners frequently use the excuse of no longer being "in love" with their mates as a license to seek romance with another person.

From earliest recorded history the word "love" has carried thousands of definitions and meanings. All of the world's great religions have espoused the perfect love that St. Paul defined in the thirteenth chapter of First Corinthians: "Love is patient, kind, nonenvious, never boastful, not conceited, not rude, never selfish, not quick to take offense. Love holds no grudges and delights not in sin, but in truth. It believes, hopes, and endures all things. . . . There are three lasting values: faith, hope, and love. The greatest of these is love."

A more practical definition of love is that it is a state in which one person cares as much about the security and satisfaction of another person as he cares about his own.

The word "love" has been used to cover a multitude of trivial as well as important emotions and has come to be equated with many other experiences. For example, one of the almost constant aspects of love is longing. The unwanted, unloved child silently wishes each morning that "my mother (or father) will love me today." That person is likely to carry his longing into adulthood, when it becomes "I wish that she (or he) will *desire* me today." Thus he erroneously equates sexual desire with love.

Since love has come to be associated with so many extraneous factors and to cover such a broad range of feelings, some people believe that "intimacy" may be a better word to describe the element in meaningful human relationships which is so fundamental to their growth. In order for intimacy to evolve, both time and privacy are needed. The five primary components of intimacy, in the order of their development, are: *choice, mutuality, reciprocity, trust,* and *delight.*

One chooses, on a conscious basis, those few with whom one can or shall be intimate. The choice must be a mutual one, since a unilateral choice would obviously exclude intimacy. In true intimacy one partner cannot be more intimate than the other, thus the third component, reciprocity. But none of the foregoing will prevail and thrive without the development of mutual trust, a step involving many small experiences in which each individual opens his innermost self to the other. Small revelations about himself allow the individual to test the safety of his disclosures. As trust is built on these successive, successful experiences, intimacy develops to its ultimate expression—delight in one another.

The delight of two people in one another, in an atmosphere of security based on mutuality, reciprocity, and trust, is surely what we all seek in human relationships. If this sort of intimacy develops and persists over the years, it will not be destroyed by physical infirmities, aging, fading looks, reduced sexual potency, or even infidelity. Perhaps intimacy is the force that binds "loving" someone and being "in love" with someone.

FURTHER READING

Marriage and Family Interaction, by R. R. Bell. Homewood, Ill.: Dorsey Press, 1971.

> This book on marriage and the family gives a good review of the sexual attitudes of Americans. The causes and development of the attitudes are also discussed.

The Transparent Self, by S. M. Jourard. New York: D. Van Nostrand, 1971.

> The personal and interpersonal difficulties which arise when an individual conceals his true feelings are discussed in this paperback book. Jourard believes that self-concealment leads to alienation and to emotional and physical illness. He explores self-disclosure in relation to marital adjustment, family relationships, and the male role in our society and develops the concept that sickness is a protest against the life-denying elements in our lives.

Sexuality: A Search for Perspective, edited by D. L. Grummon and A. M. Barclay. New York: D. Van Nostrand, 1971.

> Based on a colloquy held at Michigan State University, this group of papers contains a number of useful sections for further study of the issues surrounding sex roles, sex and personal identity, sexual codes and personal choice, and the new sexuality.

Sexual Behavior in the Human Male, by A. C. Kinsey, W. B. Pomeroy, and C. E. Martin. Philadelphia: W. B. Saunders, 1948.

> This book is the summary of the Kinsey research into the sexual behavior of the American human male. Chapters 10, 11, and 17 are particularly related to sexual attitudes.

Sexual Behavior in the Human Female, by A. C. Kinsey, W. B. Pomeroy, C. E. Martin, and P. H. Gebhard. Philadelphia: W. B. Saunders, 1953.   •

> Chapters 1, 3, 5, 8, 10, and 11 are most pertinent to the question of sexual attitudes.

Human Sexuality, 2d ed., by J. L. McCary. New York: D. Van Nostrand, 1973.

> Chapter 16 consists of a thorough review of American attitudes toward sex.

8 THE SEXUAL ACT

The current "realistic" trend in movies has led to a proliferation of films that prominently feature nudity and sexual activity. There is almost always a scene in which a man and a woman enter a bedroom, shut the door, peel off their clothes, and fall into bed. The camera focuses on the facial expressions of the couple; by various sounds and movements, they convey the passion of a mutual, ecstatic orgasm. The only realistic thing about such depictions of sexual experience is that the actors are real people.

A man and a woman who are trying to develop a close, satisfying sexual relationship will learn very little from the abrupt intimacy portrayed in such films. In real life, the sexual act is rarely accomplished with such mechanical dispatch or with such instant expertise. Indeed, sex would quickly become a very dull and monotonous activity if it were.

Films which emphasize the ecstasy of orgasm convey a distortion of the sexual act because they omit the many activities and levels of feeling which precede orgasm and are among the greatest pleasures of sexual experience. The sexual act consists of three distinct phases: the period of sexual arousal, or *foreplay*; the period of *coitus* (during which the male penis is inserted into the female vagina) which leads to orgasm; and the period following orgasm, called the *aftermath*, or *resolution*. In this chapter we will consider the various techniques and positions involved in the sexual act, and the influence of various substances on sexual desire. Chapter 9 will go into more detail on the physiological and psychological aspects of orgasm.

The sexual act has long been surrounded by a number of myths, including the belief that there is a marked difference in the sexual responsiveness of men and women. Research has shown, however, that a woman's sexual response can be just as intense as that of a man. The physiological and psychological experiences of men and woman during the sexual act are more similar than dissimilar, and there is little difference in the degree to which men and women respond to *erotic,* or sexually arousing, stimuli. While women may respond in a slightly different manner and to slightly different stimuli than men, both are equally aroused by erotic literature, films, and fantasies and other psychological stimuli. Furthermore, a woman's responsiveness to direct physical stimulation, like a man's, is dependent only on her receptiveness to sexual activity and to the technique employed by her partner.

Too often, a young couple who sincerely wish to give each other an enjoyable sexual experience are hampered by their mutual ignorance and inexperience. Young men are expected somehow to possess skill and finesse and to be able to take the lead in sexual encounters with smooth confidence. Young women, on the other hand, frequently feel that naiveté and femininity go hand in hand, and they therefore may place unrealistic demands on their partners to teach them "all about sex."

Acquiring information about effective techniques of sexual stimulation will lead to confidence in both partners and to a more equal responsibility for the enjoyment of sex. A knowledge of technique, however, is not enough to establish and maintain a rewarding sexual relationship. There must also be a genuine, unselfish concern for the sexual enjoyment of one's partner.

TECHNIQUES OF SEXUAL AROUSAL

Much of the enjoyment of sexual activity, for most men and women, is in the initial stage when each partner contributes to the sexual arousal of the other. The act of arousal, in fact, is a rewarding and pleasurable experience in itself and should not be looked upon as a series of "preliminaries" preceding the "real thing."

Some of the elementary requirements for sexual arousal are

patently obvious, but they are overlooked with distressing frequency. The most important of these is personal attractiveness. Sexual happiness is not reserved only for the "beautiful people," but visual stimulation is extremely important in a sexual relationship. Clean, shiny hair, a clean body that is supple and healthy, neatly trimmed nails, and clean, appropriate clothing are the first steps in being desirable to the opposite sex.

The sense of smell is also very important in sexual activity. The man whose sexual technique is absolutely flawless will fail to excite the most receptive woman if he has bad breath, offensive body odor, or unclean hair. Similarly, the woman whose sexual response is uninhibited and enthusiastic will be unappealing if she does not present a body that is clean and fresh. Odors in the genital area are particularly unappealing and sexually inhibiting. Both men and women should take care to remove, with soap and water and cloth, the malodorous smegma which collects under the prepuce of the penis and the clitoris. Also, the entire genital area should be given careful attention to remove the secretions that normally accumulate each day.

Just as the senses of sight and smell are important to sexual arousal and enjoyment, so is the sense of sound. Music, of course, is frequently associated with lovemaking, and enterprising music companies have even issued records "to make love by." Talking can also be an enhancing factor in sexual activity, and both men and women find the verbalization of feelings and desires highly enjoyable and stimulating during lovemaking. Tender expressions of love, exclamations of delight, requests for particular movements, admiration for the partner's body, and earthy expressions of desire all add immensely to the sexual satisfaction of both partners. Women, especially, desire to be "talked to" during the sexual act.

Pace and duration, as well as style, are matters of individual taste. Generally speaking, however, an unhurried pace is most likely to bring the greatest satisfaction to both partners. Women are more likely to enjoy sex—and therefore to make it more enjoyable for their partners—if there is ample time (at least 15 or 20 minutes) for them to reach a peak of excitement before intercourse. A woman's orgasmic capacity and enjoyment are further heightened if her partner is able to continue intercourse for an extended period of time.

A man usually achieves orgasm within about 4 minutes after *intromission* (the insertion of the penis into the vagina), while the average woman requires over 10 minutes of sexual intercourse before she attains an orgasmic response. With manual, electric vibrator, or oral-genital stimulation, however, a woman can usually reach orgasm in less than 4 minutes. Studies have shown that if intercourse lasts longer than 11 minutes, almost every woman will reach an orgasm. By contrast, only about 25% of women are able to achieve an orgasmic response if intercourse lasts less than a minute. A revealing fact which every man should carefully consider is that many broken marriages have histories of sexual intercourse of short duration. The muscle control necessary for a man to engage in lengthy acts of coitus is developed through training and exercise, just as any other muscle control is developed.

A man can often condition himself, during masturbation, to delay ejaculation for longer and longer periods of time. If premature or early ejaculation persists in sexual intercourse, training in methods of ejaculatory control (which are described in Chapter 10) can overcome the problem in almost all cases. The rewards to his partner—present or future—and to himself will be well worth the effort expended in such training.

The Erogenous Zones

Erogenous zones are areas of the body, genital and non-genital, that are rich in the nerve endings whose stimulation causes sexual arousal. The most sensitive erogenous zones for both sexes are the genitals, the inner and outer regions of the thighs, the breasts (particularly the nipples), the buttocks, and the abdomen. Other erogenous areas are the armpits, small of the back, shoulders, neck, earlobes, scalp, eyelids, and especially the mouth, tongue, eyes, and nose. Although stimulation of any of these areas is sexually arousing under favorable conditions, response can be obstructed by fear, pain, guilt, or distaste.

In addition to those zones that are generally common to all people, other areas of the body can take on erogenous sensitivity through conditioning. For example, if a man were to tickle the sole of his partner's foot each time they had enjoyable intercourse, foot-tickling would come to be associated with pleasurable intercourse, and the sole of the foot would become a conditioned erogenous zone for that particular woman.

A knowledge of the erogenous zones of one's own body is essential for the development of one's full capacity for sexual responsiveness. Sexual responsiveness is learned through experience and experimentation, beginning with one's own body. The person who is most sexually responsive has developed a sensuous enjoyment and appreciation for the sight, smell, taste, feel, and use of his body in all its infinite capacities.

Learning About One's Own Sexuality

Probably the most successful way of learning to respond to one's full sexual capacity is through *masturbation,* the self-stimulation of the genitals through manipulation. A healthy and beneficial means of reducing sexual frustration and tension, masturbation (which will be discussed at greater length in Chapter 13) is practiced by the majority of both men and women, married and single. Men usually masturbate by gripping the penis and moving the hand back and forth, so that the glans is stimulated in much the same manner as it is in the in-and-out movements of coitus. The degree of pressure and the speed of movement vary from man to man. Women usually masturbate by stroking the clitoris, again varying the intensity of pressure and the speed of movement to suit their individual preferences. Most women prefer stroking the side of the clitoris rather than its glans. Some women prefer vaginal stimulation and insert phallus-shaped objects or a finger into the vagina during masturbation. A few women prefer stimulation of the urethral opening, and a small percentage are able to attain orgasm by rhythmically pressing their thighs together.

Other masturbatory techniques useful in heightening women's genital sensitivity include directing a stream of water onto the vulval area while bathing or showering, and applying an electric vibrator directly to the clitoral area. Women report that the continuous pressure of running water produces an orgasm just slightly less intense than that produced by an electric vibrator. Of the vibrators, most women prefer the type which has rubber-knobbed attachments that can be applied to the side or glans of the clitoris. Stimulation of this intensity seldom fails to bring a woman to multiple orgasms, and the orgasms she experiences are usually of a much greater intensity than those she experiences by any other means. Some women who enjoy vaginal stimulation insert a battery-driven penis-shaped vibrator directly into the vagina (although usually only slightly penetrating the opening), either as the sole masturbatory technique or in conjunction with manual or electric-vibrator stimulation of the clitoral area.

By employing these masturbatory techniques, men and women can discover what is most stimulating to them and they can, in turn, give this information to their sexual partners. There are wide differences in individual reactions to various arousal techniques. Sexual partners cannot be clairvoyant; it is impossible for anyone to know what is most enjoyable for another person unless he is told.

Although there are many myths about the dangers of masturbation to body or mind, none of these myths has any foundation in fact. Masturbation does not "weaken" a man, nor does it lead to insanity, moral depravity, or hair on the palms of the hands! The only thing that masturbation leads to is pleasurable sensations including orgasm, and, in a man, ejaculation, with an accompanying release of sexual tension. In addition, there is no such thing as "excessive masturbation." The body regulates itself by refusing to respond when a state of sexual satiation is reached. Therefore the amount of sexual activity engaged in by any one person is normal for that person.

A young couple who have fondness and sexual attraction for one another may feel that sexual intercourse should be postponed until marriage—either to each other or to others. For these couples, mutual masturbation allows them relief from the uncomfortable congestion of the genitals which can occur when sexual tensions are not released by orgasm. Mutual masturbation also gives them the emotional fulfillment of providing sexual pleasure to each other. Young people are sometimes warned that petting to orgasm will prevent their being able to achieve orgasm through intercourse when they marry. On the contrary, those people who enjoy petting and who are capable of freely responding to it are most capable of freely responding to sexual intercourse and of deriving the most pleasure from it.

Foreplay

Although the entire body can and should be used in sexual arousal, the hands are of primary importance. A lover's hands should seldom be motionless during the entire sexual act. Each partner should use both the palms and fingers to touch, stroke, massage, and fondle all parts of the other's body. Thus each has the dual satisfaction of receiving stimulation and of enjoying the tactile exploration of the other's body.

During the first stages of sexual arousal, both men and women are stimulated by gentle, slow, generalized stroking, but the caressing should become more specific as sex play progresses. Lightly and gently at first, and then more boldly, the hands should dart and slide over the partner's body—stroking, holding, caressing, squeezing, and massaging—alternating strokes with the palms of the hands with light, silky stroking of the fingertips. The stroking should gradually move toward the genital area in an advance-retreat-advance approach.

The man should be aware of the sensitivity of the woman's skin, and of the thinness and delicacy of the tissue of the vulva and vagina. These areas should not be manually stimulated unless the man's fingernails are clipped and smooth, and unless the vulval region is well moistened with either bodily secretions or with a commercial lubricating product such as K-Y Sterile Lubricant. The clitoris is especially sensitive and cannot long tolerate direct and uninterrupted manipulation.

Both men and women are sexually aroused by breast stimulation. The man can gently massage his partner's breasts, interspersing the manipulation with a light brushing of the nipple and an occasional gentle pinch of its sensitive tip. Caressing of the breast with the hands may be alternated with soft moist kisses and an exploring tongue. The tempo of the tongue's movements should be changed occasionally, allowing it to dart back and forth across the nipple in a firm, rapid manner, before resuming once more the soft moist stimulation. This kind of oral contact is equally pleasing to both men and women. Men are also sensitive to stimulation of their nipples. The woman may gently roll his nipples between her thumb and finger or lightly rake her fingernails across their tips.

Kissing, the usual forerunner of all sexual activity, should be continued during sex play. Like caressing, kissing should be varied in a teasing manner: open mouth, closed mouth; light lip pressure, heavy lip pressure; moist lips, dry lips; soft lips, nibbling teeth and lips; a darting tongue, a soft sensuous tongue. The lover's face and body should be covered with kisses, and the tongue should participate in this exploration. Ordinarily, kissing of the mouth should precede kissing of other parts of the body, except perhaps the hands. The woman may be particularly pleased if the man tenderly kisses her hands or nibbles her fingertips.

Sexual stimulation should continue until both lovers are ready to proceed with intercourse. Because both men and women have traditionally used the man's sexual response and capability as the gauge of "the way it is done," many women—and men, too—fail to realize that women are capable by natural endowment of multi-orgasms, and, in fact, frequently require such multiple responses during a single sexual episode in order to be sexually satisfied. Many women, for example, are able to have six or more orgasms during a single period of sexual activity; about 15% of women regularly have multiple orgasms. By contrast, only about 6% to 8% of men are able to have more than one orgasm during each sexual experience; when the capacity for multiple orgasm exists, it is usually found only in very young men.

Since women are multi-orgasmic and since each successive orgasm is more intense than the preceding one, many women find that they achieve greater satisfaction if they are brought to orgasm one or more times before coitus. In this way, they are not left unsatisfied after the man has ejaculated and is no longer able to continue intercourse. Some men, of course, are capable of delaying their own orgasm in prolonged sexual intercourse; their sexual partners can therefore experience multiple orgasms during a lengthy coital act.

Keeping the man sexually excited and pleasurably engaged in bringing her to orgasm as often as she requires for complete satisfaction will necessitate timing and finesse on the woman's part. With her caresses and kisses, she should keep him just below the point of greatest sexual excitement, with an occasional teasing stimulus that will momentarily heighten his arousal level. She should be aware, for example, that stimulating the glans and frenum of his penis for any length of time may cause ejaculation to be imminent, and she should therefore avoid such intense stimulation unless she is ready for penetration. By enthusiastic response and pleasurable manipulation of her partner's body, she can, with practice, keep him at a prolonged state of erection, adding to the enjoyment of both.

Oral-Genital Stimulation

A form of sexual activity that is intensely pleasurable for both sexes is *oral-genital stimulaton.* This stimulation is also a very effective means of bringing both a man and a woman to orgasm. *Cunnilingus,* the tongue-stroking of the woman's vulval area by the man, usually centers about the clitoris, although other parts of the vulva, particularly the labia minora, are also sensitive to oral stimulation. The sensitive glans of the clitoris can be stimulated in much the same manner as the nipples of the breasts are stimulated by the tongue. Beginning with light, teasing strokes of the tongue, interspersed with bold darting motions, the man should vary the technique to keep pace with the woman's heightening sexual excitement. As the woman's climax nears, the man should maintain a steady, constant stimulation of the clitoral area. (At the height of sexual tension the clitoris withdraws under its prepuce, and direct contact can no longer be maintained.) If the woman desires another orgasm, the same licking movements frequently will quickly bring another one about.

Fellatio, oral-genital stimulation performed by the woman on the man, is highly pleasing to a man both for its physiological stimulation and also because it indicates that his partner enjoys a part of his body that is very important to him. Starting by covering the penis with soft kisses, the woman should gradually take the erect penis into her mouth. With tongue movements similar to those used in cunnilingus, she should stimulate the penis, particularly at the glans and frenum. She can vary her technique according to the man's preferences, now lightly and softly kissing the penis, now sucking it closely, all the while stroking and fondling the testicles and scrotum. This kind of stimulation seldom fails to arouse a man to intense excitement, and a woman should be aware that the more intense and rapid her movements are, the more likely it is to bring a man to a height of arousal that can easily terminate in orgasm. She should therefore time her stimulation of the penis to coincide with her own state of sexual arousal.

Although some people have a negative attitude toward oral-genital sex, it is practiced by the majority of men and women who are college educated, and it has been recommended by many authorities in the field of sex and marriage as a desirable and vastly pleasurable form of sexual behavior. If either partner, after attempting at least some experimentation with both giving and receiving oral-genital stimulation, finds that the technique is objectionable, then that individual should abstain from this form of sexual activity for the time being.

The freedom of both partners to explore all arousal techniques freely and to refrain from any technique which causes objections in either partner is essential for the fullest pleasure of both the man and the woman.

COITAL POSITIONS

The number of possible positions that two people can adopt for sexual intercourse is almost limitless, and each couple must arrive at their own preferences through experimentation and practice. Indeed, continued experimentation and adaptation of preferred positions add spice to the sexual act and prevent it from becoming monotonous. There is no one "normal" position, and any and all positions of sexual intercourse that both partners find satisfactory and pleasurable should be used.

The four most common positions of sexual intercourse are face-to-face, man-above; face-to-face, woman-above; side position, face-to-face, and the rear-entry position. There are endless variations on these positions, of course, and with an uninhibited approach, each couple can work out their own adaptations.

The *face-to-face, man-above position* is so common in our society that it is often and erroneously referred to as the "normal" position. However, people of some other cultures consider the position uncommon and refer to it with amusement as the "missionary position." Although it is still probably the most

FIGURE 8.1 Representation of the erect penis inserted into the vagina.

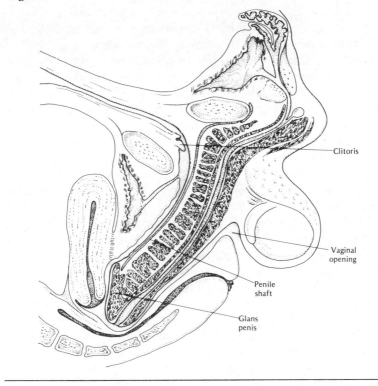

Clitoris

Vaginal opening

Penile shaft

Glans penis

familiar coital position in our society, the position is relatively rare in other cultures and is far from being a universal favorite.

Intromission is easily achieved in the face-to-face, man-above position when the woman lies on her back with legs apart and knees bent. The man, supporting himself on his elbows and knees, is largely in control of the couple's bodily movements. He should try to keep contact with the clitoris by putting pressure on the upper part of his partner's vulva. Pressure on her pubic bone is helpful to sandwich the clitoris between it and his pubic bone, thus providing clitoral friction. In this position, the woman may vary the position of her legs, sometimes closing them, sometimes pulling her knees to her shoulders or locking her legs around her partner's body.

The *face-to-face, woman-above position* offers certain advantages that the man-above position lacks. Clitoral contact is frequently easier and the friction more intense, for example, and the woman can control the tempo of movement and depth of penetration. This position is less sexually stimulating to the man because his body is less active; his muscles are more relaxed, so that he is frequently able to delay ejaculation for a longer period. Since the woman has primary control of coital movement, the man can relax and abandon himself to the pleasures of his partner's caresses and of erotic fantasy. This position may be varied by the man's resting on his elbows and raising his bent knees for the woman to lean back against as she sits astride him. She can also lie full length against him, thus maintaining full body contact.

In the *face-to-face side position,* both partners lie on their sides facing each other. In this position, they can share control of the movements of intercourse. This position is sometimes assumed after the partners have achieved intromission in another position and have rolled onto their sides, giving them complete freedom to maneuver their legs, arms, and hands. Often the couple can go to sleep without losing contact after the completion of intercourse. One of the chief advantages of this position is that neither partner is supporting the weight of the other. It is therefore especially helpful to assume this position when either partner is fatigued or in ill health or if one partner is considerably taller than the other. Since both partners can easily regulate their pelvic thrusts, sexual activity before orgasm can often be prolonged.

One variation of the basic face-to-face side position is the *lateral coital position,* the position which Masters and Johnson declare to be the most satisfactory for the vast majority of couples who try it. In this position the man can best develop and maintain ejaculatory control, and the woman is free to engage in slow or rapid pelvic thrusting. Thus, it allows the greatest flexibility of free sexual expression for both partners.

The *rear-entry position* may be assumed in a variety of ways. Both partners can lie on their sides, or the woman can kneel, lie on her stomach, or sit on the man's lap with her back to him.

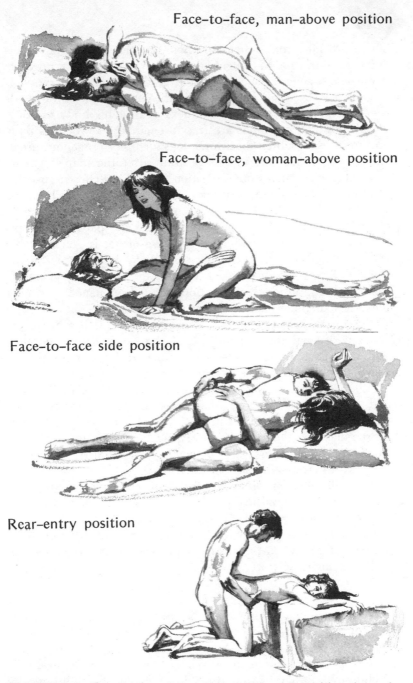

Face-to-face, man-above position

Face-to-face, woman-above position

Face-to-face side position

Rear-entry position

FIGURE 8.2 Four basic coital positions. The side position shown is termed the lateral coital position by Masters and Johnson.

There are numerous other variations. In the side-by-side rear-entry position, the placement of the woman's buttocks prevents deep penile penetration, but whatever degree of penetration is possible can be easily regulated by the man. A man often finds the pressure of his partner's buttocks against his body exciting. In this position, his hands are free to encircle the woman's body and to caress her breasts, clitoris, legs, or other erogenous areas. Contact is usually lost in this position after the man's orgasm.

A more vigorously active position is the knee-chest rear-entry position in which both partners assume a kneeling position, the woman with her head and arms on the bed. The position in which the woman lies on her stomach and her partner attempts rear-entry penetration while lying on top of her is generally too awkward and insufficiently pleasurable to be used by many couples. Sitting positions offer variety and novel enjoyment to some couples, although they allow such deep penetration that they are sometimes uncomfortable for the woman.

One of the chief factors which affects a couple's choice of coital position is their feeling about the psychological implications of the various positions. Some men feel uncomfortable in coitus involving any of the woman-above positions because having the woman in a "superior" position makes them feel passive and controlled. Conversely, some women are uncomfortable in woman-above positions because they prefer to be "dominated" by the man and the woman-above positions seem too aggressive to them. These feelings are, of course, related to the sex roles which are perpetuated by our society.

It is a burden for either partner to *always* have the responsibility of initiating and leading in a sexual relationship. Although it is important to recognize one's own feelings in this regard, the ideal relationship permits both the man and the woman to be active and passive in turn as their own needs and the needs of their partner vary.

A knowledge of the variety of possible sexual positions is helpful to facilitate experimentation and avoid monotony; however, a couple should not be overly concerned with the techniques of sexual intercourse while they are engaging in it. Coital mobility is very important, but movement uninhibited by any conscious thought processes is probably of greater importance. It has been found, for example, that women who can consciously control their coital movements at the height of intercourse are not so likely to reach orgasm as are those who lose control of their movements.

Coitus should not be approached as a gymnastic feat, an endurance contest, or one of a series of laboratorylike experiments. Rather, it should be approached as an act designed to bring mutual pleasure through a variety of techniques and postures. Any technique of sexual arousal or position of sexual intercourse that affords mutual pleasure to a couple should be freely enjoyed by them.

APHRODISIACS AND ANAPHRODISIACS

Man has sought to regulate his sexual appetite since the beginning of civilization through a variety of foods, drugs, mechanical devices, and physical activities. Most often the search has been for means of increasing his sexual desire, but in some instances, means of decreasing his desire have also been sought. An *aphrodisiac* is anything which increases sexual desire; an *anaphrodisiac* has the opposite effect.

Certain foods have long been thought to have sexually stimulating properties. The rarity or newness of some food (such as the potato when it was first brought to England) may arouse the hope that a sexual stimulant has been discovered. In other cases, certain foods have shapes or properties which resemble a particular sex organ, and the superstitious belief arises that sexual strength can be gained by eating such food. This belief, called the "doctrine of signatures," leads to the consumption of certain foods for their assumed erotic properties.

One well-known example is the idea that the oyster (which resembles the testicles) contains sexually arousing properties. Chemical analysis, however, shows that the oyster consists of water, protein, and carbohydrates, plus small amounts of fat, sugar, and minerals—none of which can directly affect sex drive or performance.

Other cultures have their own applications of this theory. Many Chinese, for example, place unshakable belief in the potency of powdered rhinoceros horn. It is not difficult to recognize how the succinct word "horny" has come to mean having strong sexual desire, in the vernacular.

Very recently, the lowly peanut was alleged by a story circulated in the press to have aphrodisiac qualities. As a result of the story, the headmistress of a South African high school promptly banned peanut-butter sandwiches from her girl students' lunch boxes!

The persistence of such absurd myths is undoubtedly due to the fact that the psychological impact of *believing* that certain foods are aphrodisiacs is sometimes strong enough to produce, temporarily at least, an elevation in sexual desire and performance. The result is that the person believes that his sexual triumph is directly related to eating raw bull's testicles ("prairie oysters") or clams or celery or tomatoes or any one of the other foods that are reputed to be aphrodisiacs. Thus, the individual's belief tends to perpetuate itself, and he often passes along his superstition to other people.

Another reason for the widespread belief in the aphrodisiac qualities of certain foods is the fact that there is a strong association in the minds of most people between hunger for food and sex. It is certainly true that highly nutritious food is essential to physical well-being and that the well-nourished person is likely to have a more satisfying sex life. It is also true that certain sensuous people derive a distinct aphrodisiac effect from a gourmet meal that is served leisurely and elegantly in an atmosphere of candlelight and lovely music. The effect is psychological, however; food in itself cannot be an aphrodisiac.

Alcohol is probably the most famous of the alleged sexual stimulants, but the truth is that alcohol is a depressant. In sufficient quantities, it narcotizes the brain, thus retarding reflexes, and dilates the blood vessels, thus interfering with the capacity for erection. However, in small quantities, alcohol acts to remove an individual's sexual inhibitions, and many men and women report that their sex drive and sexual enjoyment are increased by alcohol consumption. If sexual drive and ability habitually increase after the use of alcohol, or if the person is unable to function sexually without the use of alcohol, one of two forces (perhaps both) is at work: either the stresses of daily living have acted as temporary inhibitors to sexual impulses, or some real emotional block exists in the area of sex. Thus, any increase in sex drive following consumption of alcohol is based on temporary removal of psychological barriers rather than an increase in physical prowess. Ridding oneself of emotional conflicts concerning sexuality will do more to increase sexual capability and enjoyment than will consumption of alcohol.

Drugs as Aphrodisiacs

The most popularly known drug associated with sexual drive is *cantharides,* or "Spanish Fly." Derived from a beetle native to southern Europe, the drug is produced when the insects are dried and heated until they disintegrate into a fine powder. When this powder is taken internally, an acute irritation of the genitourinary tract accompanied by an increase in the dilation of the associated blood vessels results. The increased blood supply to the irritated tissue can produce penile erection but without an increase in sex drive. Taken in excessive doses, Spanish Fly can cause violent illness or even death.

Africans have long used another drug for sexual arousal. Taken from a tree which is native to that region, *yohimbine* is primarily used in most nations as a diuretic (a drug which increases urine flow) and in the treatment of disorders such as neuritis and meningitis. Its aphrodisiac qualities are reportedly due to the fact that it stimulates the nerve centers which control erection. While there is some doubt about its effectiveness, yohimbine is generally conceded to be the most widely used drug for increasing sexual drive.

Claims are also made for the aphrodisiac effects of various addicting or illicit drugs such as opium, morphine, cocaine, LSD, hashish, and marijuana. Like alcohol, these drugs release inhibitions; but, also like alcohol, they tend to have an anaphrodisiac effect if taken in large enough quantities.

Marijuana has gained many devotees as a sexual stimulant. Its effect appears to be to enhance the enjoyment of sexual activity rather than to increase the sex drive. Because the drug heightens sense perception and distorts time perception, orgasm is subjectively prolonged and seems more pleasurable. No evidence exists, however, that marijuana is sexually stimulating in and of itself. Sexually inexperienced users are more apt to be "turned off" by marijuana, while those who report the greatest enhancement of their sexual feelings are those who have regular sexual intercourse with one partner. For them, marijuana's effect offers novelty and change, with resulting heightened excitement. Heavy marijuana users tend to lose their ability to discriminate between a "high" and a new sensory experience, and frequently become temporarily impotent. Their potency returns when they discontinue using marijuana for a period of several weeks. This dual effect of marijuana, to heighten sexual enjoyment and to cause impotence, has led to its reputations as both an aphrodisiac and an anaphrodisiac.

Like marijuana, any aphrodisiac effect of LSD is due to its distortion of perception and the heightened suggestibility of the user, not to any sexually stimulating properties of the chemical itself.

Two new drugs have recently been discovered to have possible aphrodisiac effects. One, PCPA, has been used experimentally to treat schizophrenia and certain types of tumors. The other, L-dopa, is used in the treatment of Parkinson's disease. Many patients who have been treated with L-dopa have shown dramatic relief of their disease symptoms, with a side effect of hypersexuality in 2% of them. Similar results have been reported in the use of PCPA. Neither the effects nor the side effects of these powerful drugs have yet been fully measured, however. Large-scale experimentation is needed to determine their specific aphrodisiac potentials, and optimism about both must be tempered with caution.

A drug which is alleged to be an intensifier of orgasmic pleasure is *amyl nitrite*. Inhaling this drug at the instant of orgasm is reported by some individuals to enhance the pleasure of the experience. (One wonders, however, how they can avoid being distracted by the mechanical operations necessary for amyl-nitrite sniffing at such a moment!) The drug apparently acts to relax the smooth muscles and consequently produces dilation of the veins in the genitourinary tract. Some of the side effects of amyl nitrite are dizziness, headache, fainting, and, in rare cases, death. Obviously, its use should be under the direction and prescription of a physician, as should that of any other drug mentioned.

Eating, drinking, and using drugs are not the only experiences alleged to be aphrodisiac. Erotic pictures, songs, and literature, as well as recordings of squeaking bedsprings accompanied by heavy breathing, moans, and gasps, have been used to titilate sexual interest and drive. Pornographic films or books are sometimes prescribed by marriage counselors for couples whose sex life has become lackluster and apathetic. While new sexual excitement can occur when one is exposed to erotic stimuli, immunity to such stimulation rapidly develops if the exposure is overdone.

All in all, the most effective aphrodisiacs for man remain good health, plenty of rest and sleep, adequate diet and exercise, and freedom from emotional tension.

Anaphrodisiac techniques have varied through the ages: from taking cold baths, as suggested by Plato and Aristotle; and wearing chastity belts and penis cages, as suggested by the Romans and the British at one time; to using tranquilizers and other chemicals in the present day.

The substance which is best known as a reputed anaphrodisiac is *saltpeter,* or potassium nitrate. In spite of frequent stories about its being sprinkled on the food in school cafeterias, boys' and girls' camp dining halls, and army mess halls, it is an almost completely neutral chemical and is an absolute failure as an anaphrodisiac. Its only physical effect is that it is a fairly effective diuretic, and this may account for its far-flung but undeserved reputation as a sex deterrent.

Recent reports indicate that the drug *Ismelin* is a fairly effective anaphrodisiac, but side effects of stomach cramps, diarrhea, and general loss of physical energy are also reported. One drug, *cyproterone acetate,* has been used in England, Germany, and Switzerland to reduce the sexual desire of aggressive sex offenders. Success has been reported, but it is too early to determine if the drug is truly effective and whether it produces harmful side effects.

Limited success has been reported from prescribing certain tranquilizers and other drugs in an attempt to decrease sexual desire. Some physicians are reluctant to use these drugs, however, fearing that removal or reduction of emotional blocks may result, producing aphrodisiac effects or unusual sexual behavior.

Men who are treated for various illnesses with the female

hormone estrogen almost always experience a decrease or cessation in sexual drive and interest. In contrast, male hormones have the opposite effect in women.

Most information regarding aphrodisiacs and anaphrodisiacs is based more on folklore than on scientific evidence. In those cases in which there seems to be a change in sexual desire or ability, the cause is usually psychological rather than physiological. Although the desire for a bottled cure for faltering sex interest is understandable, positive changes in sexual adjustment arc almost always the result of the individual's increased understanding of his own feelings about sex.

FURTHER READING

The Joy of Sex, by A. Comfort. New York: Crown, 1972.

Subtitled "A Gourmet Guide to Love Making," this book contains much material for both the sexually experienced and the sexually inexperienced who wish to develop their sex lives. Sexual positions are tastefully shown with excellent art work.

The Art and Science of Love, by A. Ellis. New York: Lyle Stuart, 1960.

This book is one of the all-time classic sex manuals. It is candid and the reading is enjoyable.

The Sensuous Woman, by J. New York: Lyle Stuart, 1969.

Now in paperback, this book is probably the best in the field for awakening and developing the sexuality of women.

The Sensuous Man, by M. New York: Lyle Stuart, 1971.

This book is also now in paperback. It was written and published as a sequel to *The Sensuous Woman* in order to provide similar awakening and development of the sexuality and sexual techniques of the man.

The Pictorial Guide to Sexual Intercourse, by I. Schwenda and T. Leuchner. New York: Pent-R-Books, 1969.

Tastefully done in good color, this paperback book shows the basic coital positions and dozens of variations of those positions.

Human Sexuality. 2d ed., by J. L. McCary. New York: D. Van Nostrand, 1973.

Chapters 10 (Techniques in Sexual Arousal), 11 (Aphrodisiacs and Anaphrodisiacs), and 12 (Positions in Sexual Intercourse) form the foundation for the material in this chapter.

9 ORGASM

Orgasm is the highly pleasurable, tension-relieving experience that is the summit of physical and emotional gratification in sexual activity. The physiological responses leading to orgasm are the same whether the sexual stimulation arises from sexual intercourse; manual, oral, or mechanical manipulation; or fantasy. In both sexes, the approach of orgasm is marked by a rise in blood pressure and pulse rate, faster and deeper breathing, engorgement of special tissues with blood, and, finally, an explosive release of muscular and nervous tension. This release is followed by a rather quick return to the nonstimulated state.

Orgasm is a short-lived experience (usually lasting about 3 to 10 seconds, ordinarily longer for women than for men), but it is among the most intense of human experiences. This intensity may be difficult to understand. However, if another body need—for example, hunger—were to be satisfied in an equally short period of time, perhaps a similar intensity of reaction would be experienced.

The subjective sensation of orgasm is centered in the pelvic region for both men and women: the penis, prostate, and seminal vesicles in men; and the clitoris, vagina, and uterus in women. The response area is considerably more generalized among women, however, than among men.

Many physiological changes occur in men and women as their sexual tension mounts to orgasmic release. Orgasm in the man is ordinarily accompanied by ejaculation, for which there is no parallel response in women. Researchers have discovered, however, that there are few other differences between male and female orgasm. The sexual responses of a man and a woman are very similar and often parallel one another.

Through carefully controlled laboratory studies spanning an 11-year period, bodily changes during the various phases of the sexual response cycle have been observed and recorded by the internationally famous team of sex researchers, William Masters and Virginia Johnson. Masters and Johnson divide their description of the sexual response cycle into four phases: the excitement phase, the plateau phase, the orgasmic phase, and the resolution phase. They have found that a variety of physical and psychological stimuli will encourage the development of these phases, and that adverse stimuli can interrupt their development.

No one is consciously aware of all the many physiological events which take place during the sexual act. But anyone wishing to understand orgasm, to heighten his or her awareness of the experience, and to know something of what his or her partner is experiencing will want to look at the orgasmic responses of men and women in some detail as we shall do in this chapter.

THE EXCITEMENT PHASE

The *excitement phase* is the initial stage of the sexual response cycle. Any form of sexual stimulation that is appealing to an individual will initiate the excitement phase, and if the stimulation is continued, it leads to the other phases of response and usually produces an orgasm. The excitement phase can be extended by interruption and subsequent resumption. It can also be stopped completely by totally withdrawing the stimulation; if the stimulation becomes objectionable or if extraneous factors interfere with the stimulation, the excitement phase may be stopped. Under any of these circumstances, the bodily changes that have occurred disappear in a relatively short time.

Sexual stimulation produces basically the same bodily reactions in both the man and the woman. Among these reactions are increased muscular tension (called *myotonia*) and an engorgement of the blood vessels (called *vasocongestion*) which causes the surrounding tissue to swell. Vasocongestion is especially pronounced in the genital organs.

A woman's physiological response to sexual stimulation in the excitement phase includes marked vasocongestion in both the external and internal genital areas. It causes the labia majora (also called the major lips or outer lips) to become congested with blood. If the woman has not borne children (in which case she is referred to by scientists as a *nullipara*), the lips thin out and become somewhat flattened. As they flatten, the lips also elevate slightly, upward and outward, flaring away from the vaginal opening to allow the man freer access. This flattening process is not usually complete until late in the excitement phase, or until the beginning of the plateau phase.

In a woman who has borne children (she is called a *multipara*) the major lips become greatly engorged, often increasing in size by two or three times. Although the lips hang in a rather loose and pendulous manner, there is a marked gaping away

FIGURE 9.1   The female pelvic region, showing organs and tissue in a normal, unexcited state.

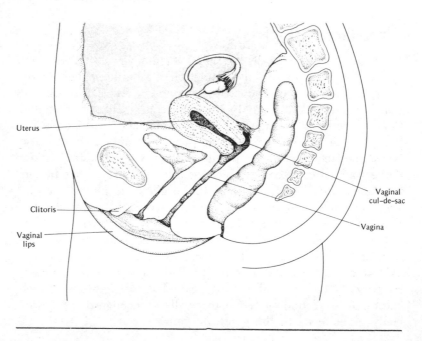

from the vaginal opening so that the man will not be impeded in penetration.

The labia minora (also called the minor lips, inner lips, or sex-skin) also begin enlarging in the excitement phase. By the end of this phase, or perhaps early in the plateau phase, they are two to three times thicker than their normal size. This thickening of the inner lips adds a centimeter or more to the length of the vaginal barrel and is further preparation for reception of the erect penis.

The clitoral shaft also swells during this phase, and the loose, wrinkled external skin that surrounds the clitoris fills out as the glans tissue beneath it expands. There is an increase in both the diameter and the length of the clitoral shaft, but the increase in size of the clitoris is usually not visible to the naked eye. If the increase in clitoral size becomes observable, it will be only after sexual tension has progressed into the late part of the excitement phase. Direct manipulation of the clitoral region will produce more rapid and greater enlargement of the clitoral glans than will other stimulation such as fantasy, breast manipulation, or sexual intercourse.

Within 10 to 30 seconds after sexual stimulation—whether psychological or physiological—has begun, the vagina begins to lubricate itself through a "sweating" phenomenon. Small droplets of clear fluid appear on the walls of the vagina; as sexual tension increases, the droplets coalesce to form a moist coating of the entire vaginal wall, completely lubricating the vaginal barrel.

The vasocongestion that causes the "sweating" in the vagina also causes a color change in the vaginal tissue. From its usual purple-red color, it changes slowly to a darker, rather patchy deep purple. The entire vaginal barrel becomes consistently darker in the subsequent phases.

Under nonexcited conditions the walls of the vagina—especially in women who have never borne a child—are touching. During the excitement phase, the wrinkled surface of the vagina stretches and flattens, and the vaginal mucosa thins with the expansion. Towards the end of the excitement phase, the entire uterus is drawn upward, pulling on the vagina and making its inner two-thirds much wider and longer in a ballooning or tenting effect which helps to prepare the vagina for the penetration of the penis. The entire vagina becomes dilated, but the marked expansion is limited to its inner two-thirds.

During the early part of the excitement phase, rapid and irregular contractions begin in the uterus. The uterus also responds with vasocongestion during this phase. The longer the phase lasts, the greater the increase in the size of the uterus over its unstimulated state. If the excitement or plateau phase is sustained for an excessively prolonged period, the uterus may become 2 or 3 times larger that its normal size.

Male genitalia show the same marked engorgement of the tissues with blood. A man's first physiological response to sexual stimulation is erection of the penis as its three spongy cylindrical bodies of erectile tissue fill with blood. This is a parallel response to vaginal lubrication in women. When the excitement phase is prolonged with varied stimuli, an erection may be lost and regained many times. Distractions such as loud noises, noticeable changes in lighting or temperature, or feelings of anxiety or fear can cause a partial or a complete loss of erection, regardless of the amount or type of stimulation. With penile erection, the

---

FIGURE 9.2   The male genitalia in the preexcitement phase. The dotted lines represent the organ positions in the excitement and plateau phases. Note that the testis and the scrotum move up and toward the body cavity .

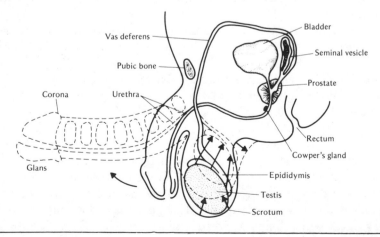

urethra, of course, also lengthens. As the excitement phase progresses, the penile urethral passage becomes twice as large in diameter as it is in an unstimulated state, and the urethral opening widens.

Sexual excitement causes the skin of the scrotum to become thick and congested, limiting the space within the scrotal sac. The testes rise higher in the scrotum, with a slight rotation of the axis of the testes. If the excitement phase is prolonged more than 5 to 10 minutes, the scrotal sac may relax again and the testes descend, but when sexual tension progresses to the plateau phase, they will quickly elevate again and the scrotal wall will rethicken.

Erection of the nipples occurs during the excitement phase in almost all women and in about 30% of men. This erection is maintained throughout the entire cycle for women, and eventually nipple erection will occur in an additional 30% of men. Nipple erection is not necessarily an indication of sexual arousal, however, since it can also be caused, in women, by cold weather, cold baths, or the removal of an excessively binding brassiere.

In women, increased sexual tension causes the *areolae*, the pigmented areas of the breasts surrounding the nipples, to become engorged and swollen. This concentration of blood in the breast tissues during the excitement phase causes the breasts to swell by 20% to 25% in women who have not nursed babies. There is somewhat less increase in breast size among women who have nursed babies because of the alteration of blood vessels and fibrous tissues caused by milk production. The breast size of men is not similarly affected by sexual stimulation.

A measleslike rash, called the *maculopapular sex flush*, appears in about three-fourths of sexually stimulated women and in about one-fourth of sexually stimulated men, although it may not appear in men until the plateau stage. It begins in the stomach region and at the throat and neck, and it spreads quickly to the breasts. As a rule, the intensity of the flush is in direct proportion to the intensity of the stimulation received.

Myotonia of voluntary muscles—and to a limited extent, of some involuntary muscles—is observable during the excitement phase, especially the latter part. There is muscle tension in the abdominal region and in the long muscles of both legs and arms. As excitement increases, the movements of both men and women become more restless, forceful, and swift. As sexual tension builds, there is a corresponding increase in heart rate and an elevation of blood pressure.

THE PLATEAU PHASE

During the *plateau phase,* sexual tension continues to mount, and physiological changes are intensified. If sexual stimulation is withdrawn during this period, an orgasm will not occur and the built-up sexual tensions will decrease very gradually over a prolonged period of time.

Several marked changes occur during this phase in the genitalia; most of the changes are elaborations of the changes that began during the excitement phase. In women, there is a vivid color change, called the *sex-skin reaction,* in the engorged labia minora. In nulliparous women, the color change ranges from ashen pink to a scarlet hue. A multiparous woman experiences a greater dilation of the veins, so that the sex-skin coloration is deeper, varying from scarlet to a dark red wine color. There is a definite correlation between the intensity of the color change and the degree of sexual excitation. The marked color change is evidence of an impending orgasm.

The clitoris exhibits its most singular response to sexual stimulation during the late plateau phase. The body and glans of the clitoris withdraw and pull back deeply underneath the foreskin or hood, so that there is a 50% reduction in total length of the clitoris just before orgasm. If sexual stimulation is removed during the plateau phase, the clitoris will resume its normal position; if stimulation is reapplied, the clitoris will withdraw again.

The outer third of the vagina, which had become slightly dilated during the excitement phase, becomes so congested with blood during the plateau phase that the vaginal opening decreases by at least a third. The distended muscles involuntarily contract, causing the vagina to tighten around the penis as the woman nears orgasm. The congested outer third of the vagina and the engorged labia minora have been given the name *orgasmic platform* by Masters and Johnson.

The uterus continues to elevate during this phase, producing a further enlargement of the inner portion of the vagina through a tenting effect. The rapid and irregular contractions of the uterus intensify as the response cycle progresses from early excitement to late plateau phase, and further vasocongestion of the uterus produces additional enlargement.

Genital reactions in the male during the plateau phase are mostly an intensification of the reactions begun in the excitement phase. Late in the plateau phase the corona of the glans of the penis becomes more swollen, and there may be a deepening of the mottled reddish-purple color of the glans and the area just below the corona, but this color change is not as marked as the sex-skin color change in women. A few drops of secretion from the Cowper's glands are usually discharged from the penis during this phase, especially if the excitement phase has been prolonged and orgasm has been delayed. This fluid is in advance of the true ejaculate.

By the end of the plateau phase, the testes are fully elevated in the scrotum, indicating that orgasm is imminent. Vasocongestion in the testes causes them to increase in size, sometimes as much as doubling. The more protracted the plateau phase is, the more vasocongestion there is and the more marked the increase in testicular size. In nearly all men, one testicle always hangs slightly lower than the other. The lower testicle, usually the left one, may move up and down in the scrotum by muscular contractions during the first two sexual phases before it finally elevates completely to join the other testicle, which usually becomes elevated early in the plateau phase.

Women's breasts reach their peak of expansion during the plateau phase. The areolae become so enlarged that they partially cover the erect nipples, giving the illusion that there is a loss of nipple erection. This is especially true of breasts that have never suckled a baby.

If a sex flush appeared on the woman during the excitement phase, much of her body will now be flushed. Late in this period, the intensity of the color and the expanse of the flush reach their peak. The man may now show the first signs of a sex flush, beginning under the rib cage and spreading over the chest, neck, and face. Fewer men than women have this response, and in those men who do, it may not occur during every response cycle.

Increased muscular tension is the most marked bodily response in both sexes during this period, but it is perhaps more pronounced in the man. Both voluntary and involuntary muscles are involved. There may be strong contractions in the muscles of the neck, face, and abdomen. The cords of the neck become rigid and stand erect (especially among women) with the approach of orgasm, and the long muscles of the thighs become very tense. Late in the plateau phase there are involuntary spastic contractions of hand and foot muscles which develop into grasping, clawing movements. Involuntary muscle contractions lengthen the vaginal barrel. Both sexes often purposefully make the muscles in the buttocks more tense in their striving for orgasm. Pelvic thrusts are at first voluntarily controlled by both men and women during this phase, but as excitement mounts, their motion becomes a rapid, forceful thrusting, which is essentially an involuntary reaction, especially in men.

As the plateau phase continues, the heart rate elevates, sometimes increasing to more than twice the usual rate of about 70 beats per minute. During the latter part of this phase, there is also a marked elevation of blood pressure. Hyperventilation (increase in respiratory rate) begins during the plateau phase.

THE ORGASMIC PHASE

The *orgasmic phase* consists of those few seconds when the sexual tension evidenced by muscular spasm and engorgement of blood vessels reaches its maximum intensity and is discharged in the orgasm—a highly pleasurable, totally involuntary response.

The vagina shows a unique response during the orgasmic phase. The orgasmic platform, first noticeable during the plateau phase, contracts strongly in intervals of about 0.8 second. There are at least 3 or 4 of these contractions, and there may be as many as 15. They decrease in frequency and intensity after the first few, and their strength varies from woman to woman, with variations in individual experiences.

Beginning about 2 to 4 seconds after a woman first experiences orgasm, the rapid uterine contractions noted in the earlier phases become stronger and more regular. Like the contractions of labor in childbirth, these contractions typically begin at the top of the uterus and work their way downward to the lower section of the cervix. Uterine contractions are more pronounced when orgasm has been brought about by masturbation than by coition.

FIGURE 9.3 The female pelvic region, showing the changes in the size and position of organs and tissue during increasing sexual excitement and orgasmic response. Note the ballooning and tenting effect of the inner portion of the vagina. The dotted lines show the organ positions during orgasm.

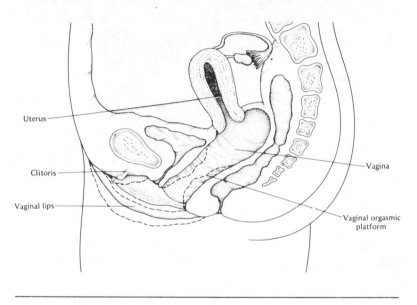

At about the same time that the sexual response cycle advances from the plateau to the orgasmic phase in the man, contractions of the accessory organs of reproduction—the vas deferens, the seminal vesicles, the ejaculatory duct, and the prostate—work to collect sperm and seminal fluid, which are compressed into the entrance to the prostatic urethra. The urethral bulb becomes greatly distended, and this signals the inevitability of orgasm in the man. He is unable to hold back from the climax after this moment.

Ejaculation of the seminal fluid is caused by regularly recurring contractions of the urethra and of muscles at the base of the penis and around the anus. The intervals between contractions are roughly the same as those between orgasmic vaginal contractions—0.8 second between the first 3 or 4 major responses, with a gradual lengthening of intervals after that. The urethra

FIGURE 9.4   The male genitalia in the orgasmic phase. The dotted lines represent the organ positions in the completed resolution phase. Note that the testis and the scrotum move down and away from the body cavity during the resolution phase.

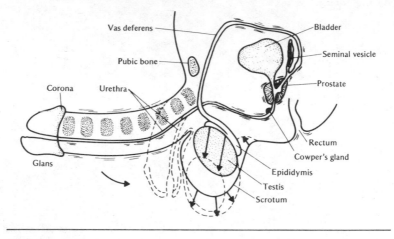

continues to contract slightly and irregularly for several seconds after the initial expulsive responses, the interval between the final contractions lasting perhaps several seconds.

In both males and females, the sphincter muscles of the rectum may contract involuntarily at approximately 0.8-second intervals, although the number of such contractions is usually only 2 to 4. This is more likely to occur in men, but it is also experienced by women whose orgasm has been intense. It is most often experienced during masturbation rather than during sexual intercourse.

Women sometimes have an involuntary distention of the external opening of the urethra during orgasm. The distention disappears and the opening returns to its normal state before the orgasmic phase is over. Women also occasionally feel an urge to urinate during or immediately after orgasm, and there may be a loss of urine as sexual tension mounts. More multiparous than nulliparous women have a tendency to urinate involuntarily at this time because their sphincter muscles are more flaccid.

If there has been a sex flush, the intensity of the flush during the orgasmic phase is proportionate to the intensity of the orgasm.

There is a loss of voluntary control, and great involuntary-muscle tension throughout the body. Muscular strain may be so severe as to cause aching and soreness the following day. Both superficial and deep muscles are involved. The neck, hands, arms, feet, and legs exhibit individual responses at the time of orgasm. In women, corded neck muscles are an easily observable reaction just before and during orgasm, indicating the marked and generalized muscular strain that the body undergoes at this time. There may also be flushing and slight swelling of the face and expansion of the rib cage. The more effective the stimulation has been, the more completely the whole body becomes involved in the release of tensions.

At the moment of orgasm, breathing is at least twice as fast as it normally is. The increase in intensity and duration of any respiratory changes is directly correlated with the intensity and duration of sexual tension. If the orgasm is mild or of short duration, there may be no increase in the respiratory rate at all. Heart rate increases to 110 to 180 beats per minute, and blood pressure increases by a third or more. The increase in women is usually greater through masturbation than through sexual intercourse.

The Question of
Simultaneous Orgasms

Whether it is desirable for a couple to have simultaneous orgasms has long been a subject of speculation. Naturally, if both partners prefer orgasms at the same time—and many couples do—then they should strive for this goal. However, there are some aspects of sexual response that should be considered before a couple embark upon the uneven struggle toward simultaneous orgasm, or before they accept the premise that it offers the ultimate in sexual achievement.

The effort to give one's partner the fullest measure of concern and satisfaction is essential to rewarding sexual activity. If either person is primarily concerned with gratifying himself or is caught up in his own impending orgasm, he cannot give full attention to his partner. Similarly, if one is concentrating only on the partner's sexual gratification, appropriate concentration on one's own responses and pleasure is impossible.

Furthermore, men and women react quite differently in bodily movements at the time of orgasm. The man's tendency is to plunge into the vagina as deeply as possible at the moment of orgasm and to hold this position, followed perhaps by one or two deep, deliberate thrusts. The woman's tendency, on the other hand, is to want the same stroking, plunging movements of the excitement and plateau phases continued during the orgasmic reaction, with perhaps an acceleration of the thrusts and an increase of pressure in the vulval area. These two highly pleasurable patterns of movement are obviously incompatible. Since both cannot be executed at the same time, whichever pattern is carried out during simultaneous orgasm must detract from the full pleasure of one of the partners.

The arguments would appear to be stronger against than for simultaneous orgasm. It is easier for a man to achieve orgasm, but he is usually capable of only one. The sensible approach to orgasm would therefore seem to be that the man delay his own climax until his partner is fully satisfied. The couple can thereby devote full attention to giving the woman as many orgasmic responses as she wishes, and both can then concentrate wholly on providing the man with as satisfying an orgasm as possible.

The quality of an orgasm—that is, its intensity, length, and overall pleasure—varies from person to person and within the same person from one act of coition to another. Recency and frequency of occurrence can influence the quality of the next sexual experience, as can such factors as anxiety, guilt, depression, anger, indifference toward one's partner, and distaste for one's surroundings. These factors not only can affect the quality of the orgasm but also, if strong enough, can block the response altogether. As would be expected, women, because of their being subjected to the double standard, report a greater variability in the subjective quality of their orgasms than men do.

Sigmund Freud advanced the mistaken idea that women who are only capable of orgasms which result from clitoral stimulation are sexually immature, while mature women have orgasms in response to vaginal stimulation. The myth has persisted that there are two different kinds of female orgasms: clitoral and vaginal. Masters and Johnson proved conclusively that the orgasmic contractions that take place in the vagina and uterus are identical regardless of the technique used to bring them on. An orgasm is an orgasm, and there is only one kind. External stimulation of the clitoris and other areas of the vulva produces the strongest physiological reactions during orgasm for women. Furthermore, whether a woman has orgasms resulting from clitoral stimulation, vaginal penetration, or both, her response has nothing to do with her emotional maturity.

THE RESOLUTION PHASE

The *resolution phase* is a period of return to the nonstimulated state. During this phase, women are capable of continued orgasms if there is continued stimulation, but for men this phase includes a time (*refractory period*) during which restimulation is impossible.

As vasocongestion disappears in nulliparous women, the labia majora quickly return to normal size and resume their midline positioning that partially covers the vaginal outlet. In the multiparous, engorgement of the major lips may persist for 2 to 3 hours before complete detumescence. As the excess blood drains from the labia minora, they usually return to a light pink color within 10 to 15 seconds, and the sex-skin color is usually totally normal within 5 minutes after orgasm.

The clitoris, which was retracted and invisible during the late plateau and orgasmic phases, now returns to its normal position within 5 to 10 seconds after orgasm. Congestion of the clitoral glans and shaft may remain, however, for 5 to 10 minutes after orgasm, and occasionally may persist for as long as 30 minutes.

The outer third of the vagina quickly returns to normal as the vasocongestion that produced the orgasmic platform disappears, and the opening of the vagina therefore returns to its normal size. As the elevated uterus returns to its normal position and the cervix descends, the inner two-thirds of the vagina is no longer pulled upward, and it slowly reverts to its normal collapsed state. The vaginal walls regain their rough, wrinkled surface, and the deep color of the vagina fades. The entire vagina returns to a normal state within 10 to 15 minutes after orgasm.

During the first 5 to 10 minutes immediately following orgasm, there is a slight spreading apart of the opening of the cervix as the uterus ceases to contract and resumes its normal position and size. If the plateau phase has been excessively prolonged, the uterus may remain enlarged for 10 minutes in nulliparous women and often for 20 minutes in multiparous women. If the buildup of sexual excitement does not culminate in orgasm, the increased uterine size may persist for as long as an hour.

In men, return of the penis to its normal flaccid state occurs in two stages. In the first stage, about 50% of the erection is quickly lost soon after ejaculation. During the second stage, the remaining erection is lost at a slower rate which varies according to the amount of continued sexual stimulation. If the penis is kept in the vagina or if the partner is held close for a time after ejaculation, the penis may retain a partial erection for a longer time. If the man stands up, urinates, smokes, or does some other sexually unrelated act, detumescence will occur rapidly in both the primary and secondary stages.

In most men, the scrotal skin rapidly returns to its relaxed, loosely wrinkled, prearousal state as congestion disappears. In a few men, the return to a nonstimulated state is a slower process and may last for an hour or two. The testes return to their normal lowered position according to the rate of decongestion of the scrotum. The testes also lose their vasocongestion and return to normal size. The longer the plateau phase, the slower the return to normal size in the testes during the resolution phase.

The swelling around a woman's nipples disappears rapidly after orgasm, and the nipple erection that had persisted since the excitement phase becomes observable again, giving the impression that the nipples are becoming erect once more. Nipple erection is lost in women more quickly than it is in men. It may take an hour after ejaculation for a man to lose his nipple erection, while a woman's is usually lost before her breasts return to normal size. In a nulliparous woman, the breasts may remain enlarged for 5 to 10 minutes after orgasm, but multiparous women quickly lose any swelling in their breasts.

The sex flush of both men and women disappears rapidly during the resolution phase in reverse order of its appearance. It quickly fades from the buttocks, arms, thighs, abdomen, and back but is much slower to disappear from the neck, chest, breasts, face, and upper abdomen or stomach area.

The muscular tension built up during the excitement, plateau, and orgasmic phases relaxes during the resolution phase and usually disappears completely within 5 minutes after orgasm. In men, the contracted sphincter muscles of the rectum are relaxed by the time that ejaculation is completed.

Heart rate, blood pressure, and respiratory rate quickly return to normal after orgasm. About a third of all men and women develop a perspiratory reaction immediately after orgasm. This perspiration may cover the entire body in both sexes, but it is usually confined in men to the soles of the feet and the palms of the hands. In women, it frequently covers the back, thighs, chest, underarms, upper lip, and forehead. This film of perspiration is not related to the physical exertion of coitus, since the response occurs regardless of the degree of physical activity in the first three phases. The amount of perspiration parallels the strength of the orgasm.

THE AFTERMATH

Just as the buildup of sexual arousal is an integral and pleasurable part of the sex act, so is the aftermath an important part of the act, as well as an emotionally fulfilling experience. Indeed, some regard the aftermath of one sexual encounter as the beginning of the next. The man who has an orgasm and then perfunctorily turns his back and falls asleep should not be surprised if his partner is not receptive to his next advances. Similarly, a woman who immediately leaps from the bed after intercourse to douche or bathe leaves hurt feelings behind her. To hold each other in a close and lingering embrace, to discuss softly the delights of the experience they have just shared, to caress one another, to relax and doze with intertwined bodies—all add to the emotional fulfillment.

While it is advantageous for a couple to read and discuss the various sexual techniques recommended and described by all authorities, it is ultimately up to each couple to discover for themselves what their individual likes and dislikes are. A technique that enhances sexual pleasure for one might be considered physically painful or ludicrous by another. Only by uninhibited experimentation and frank and open discussion can a couple find what brings them the greatest erotic pleasure. Whatever the sexual activity, it should be mutually satisfying to both.

Although the material in this chapter has focused on the physiological aspects of the sexual act, the importance of the emotional aspects must not be overlooked. A close relationship and deep emotional involvement—love, if you wish—are of paramount importance to a complete and fulfilling sexual experience. Physiological sexual needs can be relieved without love, closeness, or even understanding. But no one can really attain complete emotional, physical, and sexual satisfaction, in all its beauty, without the intermingling of those elements. Ask any person who has had sexual intercourse in both circumstances.

A. H. Maslow described a healthy love relationship perceptively when he wrote, in *Motivation and Personality:*

> It is quite characteristic of self-actualizing people that they can enjoy themselves in love and in sex. Sex very frequently becomes a kind of game in which laughter is quite as common as panting. It is not the welfare of the species, or the task of reproduction, or the future development of mankind that attracts people to each other. The sex life of healthy people, in spite of the fact that it frequently reaches great peaks of ecstasy, is nevertheless also easily compared to the games of children and puppies. It is cheerful, humorous, and playful.

FURTHER READING

Human Sexual Response, by W. H. Masters and V. E. Johnson. Boston: Little, Brown, 1966.

> This is the original and detailed presentation of the psychosexual response of both men and women as they progress through the four phases of the human sexual response cycle.

An Analysis of Human Sexual Response, edited by R. Brecher and E. Brecher. New York: New American Library, 1966.

> This paperback book gives a much simplified, but accurate, picture of the human sexual response in the four phases of the response cycle. The book also includes articles on other aspects of human sexual behavior.

Sexual Behavior in the Human Female, by A. C. Kinsey, W. B. Pomeroy, C. E. Martin, and P. H. Gebhard. Philadelphia: W. B. Saunders, 1953.

Chapters 9, 13, 14, 15, and 17 are directly related to the topic under discussion in this chapter.

Human Sexuality, 2d ed., by J. L. McCary. New York: D. Van Nostrand, 1973.

Chapter 13 summarizes the scientific work on the human sexual response developed and reported by Masters and Johnson and other researchers in the field.

Sexual Myths and Fallacies, by J. L. McCary. New York: D. Van Nostrand, 1971.

Special topics in the section on Sexual Physiology and Functioning are related to the matter of orgasm.

10 SEXUAL DYSFUNCTION

Feelings of sexual inadequacy may trouble an individual for many reasons. A relaxed and playful attitude about sex is sometimes difficult to achieve in a culture which is as self-conscious about sex as ours. Our society also encourages sexual competition; both men and women are conditioned to compete with other members of their own sex for the attentions of the opposite sex. Under such circumstances, sexual attractiveness and performance can assume a disproportionately large role in one's evaluation of himself as well as in his judgments of others. Descriptions of sexual experiences in the mass communication media can easily encourage unrealistic expectations; if an individual expects every orgasm to be accompanied by movements of the earth and the ringing of bells, he is bound to be disappointed!

Nevertheless, some objective criteria do exist for measuring satisfactory sexual experience, and some individuals do suffer from *sexual dysfunction,* problems that interfere with a smooth and adequate sex life. A person is considered sexually dysfunctional if his efforts to gratify his sexual desires are continually frustrated in spite of an available and sexually functioning partner. The man who cannot achieve an erection and the woman who has never experienced orgasm are examples of such individuals.

The most common sexual dysfunctions are impotence, premature ejaculation, dyspareunia, and female orgasmic dysfunction. Fortunately, methods of treatment are now available for each of these dysfunctions.

IMPOTENCE

Sexual *impotence* (from the Latin: "without power") can be defined as a man's inability to attain or maintain an erection of sufficient strength to enable him to perform the act of intercourse. Three types of impotence are recognized: organic, functional, and psychogenic.

The first of these, *organic impotence,* is relatively rare and is caused by some anatomical defect in the reproductive or central nervous system. *Functional impotence* may be caused by a nervous disorder, excessive use of alcohol or certain drugs, deficient hormonal functioning, circulatory problems, the aging process, or physical exhaustion—any of which can interfere with the functioning of the various sex organs. *Psychogenic impotence* is by far the most frequently encountered type of impotence. This malfunctioning is usually caused by the emotional inhibition or blocking of certain impulses from the brain that act upon the neural centers of the spinal cord controlling erection. Psychogenic impotency has been classified as either primary or secondary.

Primary impotence means that the man has *never* been able to achieve or maintain an erection of sufficient firmness to engage in coitus. *Secondary impotence* is a sexual dysfunction in which the man has had at least one successful coital experience but is now incapable of coital performance. A single failure to achieve erection does not mean that a man is impotent. Virtually all men at one time or another, particularly when they are upset or very tired, are unable to attain an erection or maintain it long enough for penetration. When a man fails to achieve penile erection in 25% of his sexual attempts, however, the condition may be correctly diagnosed as secondary impotence.

The man who suffers from secondary impotence is typically successful in his first attempt at sexual intercourse and continues to be effective in dozens or perhaps thousands of coital encounters thereafter. But the day arrives when, for one of many reasons, he fails to achieve an erection. A first-time failure or several failures occurring within a short period of time can generate such fear and apprehension that the man can no longer function sexually. As he puts more and more pressure on himself to perform and becomes more and more anxious about possible failure, he becomes increasingly tense and less likely to be able to achieve an erection. Thus, fear of failure becomes a self-fulfilling prophecy, and a pattern of failure is established.

College-age men are not usually concerned about the effects of the aging process on their sexual ability, but older men are often led to believe that they have grown too old to function sexually. They may become so convinced that their age prevents them from having erections that they do indeed become impotent, despite the fact that they continue to have morning erections and erections during sleep. Any man who can achieve a morning erection *is* capable of having an erection; his failure at other times is psychological rather than physical. Almost all men have erections every 60 to 80 minutes during sleep (and sleeping women develop vaginal lubrications at about the same time intervals), whether or not they are capable of erections during the waking state.

Some Causes of Impotence

Masters and Johnson have listed these causes of secondary impotence, in descending order of frequency: a history of premature ejaculation (in older men), intemperate alcoholic consumption, excessive maternal or paternal domination in childhood, inhibitory religious orthodoxy, homosexual conflict, inadequate sexual counseling, and certain physiological inhibitors.

In those cases in which premature ejaculation is the herald of impotence, the evolution of the problem usually follows a predictable course. The man regularly ejaculates prematurely. At first his partner is tolerant. But as time passes she complains more and more. She feels that the condition is solely her lover's "fault" and demands that he do something to correct it—immediately! The man, who perhaps has been insensitive to the severity of his partner's sexual frustration, finally internalizes her accusations. He comes to view himself as a grossly inadequate lover and decides that at all costs he must learn to delay ejaculation.

He tries all manner of techniques to take his mind off the pleasurable sensations of coitus, but he succeeds only in blocking his full emotional involvement in coition. In his anxiety and overconcern about satisfying his lover, he typically cannot control his ejaculation any more successfully than he did in the past. Not wishing to risk additional failure, he begins to avoid coition altogether, using any excuse possible. Sooner or later, however, his partner approaches him sexually and he discovers to his horror that he does not respond with an erection. Now he has a problem of considerably greater magnitude than premature ejaculation—he is totally incapable of coitus. Thus failure generates fear, and fear generates further failure.

An adequate masculine self-image, usually acquired by a boy through identification with his father, is quite obviously linked to successful sexual functioning. But either parent can undermine a young man's confidence in his masculinity and, hence, in his potency—the mother, by mercilessly domineering her husband or otherwise trying to destroy him; the father, by establishing unattainable goals for his son.

Secondary impotence may also have its foundation in unhealthy relationships between a boy and his mother, which may lead him to see in all women the mother for whom he felt unconscious incestuous desires. Other men become sexually incapable because of conscious or unconscious disgust, anger, or hostility toward their wives.

Religious training may be related to several forms of sexual dysfunctioning, including impotency. Masters and Johnson have observed that "severe religious orthodoxy may indoctrinate the teen-ager with the concept that any form of overt sexual activity prior to marriage not only is totally unacceptable but is personally destructive, demoralizing, degrading, dehumanizing and injurious to one's physical and/or mental health."

Homosexual conflict can contribute to secondary impotence in two ways. The individual may be caught in an unconscious tug-of-war between homosexual and heterosexual desires. Or he may have had one or more homosexual experiences. Although he is basically heterosexual, these experiences may confuse his sexual self-image and he may become heterosexually impotent.

The ills resulting from inadequate sexual counseling have already been firmly established in this text. Guilt and shame, usually relating to some childhood experience or stemming from faulty sex education, are common contributors to sexual inadequacies.

The Treatment of Impotence

A trained therapist is necessary for the treatment of impotence. Both the impotent man and his sexual partner receive help, and the most successful results are obtained from a therapist team of a man and a woman. The initial treatment involves efforts to teach the impotent man to resist the temptation to make a direct attack on the problem of inadequate erection. He must instead be convinced by the therapists that he does not have to be *taught* to have an erection. He is encouraged to learn to relax and enjoy the physical pleasures of body contact and the emotional interaction with his sexual partner without feeling a compulsion to achieve a firm erection. The couple must become attuned to one another's sexual needs and learn to fulfill those needs, for it is only through giving pleasure to the other that either partner can receive it. The couple learns this process of giving-to-receive from the therapists.

The main therapeutic goals in the treatment of impotence are: to remove the man's fear of failure; to divest him of a spectator's role in sexual activity by reorienting his emotions and sensations toward active, involved participation; and to remove the woman's fear of her lover's being sexually ineffective. All concerned must recognize that fear is causing the problem and that, in a very real sense, there is "nothing to fear but fear itself."

The importance of the woman's role in helping the man to overcome his (actually, their) sexual difficulties cannot be overemphasized. If she expresses disappointment over the man's failure, she will increase his anxiety and guilt feelings, which will only intensify his inhibitions. She should offer compassion and reassurance, as well as any physical stimulation that he needs to attain and maintain an erection.

After the couple learn the art of giving pleasure in order to receive pleasure, overcoming the specific problem of impotence is relatively simple. They are instructed to fondle and caress one another's genitals and breasts. Erection is still not the specific goal at this point. The couple are told to relax and to do whatever is sexually pleasurable; erection will occur in time because neither feels compelled to produce it. Once the man does have an erection, the couple are encouraged to let the penis become flaccid again, then to stimulate it once more into another erection, and to repeat this cycle several times. This procedure allows both partners to observe for themselves that if the man has one erection, he can have another one, and that the loss of penile firmness is not necessarily a permanent one.

At no time are the couple encouraged by the therapists to attempt intercourse. The old pervasive fears of many couples can be rearoused by a therapist who tells them, "You are ready, so tonight's the night!" The couple must refrain from attempting intercourse during the early days of therapy, no matter how ready or confident the man feels. After about 10 days, the woman is instructed to initiate the first coital attempt.

The man lies on his back and the woman assumes the woman-above coital position. She manipulates his penis into an erection and at the appropriate time guides the penis (still manipulating it) into her vagina as she very slowly moves her hips. If the penis becomes soft after insertion, it is withdrawn; she again manipulates it into an erection and reinserts it. But if it again becomes flaccid, the couple are instructed to desist from further sex play at that particular time. Once the penis remains firm after intromission, the woman is still and allows the man to do the pelvic thrusting. In the final days of treatment, both share in the pelvic movements. Ejaculation and orgasm will follow if the couple do not attempt to force the response.

The prescribed treatment is considered to be a success if impotence fails to recur for at least five years. In treating cases of secondary impotence, Masters and Johnson report a success rate of 73.8%.

PREMATURE EJACULATION

Premature ejaculation is a condition in which a man cannot delay ejaculation long enough after penetration to satisfy his sexual partner in at least half of their acts of sexual intercourse together. It is a condition which causes anxiety and stress for many men and women, and it can seriously impair a sexual relationship. Many men expect a great deal of themselves as lovers, and hence feel ashamed and sexually inadequate if their "staying power" after penile penetration is minimal. Yet the Kinsey group found that perhaps 75% of all men ejaculate within 2 minutes after intromission. This is not to say, however, that because such men constitute the vast majority, they should not work at learning techniques for delaying ejaculation.

Sexually aroused lovers will both feel cheated if orgasm occurs within mere seconds of penile insertion. Not only is the man's confidence in himself as a lover weakened, but he has also been denied the intense pleasure of prolonged penile plunging. If the couple depend upon intercourse to bring the woman to orgasm, she is left almost completely unfulfilled and most assuredly will feel frustrated. Repetition of this sort of bad timing can understandably prevent the development of what might otherwise have been a thoroughly satisfactory sexual relationship.

Some Causes of Premature Ejaculation

Many people assume that premature ejaculation is primarily the result of a physical condition, such as a penis made "abnormally sensitive" by circumcision. One assumption is that the glans of the circumcised penis is more sensitive to the friction of masturbation or coitus than is the uncircumcised penis, and that the circumcised man cannot, therefore, delay ejaculation as long as the man whose foreskin is still intact. Neurological and clinical testing of tactile discrimination (sensitivity to touch) has failed, however, to reveal any differences in the sensitivity of a circumcised and an uncircumcised penis. Control of ejaculation, or lack of it, is related far more to self-training and to emotional factors than to such physical conditions as an overly sensitive penis.

The penis does not control ejaculation, premature or otherwise. The brain does—usually unconsciously, via the spinal cord. The best evidence of this fact is that ejaculations can occur during sleep or while a man is unconscious. The psychological forces in premature ejaculation are legion, as we have seen. An element of revenge is often present in it—toward the particular woman or toward women in general. Or the man may be unduly tense, tired, or lacking in self-confidence in his sexual abilities. Premature ejaculation may result when intercourse has been preceded by an overlong period of sexual abstinence; or when the man has experienced a prolonged period of sexual excitement before intromission is attempted.

A wide array of other factors can cause premature ejaculation. One of the most common causes is the conditioning of the man during his early sexual experience. These experiences often take place under less than ideal circumstances; for example, in a parked car (in the imminent danger of being spotlighted by the police) or on a couch in the living room of the girl's parents (where at any moment her father is liable to bound into the room, a shotgun in his hand and blood in his eye). The anxiety engendered by these settings serves to condition many younger men to the pattern of quick ejaculation.

Another form of teen-age sexual behavior can also help to condition the man to premature ejaculation. After extensive petting, the boy, possibly fully clothed, lies ón top of the girl and rubs his penis over her vulval region by moving his body back and forth as is done in intercourse, until he ejaculates. (Aside from the unfortunate conditioning of both partners, the girl's unrelieved sexual tensions, and additional cleaning bills, about all one can say of this technique is that it prevents unwanted pregnancies, preserves the girl's virginity, and affords the boy some sexual release.)

The Treatment of Premature Ejaculation

Given the cooperation of his lover, a man can train himself (except when the cause is purely physical) to withhold orgasm until both want it to happen. The main enemy is the fear and anxiety engendered in the man by previous failures. Once he gains confidence in his "staying power" and accepts the fact that all men face the problem at one time or another, the battle is half won. To assist him toward confidence in his abilities, several routes can be taken.

Some counselors recommend that a local anesthetic (for example, Nupercainal) be applied to the penile glans—care being taken not to smear any of the ointment on the woman's vulva—a few minutes before the beginning of intercourse. The assumption is that the deadening effect of the anesthetic will decrease the sensitivity of the penis and delay ejaculation. Others prescribe the wearing of one or more condoms to reduce the stimulation generated by the friction of intercourse and the warmth and moisture within the vagina. Since muscular tension is a notorious catalyst in ejaculation, premature ejaculation may be prevented by the man's lying beneath the woman and thus taking a more passive role in coitus. (Sexual intercourse in the cramped confines of an automobile is unsatisfactory for many reasons, one of which is that it often creates muscular tension that terminates in early ejaculation.)

Some men also find that taking a drink just before coitus helps, since alcohol is a deterrent in all physiological functioning. Other men claim similar success through concentrating on singularly unsexy thoughts, such as their income tax payments. (It is suggested, however, that these men take care not to let their partners know of their diversionary thoughts, lest they be dumped from the bed before ejaculation, premature or otherwise!) Having an orgasm and, after a short rest, attaining another erection often permit a man to experience a more prolonged act of coitus the second time. Some men masturbate shortly before they expect to have sexual intercourse; because their sex drive will thereby be decreased, they can then prolong intercourse later.

The technique of delaying the man's orgasm can be learned, and probably the best method is one requiring the cooperation of both the man and his sex partner. The best chance of success lies in both partners' consulting a psychotherapist who will, first of all, assure the couple that premature or early ejaculation is a reversible phenomenon. The couple will then be instructed in the somewhat complicated technique of bringing about the reversal of premature ejaculation.

The technique requires that the woman manually stimulate her partner's genitals until the point that he feels the very earliest signs of "ejaculatory inevitability." (This is the stage of a man's orgasmic experience at which he feels ejaculation of seminal fluid coming, and can no longer control it.) At that moment he signals the woman with such a pre-agreed word as "now," and she immediately ceases her massage of the penis. She then quickly squeezes its glans, or head, by placing her thumb on the frenulum (on the lower surface of the glans) and two fingers on top of the glans, applying rather strong pressure for 3 or 4 seconds. The pressure will be uncomfortable enough to cause the man to lose the urge to ejaculate. Such "training sessions" should continue for 15 to 20 minutes, with alternating periods of sexual stimulation and squeezing.

In later sessions, the man inserts his penis in the woman's vagina as she sits astride him until he senses impending orgasm, at which point he withdraws and she once more squeezes the penis to stop ejaculation. Use of these techniques is continued in further sexual encounters until, progressively, the man is capable of prolonged sexual intercourse, in any position, without ejaculating sooner than he wishes.

Two notes of caution should be sounded to those using this technique. First, the technique will be unavailing if the man himself applies the pressure to his penis; and, second, the couple must not treat this new-found sexual skill as a game and overdo it. If the technique is overused, the man may eventually find that he has become insensitive to the stimulation and unable to respond to it. He may then develop new fears, this time about his potency, and risk developing secondary impotence. The guidance of a therapist is strongly recommended in the treatment of premature ejaculation to prevent such secondary problems.

Masters and Johnson report a 97.8% success rate in the treatment of premature ejaculation.

In any discussion of premature ejaculation, a word of caution must be injected. It is important to understand that at any one time or another almost every man has experienced ejaculation more swiftly than he or his partner would have liked. The essential thing is that the man not become anxious over possible future failures. Otherwise, what is a normal, situational occurrence may become a chronic problem.

DYSPAREUNIA

Dyspareunia is painful coitus. It can be a problem for either men or women, although women are affected far more frequently than men are. Men sometimes experience acute pain at the time of erection, but that is not actually dyspareunia. It can be said to occur in men only when orgasm causes severe, jabbing pain. The pain is commonly the result of congestion of the prostate, seminal vesicles, or ejaculatory ducts, or an inflamed verumontanum. In other cases, the pain may be caused by an irritation of the glans penis arising from poor hygienic habits in the uncircumcised male. Peyronie's disease (described in Chapter 12) can also make coitus painful for a man. Otherwise, dyspareunia in men is extremely rare.

Dyspareunia in women frequently has its inception in tension, fear, or anxiety over initial sexual intercourse. The pain can involve vagina, cervix, uterus, or bladder. The vaginal muscles become taut, and coitus can be painful, especially if the man is clumsy or insensitive. Furthermore, depending upon the type and thickness of the hymen, pain may be experienced when the tissue is ruptured by penile penetration.

Coitus may be painful because of lesions (injuries) or scar tissue formed in the vaginal opening as a result of an episiotomy, a crude nonprofessional abortion, or rape, especially gang rape (rape is quite predictably capable of causing emotional as well as physical trauma productive of dyspareunia). An accumulation of smegma under the clitoral foreskin may harden and cause a painful burning sensation when the clitoris enlarges during sexual excitation. Some women suffer considerable pain when the cervix is touched and moved by the penis during sexual intercourse; coitus, in fact, becomes impossible at times.

A displaced uterus is another persistent cause of painful coitus in women. So also are polyps, cysts, and tumors of the reproductive system. Some women suffer pain during sexual intercourse because the vaginal barrel is irritated by the chemicals contained in contraceptive creams, foams, jellies, and suppositories. Other women react painfully to the rubber or plastic that condoms and diaphragms are made of, or to excessive douching.

Still other women produce insufficient vaginal lubrication during coition, so that coital movements produce a painful or burning sensation. In this last case, coital discomfort can be avoided by using a commercial lubricant.

Medical opinion is that if dyspareunia persists over a period of time, small undetected lesions in the vagina (which cause 85% of the cases) are to be suspected. Furthermore, any infection of the vagina, uterus, bladder, or surrounding areas can obviously make intercourse painful for a woman.

Medical approaches are clearly of great value in attacking many of the causes of dyspareunia. Nevertheless, the benefits of psychotherapy should not be overlooked when the foundations of the disorder appear to lie in emotional blocks and fears.

VAGINISMUS

Vaginismus is an extremely powerful and often severely painful contraction of the muscles surrounding the vaginal tract. Anticipated pain of first penile penetration, or fear or guilt concerning sexual intercourse can cause these muscular spasms, which may persist for long periods of time. In severe cases, even an attempt to introduce the penis into the vagina will often produce agonizing pain making penile penetration impossible. In less severe cases, the vaginal spasms merely delay intromission or make it more difficult.

Masters and Johnson assert that the chief cause of vaginismus in wives is an impotent husband whose repeated attempts at sexual intercourse followed by an equal number of failures have so greatly frustrated his wife that she protects herself subconsciously by closing the vaginal doors. Other important causes of vaginismus are the inhibitions formed by emotionally traumatic experiences, such as rape; inner conflict growing out of homosexual tendencies; and physical anomalies that make intercourse extremely painful.

Men as well as women must understand the dynamics behind vaginismus and must avoid any behavior that will produce discomfort for either partner. A selfish, inconsiderate, and brutal man can do irreparable damage to the relationship by forging ahead like a battering ram in his attempts at sexual intercourse when his sex partner is suffering these muscular spasms.

In treatment, the woman is given several dilators of graduated sizes to use in stretching the vaginal muscles so that she can comfortably accommodate her lover's penis. After the largest dilator can be inserted without stress or pain, she is encouraged to retain it for several hours each night—perhaps to sleep with it in place throughout the night. Use of these dilators for 3 to 5 days is usually highly successful in helping to relieve the involuntary spasms of vaginismus. However, because the dysfunction frequently has its roots in the psychological quagmire of fear, guilt, and shame, physical efforts at overcoming it may be unsuccessful and psychotherapy is therefore indicated.

Success in treatment of vaginismus is near the 100% level. Furthermore, the vast majority of women afflicted with vaginismus are able to achieve orgasm after treatment.

FEMALE ORGASMIC DYSFUNCTION

Traditionally, the word "frigidity" has been used in association with a woman who has a total or partial lack of sex drive. But because the word has different meanings for different people, it is more confusing than useful in a discussion of sexual dysfunctioning or inadequacy. For example, a husband may desire coitus seven times a week while his wife desires it, or is orgasmic, only three times a week. This husband may consider his wife "frigid," whereas the husband who desires coitus three times a week would consider her sex drive perfectly normal. (The third husband who desires sex only once a week might well call her a nymphomaniac!)

In recent years the rather meaningless word "frigidity" has been discarded in favor of the more descriptive phrase, *female orgasmic dysfunction*. According to this concept, a woman suffers from orgasmic dysfunction when she does not go beyond the plateau phase in sexual response.

Nonorgasmic women can be placed in one of two classes: those with *primary orgasmic dysfunction* and those with *situational orgasmic dysfunction*. The woman belonging to the first category has never achieved an orgasm in her life through any method of sexual stimulation. The woman in the situational category has achieved at least one orgasm in her life—by coitus, masturbation, or some other form of stimulation—but no longer does so.

Some Causes of Female Orgasmic Dysfunction

Female orgasmic dysfunction may be caused by organic, relational, or psychological factors. Organic causes include injuries to or constitutional deficiencies in the sexual apparatus, hormonal imbalance, disorders of the nervous system, inflammation or lesions of the internal or external genitalia and surrounding areas, excessive use of drugs or alcohol, and the aging process.

Relational factors involve the woman's feelings about her sexual partner. Sometimes a man's selfishness, overeagerness, or stupidity throttles romance and fills the woman with revulsion toward sex. Resentment on the part of either partner (usually the woman), for whatever reason, can inhibit or destroy sexual functioning. So also can any of a number of other forces, realistic or unrealistic, that militate against a good overall relationship between the couple.

A common relational cause of orgasmic inadequacy in marriage is the wife's inability to accept her husband. She may find him sexually unattractive or undesirable; he may be a poor provider; he may not be the man she wanted to marry. For whatever reason, he does not fit her concept of the right man. Because a woman is typically aware that sexual capability is highly important to her partner, she can, by withholding her sexual response, express her conscious or unconscious hostility toward him and produce havoc in his self-esteem.

The most common and by far the most important causes of orgasmic dysfunctioning are psychological, typically such emotional problems as shame, guilt, and fear. Many women in our culture are indoctrinated from an early age, either directly or by implication, into a warped sexual attitude. They are taught to suppress sexual feelings, thereby formulating a negative sexual value system based on the implication that sex is bad, wrong, and dirty.

A woman thus indoctrinated comes to judge all sexual relations, whether in or out of marriage, as evil and to be avoided. Even if she cannot avoid sexual activity on the physical plane, she can minimize her participation by refusing to become involved in the interaction of sexual response. The inhibitory forces interfering with sexual warmth and responsiveness are well known. A woman may expect coitus to be physically painful and therefore dread it. She may fear rejection or condemnation by her partner if she lets herself go sexually, or be frightened of becoming pregnant. She may have homosexual tendencies, be too emotionally tied to her father, or bear a repressed hostility toward men in general. All these circumstances can inhibit her from responding warmly.

One other notable and rather sad cause of many women's inability to respond sexually is their overconcern with orgasmic response. Such women approach sexual activity with a grim determination, which is usually self-defeating, to reach a climax. What is quite obviously needed is a more relaxed attitude. These women should cease criticizing and condemning themselves because they do not experience rapid or multiple orgasms or because their climaxes are not as monumental as they fancy "modern" women's should be. Once they begin to enjoy coition for the pleasure it *does* give them (and their partners), their chances to have orgasmic responses will increase significantly.

The Treatment of Female Orgasmic Dysfunction

Stimulative methods, such as oral-genital contact and especially the use of hand vibrators, are frequently successful in producing orgasmic response in a woman. Whatever technique promises success should be used. It bears repeating that orgasm, whenever and however achieved, is the objective. Once orgasm is attained and the woman gains confidence in her ability, subsequent orgasms are usually more easily and more frequently reached.

Masters and Johnson assert that the key to successful treatment of female orgasmic dysfunction is understanding the patient's sexual value system, always bearing in mind that a woman, far more than a man, must feel that she has society's permission to express her sexuality. In a round-table discussion with both the woman and her partner, the therapists determine what the woman's sexual attitudes are. She may simply be unrealistic in what she expects from the sexual relationship or from her partner, thus committing herself to a state of constant disappointment which blocks her sexual response. Next, it must be determined what pleases her sexually and what repels her. The woman is encouraged to respond to sexual stimulation within the framework of her particular attitudes and sexual desires.

Following this clinical discussion, the couple put the woman's desires into practice, nude, in the privacy of their bedroom. The man sits on the bed with his back against the headboard and his legs spread apart. The woman sits between his legs, her back against his chest and her legs over his. In this position his hands are free to discover which tactile sensations are the most pleasing to her.

The couple have been advised that stimulation should be directed toward the inner thighs, the vaginal lips, and the clitoral area. Because of its great sensitivity and the possibility of pain or unpleasantness, direct contact with the glans of the clitoris is to be avoided at this point. Furthermore, the woman may well be striving to overcome her resistance to emerging as a sexual being. She might be overwhelmed by—and retreat from—sexual sensations that come too rapidly or are too intense. If vaginal secretions are insufficient to keep the vulval area moist, liberal use of a commercial lubricant (*e.g.*, K-Y ointment) is recommended. Through the teasing technique of advance and retreat, first one erogenous zone and then another are stimulated, care always being taken not to stimulate the genital region too long at a time.

As in the treatment of all sexual inadequacies, the partners are discouraged from attempting to reach orgasm; they are told simply to seek and sustain sensual pleasure. Once they can successfully reach one level of pleasure, they move to the next, and then to the next. On each day of the treatment, they repeat the cycle from the beginning, working through each plateau of erotic pleasure that they have previously attained.

As the next major step, the woman and her partner are advised to assume a comfortable, relaxed coital position, usually a woman-above position. Once his penis has been inserted, she remains quite still so that she can feel and enjoy the penile containment.

After full penetration she may begin slow, controlled pelvic movements to heighten her pleasurable sensation. The man remains motionless, allowing her to direct her movements to her full satisfaction. When she feels the urge to do so, she may increase the speed and force of her pelvic thrusts. She may then indicate to her partner to begin cooperative hip movements.

Having successfully progressed thus far, the couple may now enter the final phase of their self-training program—intercourse in the lateral coital position. This side-by-side position gives the man better control over his ejaculation and allows the woman more freedom to regulate her hip movements.

During any coital activity, it is recommended that the couple take several "breaks" and lie in each other's arms, quietly caressing one another. This quietude gives the woman an opportunity to think and feel sexually, something that is not often possible during actual coition. A key to ultimately achieving an orgasm is to enjoy quiet, unhurried sensate pleasure and to guard against the attempt to force or will an orgasm.

Although there are a number of physical, emotional, and societal factors which can bring about sexual dysfunction, the main cause is usually psychological. Modern techniques of treatment are effective in relieving many of these problems, and institutions whose main function is to treat sexual dysfunction are now available in many parts of the United States. Although one must beware of the untrained "therapist," an individual who suffers from a sexual dysfunction now has available the resources to obtain help.

FURTHER READING

Human Sexual Inadequacy, by W. H. Masters and V. F. Johnson. Boston: Little, Brown, 1970.

This classic in the field of human sexuality is the result of the monumental work in the area of sexual dysfunctioning by the authors. The language is often tedious and complex for the layman, but the book is necessary reading for any professional in the field.

Understanding Human Sexual Inadequacy, by F. Belliveau and L. Richter. New York: Bantam Books, 1970.

This paperback book gives a clear, simple explanation of Masters and Johnson's *Human Sexual Inadequacy.* It is authorized and endorsed by Masters and Johnson. Information on other work by the two sex researchers is also included.

Human Sexuality, 2d ed., by J. L. McCary. New York: D. Van Nostrand, 1973.

Chapter 18 summarizes the research and treatment of sexual inadequacies and forms the basis for material in the present discussion.

Sexual Myths and Fallacies, by J. L. McCary. New York: D. Van Nostrand, 1971.

The section on Sexual Disorders and Sexual Abnormalities, Real and Imagined, contains many discussions that are related to sexual inadequacies and dysfunctioning.

11 VENEREAL DISEASE

A variety of diseases, infections, and inflammations can afflict the male and female genital organs. *Venereal disease* or *VD* is a group of contagious diseases which are communicated mainly through sexual intercourse. (The word "venereal" is derived from *venus,* the Latin name for love or sexual desire.) Venereal disease attacks men, women, and children throughout the world, and is considered among the most serious afflictions of mankind.

The discovery of penicillin and other antibiotic drugs has made it possible to control VD, so that complete eradication of the diseases is medically feasible. But, because VD is usually transmitted by sexual contact, information about its nature and treatment is often stifled by public prudery. The efforts of public health officials to eradicate venereal disease are continually frustrated by the notion that "nice people don't talk about such things." In spite of the fact that VD can be successfully treated in practically all cases, the incidence of syphilis and gonorrhea, the two major venereal diseases, remains high in the United States. Gonorrhea is at an epidemic level.

ANATOMY OF AN EPIDEMIC

Controlling the spread of VD depends upon adequate treatment of the infected individual and of every person with whom he has had sexual contact. Cases of venereal disease should be reported to public health officials, who are responsible for contacting those who may have been infected by the person whose case is reported and arranging for their treatment. Many cases are not reported, however, making it difficult to locate and treat those who carry VD.

Infected individuals are often reluctant to seek treatment because of ignorance or guilt. Teen-agers, in whom the increase in VD has been the greatest, frequently do not feel free to turn to their parents with a problem of this nature, and few of them have ready access to a physician in whom they can confide.

Some individuals who contract VD are simply unwilling to disclose the identity of their sexual partners. In addition, physicians often fail to report cases which involve their private patients. As a result, the person who infected the patient—and those whom the patient has subsequently infected—are not contacted and treated. Under these circumstances, accurately judging the number of cases of active VD at any one time becomes impossible. The American Social Health Association, in fact, estimates that the incidence is perhaps 4 times greater than is reported.

The nature of the diseases themselves complicates the reporting and contacting process. Syphilis has an incubation period (the period between the infection of an individual and the manifestation of the disease)of about 3 weeks; this time lapse often permits health officials to seek out and treat those who have been infected before they become contagious. Gonorrhea, however, has an incubation period of only 2 to 8 days. Persons who become infected with gonorrhea, therefore, may have already transmitted the disease to others before they can be contacted. This, and the fact that there are no clinical symptoms of gonorrheal infection in about 80% of the women who contract the disease, have led to the current epidemic. The rate of increase in gonorrhea is 15% per year, and this pestilence shows no sign of abating.

Even if all cases were reported, adequate public funds are not available to assist medical authorities in searching out and treating infectious contacts. In the United States, public apathy continues to limit the efforts of agencies which are working to combat VD. In 1956, syphilis was almost eliminated in a drive by public health agencies, but faulty economic reasoning caused government officials to withdraw the funds that were needed to enable these agencies to eradicate the remnants of the disease.

Those relatively few persons who were still infected with syphilis caused the disease to become widespread again, and all progress was lost.

Teen-Agers and VD

The increased incidence of venereal disease in teen-agers is undoubtedly related to the acceleration of social change today. Values are changing so fast that it is difficult for a young person to develop a sense of himself and of his place in society. Old cultural patterns are abandoned from one generation to the next, leaving the young person without family traditions to guide him. Scientific, religious, and social concepts have also changed with bewildering rapidity, and adolescents are frequently left with no clearly defined ethical values or rules of behavior. Our mobile society, furthermore, encourages relationships of a transitory nature; casual sexual encounters, with the accompanying risk of VD, are therefore more frequent.

Studies have revealed that there is no "typical" teen-ager who is infected by VD. All personality types and all segments of society are affected. There is a higher rate of VD among boys than among girls since boys tend to have a higher rate of promiscuity and of homosexuality. (There is an extremely high rate of VD among male homosexuals.)

Although increased use of the Pill among teen-age girls has been blamed for the rise in promiscuity and in VD, there is no evidence that the availability of effective contraception leads to greater promiscuity. Furthermore, even though the use of condoms—the best protection against VD—has declined since the advent of the Pill, the current rise in the incidence of gonorrhea began at least 7 or 8 years before there was widespread use of the Pill.

One of the most significant facts uncovered by studies of young VD patients is that they tend to come from families in which there is a lack of mutual understanding—suggesting that close family ties and confidences foster responsible sexual behavior. Of one group studied, 64% had obtained their knowledge of sexual matters from their peers, and only 21% had obtained it from their parents. There was less promiscuity among those who had obtained sex education from adults who were meaningful to them. Regardless of their source of information, all the teen-agers in the study lacked adequate information about sex and VD, and they were all ignorant of the elementary facts of biology and hygiene.

Young VD patients frequently see themselves as worthless, unlovable victims of some force over which they have no control. These feelings cause them to seek relief in promiscuous sexual behavior. If they can be assisted toward a more satisfactory self-image, their sexual behavior will probably become more responsible.

The high incidence of VD in the United States is only one of the painful symptoms of our culture's warped attitudes toward sex. As with so many other facets of this problem, its relief—in the young as well as the adult—depends upon adequate information about sexual matters. Our society needs to acknowledge the fact that VD is rampant and to accept responsibility for eradicating the diseases. An individual who hopes to avoid VD infection and who wishes to support the efforts to bring VD under control must begin by learning about it himself.

The sex education that is so urgently needed if the VD problem is to be combatted ought to begin in the family with an emphasis on individual duty and responsibility in all areas of behavior. To insure healthy and responsible sexual behavior, sex education should be continued in the home, the school, and the church with factual information concerning all aspects of sex. While some parents fear that knowledge will lead to experimentation and promiscuity among young people, the opposite has been shown to be true in study after study. Young people who have the most knowledge about sex are the least likely to engage in promiscuous or otherwise irresponsible sexual behavior; they are also least likely to contract VD.

GONORRHEA

Gonorrhea is the most ancient and the most prevalent of all veneral diseases. A recent report estimated that the incidence of gonorrhea is second only to the common cold among communicable diseases in the United States. It is estimated that 1.5

million Americans will become infected with gonorrhea every year for the next decade.

Gonorrhea is referred to in the Bible and in Chinese writings that date back as early as 2637 B.C. Before the advent of "miracle drugs" in 1943, it was not easily cured and complications often resulted. The disease is usually considered relatively minor today and can easily be treated, although some strains of gonorrhea are apparently building resistance to the drugs used in treatment.

Primarily a disease of the young, gonorrhea's highest incidence is among men 20 to 24 years old. Its second highest incidence is among 15- to 19-year-olds. After the age of 25 the incidence declines steadily.

Although gonorrhea is almost always contracted during sexual intercourse with an infected person, a recent study revealed that, even without the use of a condom, the risk of men acquiring gonorrhea by sexual contact with an infected woman is only about 22%.

In a man, gonorrhea usually causes acute *urethritis*, an inflammation of the urethra. A thin watery discharge from the penis begins from 2 to 7 days after infectious sexual contact, becoming thicker and greenish-yellow in color within another day or two. There is usually a frequent and urgent need to urinate, and urination causes a burning sensation at the tip of the penis, which has become swollen and inflamed.

Painful and sometimes serious complications commonly result from untreated gonorrhea. One of the most agonizing is *epididymitis*, characterized by a swelling of the structures leading from the testes. The testes themselves may swell from the infection, sometimes becoming as large as an orange and extremely painful.

Other possible complications include inflammation of the joints or of the eye, skin infections, and, more rarely, inflammations of the membranes of the heart or brain. Gonorrheal infection of the prostate can become chronic, causing a man to remain infectious for a considerable length of time. Urethral stricture is another common and serious complication. The obstruction predisposes the patient to an attack of *pyelonephritis*, an inflammation of the kidney. These complications, which are typically accompanied by fever, malaise, and marked debility, caused the death of many gonorrheal victims prior to the introduction of antibiotic drugs.

In women, there are usually no symptoms of which the woman is aware. When the disease does cause symptoms, the first is a vaginal discharge beginning 2 to 7 days after infectious contact. The vulva then becomes red, raw, and irritated. There is an urgent and frequent need to urinate, and urination is often accompanied by pain and a scalding sensation.

Because women are so often unaware of the infection, and hence do not seek medical attention, and because diagnosis and treatment are more difficult in women than in men, gonorrheal complications in women are considerably more common and severe than they are in men. The two major complications that women can develop are inflammation of the Bartholin's glands (*bartholinitis*), and inflammation of the fallopian tubes (*salpingitis*). In bartholinitis, the gland on one or both sides of the vulva swells and becomes tender and painful. An abscess (a collection of pus) or cyst (an abnormal, membrane-covered sac) sometimes forms in the affected gland, requiring medical, or, occasionally, surgical attention.

Acute salpingitis often produces severe lower abdominal pain on one or both sides of the body, accompanied by fever and malaise. A tubal abscess can form on either or both sides. These conditions frequently cause severe abdominal pain, menstrual irregularity, chronic invalidism, and sterility. They often require surgical treatment.

Although the source of gonorrheal infection is almost always sexual intercourse, children are sometimes infected through mutual masturbation, sexual exploration and experimentation, or sexual assault. At one time, nearly 33% of all blindness in children was the result of infection of the eyes acquired in the birth process from mothers with gonorrhea. This problem has now been almost completely eradicated by treating the eyes of all newborn babies with a solution of silver nitrate.

The treatment of gonorrhea is usually quick and simple. For men, a single injection of 2.4 million units of penicillin is recommended. For women, the recommended dosage is double that for men, or 4.8 million units, and the dosage is divided into two injections given during a single visit to a clinic. When the patient is allergic to penicillin, or is penicillin-resistant, one of the tetracycline drugs may be successfully substituted.

SYPHILIS

In 1530 the physician Fracastoro published a poem, which achieved wide popularity, about a shepherd named Syphilis who had been stricken with a disease that, until then, had been known as "the great pox." The disease has been known ever since as *syphilis.*

It is often said that Christopher Columbus and his crew brought syphilis to America from Europe, or that they contracted the disease from West Indian women and then carried it to Europe. It seems unlikely that Columbus and syphilis arrived simultaneously in America, however, since study of the bones of American Indians has indicated that syphilis existed in America at least 500 years before Columbus's voyage. Whatever the reason, syphilis spread in epidemic proportions across the known world within a few years after Columbus and his men returned to Europe from their historic journeys. Columbus himself probably died, in 1506, from *general paresis,* one of the neurological disorders resulting from syphilitic infection. About 400 years later, in 1905, the causative organism of syphilis, the spirochete *Treponema pallidum,* was discovered, and the relationship between syphilis and paresis was subsequently recognized.

Once the villain spirochete had been identified, extensive studies were made of the disease, and effective methods of diagnosis, such as the Wassermann test of blood serum, were developed. In the past, syphilis was treated by a combination of bismuth and arsenic administered alternately and slowly for as long as 2 years or more. This treatment was coupled with fever induced either by typhoid germs or by extensive applications of heat. Since 1943, when penicillin was discovered, syphilis has been treated quickly and easily, sometimes by one powerful injection. The recommended dosage for men is 2.4 million units given in a single injection. A penicillin-sensitive patient can be treated with tetracycline or erythromycin.

It is important to recognize syphilis during its *early phase,* the 2 years following infection. At that time, irreversible tissue damage has not yet occurred and the disease can be most easily cured. This is also the period when the patient is most infectious and is the greatest menace to public health.

The early phase of syphilis is subdivided into primary and

secondary stages of infection. The *primary stage* is easily identified by a lesion or a *chancre* (sore) that appears in the anal-genital area from 10 to 40 days after infectious sexual contact. In about 10% of the cases, the sore may appear in the mouth or on the tonsils or lips, and the infection may be extragenital in origin.

FIGURE 11.1 Multiple primary chancres of the penile shaft, a symptom of the first stage of syphilis. Photograph courtesy of the Center for Disease Control, Atlanta, Georgia.

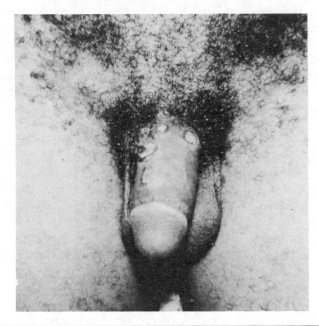

The chancre begins as a small red papule (a solid, cone-shaped lump on the skin) and then becomes eroded and moist. The only other sign at this stage is a painlessly swollen lymph gland near the site of infection. For example, if the chancre is on the penis or labia minora, the glandular swelling will be in the groin. If the disease is treated at this stage, all danger of further complications or of transmission to another person is removed. Without treatment, the primary chancre heals in 4 to 10 weeks, removing the warning signal but not the danger of internal damage.

The *secondary stage* usually begins as a nonitching rash on the trunk of the body. The rash begins after 6 weeks and usually within 3 months of infection and sometimes is so indistinct as to escape notice. Other symptoms appear at this time, but they are usually not recognizable as syphilis-related except by a physician. They include glandular enlargement, throat infection, headaches, malaise, and a low-grade fever. Sometimes there is also a loss of eyelashes, eyebrows, and scalp hair, causing a "moth-eaten" appearance. Secondary symptoms then heal, without treatment, within a few weeks or months or possibly a year. No scar tissue remains as an indication of the presence of syphilis, and the only method of diagnosis after this stage is a blood serum test.

The *third stage,* or *latent period,* of syphilis begins at least 2 years after the initial untreated infection. The disease is termed *early latent* when the patient has been infected less than 4 years or is under 25 years of age. Syphilis is considered *late latent* when infection has persisted longer than 4 years, or when the patient is over 25. During the latent period there are no symptoms associated with syphilis, and the latency may last for months or years. Syphilitics do not infect contacts during the latency period, but the results of a blood serum test are always positive. Without treatment, the disease can now progress to the destructive stage of late syphilis.

The *fourth stage,* or *late syphilis,* may manifest itself in any organ, in the central nervous system and the cardiovascular system, and, particularly, on the skin. These symptoms can appear as late as 30 years after the initial infection. Late lesions may appear in the mouth and throat and on the tongue. The lesions are usually accompanied by thickening of the tissue or by destructive ulcers and are responsible for the crippling and disfiguring effects of syphilis. A chronic inflammatory process may develop in this late stage, involving bones, joints, eyes and other organs, and, especially, the cardiovascular system.

In the United States, although the disease still rages, modern methods of diagnosis and treatment have eliminated syphilis as "the great scourge." In 1970, for example, only some 20,000 new cases were reported—although it is estimated that some 70,000 to 75,000 persons were actually infected. Deaths from syphilis numbered only 2,381 in 1967 in contrast to 9,377 in 1947. In 1947, as well, there were 6,000 first admissions to hospitals for syphilis-induced psychoses, while in 1967 there were a mere 162.

Untreated syphilis remains deadly in about 25% of those infected. About 50% of untreated cases experience no disability or inconvenience; another 25% have some residual evidence of the disease, but suffer no disability or shortening of life. Some authorities believe that the absence of severe ill effects in such a high proportion of untreated syphilitics is due to resistance to the disease built up by administration of penicillin and other antibiotics in the treatment of other earlier illnesses.

The incidence of syphilis at birth, called *congenital syphilis,* has greatly lessened in recent years due to improved prenatal care of syphilitic mothers. In 1941 there were 13,600 cases of congenital syphilis diagnosed in children under 1 year of age in the U.S. By 1970 that figure had dropped to 300. Nevertheless, congenital syphilis has not been completely eradicated. It is during the early stage of a woman's infection, the first 2 years, that syphilis may be transmitted by the mother to her unborn infant. If the mother is properly treated before her fourth month of pregnancy, the child is usually born free of syphilis.

Although there are usually pathological symptoms of congenital syphilis, the appearance of symptoms may be delayed until the child is 10 or 15 years old. In some cases they are delayed until he is as old as 30. The course of congenital syphilis is similar to that of the second and third stages in the contracted form of the disease.

Various degrees of mental defects may exist in cases of congenital syphilis, and there are sometimes developmental defects such as an increase in the cerebrospinal fluid in the skull or a decrease in the size of the brain. Hardening of the affected tissues and convulsions are also occasional developments from congenital syphilis. In other cases, pupillary signs may be the only indication of the disease.

Untreated syphilis may produce certain severely disabling disorders, the two most common being *neurosyphilis* and *general paresis.* In the past, about 5% of all untreated syphilis developed into general paresis, but the figure has recently dropped to about 3% or less.

Neurosyphilis occurs in about 25% of untreated cases of syphilis and can affect every part of the cerebrospinal system in one or a combination of any of the three forms of the disease:

inflammations of the brain membrane or of the cerebral blood vessels, partial paralysis, and hardening of the spinal column. The disease can exist without any clinical symptoms, but there are usually many physical and emotional effects.

General paresis usually appears from 10 to 20 years after the primary infection. It is more frequent in men than in women, affecting one or all areas of the nervous system, and is often fatal. Because its symptoms resemble those of various mental illnesses, general paresis is sometimes referred to as "the great imitator."

Juvenile general paresis results from congenital syphilis and usually appears between the age of 10 and the time of adolescence. This disease is rarely found today because of treatment of the syphilitic mother-to-be.

OTHER VENEREAL DISEASES

Chancroid

Chancroid is a highly contagious disease that is typically spread through sexual intercourse. The first sign of chancroid is an inflamed papule or skin eruption which appears about 12 to 16 hours after infectious sexual contact, usually at the point of physical contact. The papule soon breaks down to become a ragged-edged ulcer filled with dead tissue. Drainage from the ulcer will infect surrounding tissues, and occasionally the lymph glands of the groin may swell and rupture. If not treated, chancroid ulcerations can drain for months, causing considerably greater ill effects in women than in men.

Chancroid may be contracted in conjunction with other venereal diseases, and accurate diagnosis and treatment require expert clinical and laboratory techniques. Sulfonamides usually cure the condition in 3 to 8 days, and certain other antibiotics are also effective.

Granuloma Inguinale

Granuloma inguinale is an infectious disease which may or may not be contracted through sexual intercourse. At its onset, a small red papule appears, usually on the penis or labia, but sometimes on other parts of the body. Lesions enlarge and spread to form a large area of infection which degenerates into a red, moist, malodorous, granulated, and frequently bleeding mass. Spontaneous healing does not ordinarily occur, and much of the tissue of the entire genital region can be destroyed. The destroyed tissue is replaced by thick scar tissue. There is no lymph-node involvement in granuloma inguinale, and this feature is an excellent diagnostic aid. The disease is difficult to identify except by microscopic examination of stained slides, but it can be cured by careful treatment with antibiotic drugs of the mycin family.

Lymphogranuloma Venereum

Lymphogranuloma venereum is caused by a virus; it is manifested a few days after sexual contact by a small painless blister that soon ruptures to form a shallow ulcer with clear-cut edges surrounded by reddened skin. The blister may appear in the external or internal genital region. If the virus is contracted during cunnilingus (oral-vulval contact), it can cause the tongue of the man to blister and swell, often with an accompanying swelling in the glands of the neck.

Approximately 2 weeks after the primary lesion, the invasion of the virus progresses to a secondary stage which is characterized by pain in the groin and visible enlargement of the lymph nodes. In the third stage, enlargement of the penis, scrotum, or vulva appear.

Diagnosis of lymphogranuloma venereum is difficult, even in the laboratory. The Frei skin test has a high diagnostic accuracy, however, and should be performed in every suspected case. Antibiotic drugs have not been as effective in treatment of this disease as they have in other venereal diseases, but prognosis is more favorable with treatment.

AVOIDING VD INFECTION

When there is even the slightest suspicion of VD in oneself or one's partner, preventative measures (*prophylactics*) should be used during any act of sexual intercourse. The simplest and best prophylactics for men are the use of a condom during coition and a thorough soap and water cleansing of the genitalia afterward. Women who suspect that their sexual partner is infected should use an antiseptic vaginal douche, followed by a soap and water cleansing of the genitalia. Obviously, the most effective preventive for both sexes is to avoid sexual intercourse with any individual about whom there is even a question of possible VD.

As we have seen, venereal diseases often do not reveal themselves in clear clinical symptoms. The long-range effects of VD can be so destructive and the probability of infecting others is so great that anyone who fears that he has contracted a venereal disease should seek diagnosis as soon as possible. Treatment is almost always both fast and effective, and delaying treatment only complicates the effects of the disease.

FURTHER READING

V D Handbook, edited by D. Cherniak and A. Feingold. Montreal: Handbook Collective, 1972.

> This practical guide has a radical aim: to improve medical care by making lay people aware of information about VD which is ordinarily known only by the medical profession. Included are sections on medical examination, diagnosis, laboratory tests, and side effects of the treatment for various venereal diseases.

The Encyclopedia of Sexual Behavior, Vol. I and Vol. II., by A. Ellis and A. Abarbanel. New York: Hawthorn Books, 1961.

> This massive collection of meaningful sex-related articles, now available in one volume, is, as the title states, an encyclopedia of many aspects of sexual behavior. The article "The Venereal Diseases" (pp. 1023-1032) is meaningful to the discussion in this chapter.

The Reproductive System, by F. H. Netter. Summit, N. J.: CIBA Pharmaceutical Products, 1961.

> Sections III, V (men), and VII (women) contain discus-

sions and pictures of the symptoms of various venereal diseases.

Human Sexuality, 2d ed., by J. L. McCary. New York: D. Van Nostrand, 1973.

The first part of Chapter 20 provides the material that served as the source for this chapter.

12 NONVENEREAL DISEASES AND SEXUAL DISORDERS

In addition to venereal disease, a number of other diseases and disorders can affect various parts of the male and female reproductive systems. The organism or condition which produces these difficulties may have no relationship to sexual activity, but in each instance, some part of the internal or external genitalia is affected and may possibly be aggravated by sexual contact.

Among the *nonvenereal diseases* are numerous conditions that affect both men and women. Only those that are commonly found in younger people in our own culture will be considered here.

NONVENEREAL INFECTIONS

Trichomoniasis

Trichomoniasis, a bacterial infection afflicting 25% of all women patients, is the most common minor gynecological disease. (*Gynecology* is the branch of medicine which deals with the female reproductive system.) The first indication of infection is usually a white or yellowish vaginal discharge which is accompanied by itching and burning. This discharge frequently causes constant inflammation and soreness of the external area of the vulva. A separation of the inflamed labia often reveals a thick, smelly, bubbly discharge in the vestibule.

Trichomoniasis sometimes causes severe itching rather than soreness. In either case, the condition seems to worsen immediately before and after menstruation. The symptoms vary in women from very mild to very severe. No matter how minor the symptoms seem, a doctor should be consulted immediately if there is the slightest indication of infection.

Men also may suffer from this annoying infection, although they seldom experience the bothersome symptoms such as copious discharge, itching, and burning that are typical in women. If one sexual partner is found to be infected with trichomoniasis, the other should be examined also, since it is possible for a couple to pass the infection back and forth for many years if only one partner is treated.

Some authorities claim that trichomoniasis is a venereal infection and that it is transmitted only by sexual intercourse. Others believe that the infection is not venereal since it can be contracted in a swimming pool or a bathtub, where the organism may easily gain entry into the vaginal tract.

The drug Flagyl is reported to be almost 100% effective in the treatment of trichomoniasis. Obtainable by prescription only, it is administered orally and cures the condition within 10 to 14 days in both men and women.

Trichomoniasis is usually complicated by simultaneous infections of monilia and perhaps one or several other bacteria. Treatment of trichomoniasis and any other accompanying infection should be rigorously pursued. While the disease is not considered serious, it can be tormenting and is sexually inhibiting.

Moniliasis

Moniliasis, commonly called *monilia,* is a fungus infection of the genital region that can cause acute discomfort, primarily in women. More frequently that not, monilia accompanies other infectious organisms, such as trichomonads.

The genital area afflicted with monilia has white cheesy spots on the vulva, in the vagina, and on the cervix. There may also be minute ulcerations of the labia minora and in some cases a thick or watery vaginal discharge. All these symptoms can eventually lead to a raw, bleeding surface if treatment by a gynecologist is not prompt and careful. Women who have been overtreated with antibiotic vaginal suppositories are ready victims of the disease. A cure can be accomplished by gynecological treatment.

Venereal Warts

Venereal warts are actually benign tumors which are probably the result of a virus infection. In a man, they usually appear around the base of the penile glans and quickly develop in the moist environment of the tight prepuce. In a woman, they usually appear on or near the labia and perineum, but they can spread to cover the entire area. Veneral warts can be transmitted to another person or to other parts of one's own body, and they should be examined and treated promptly by a physician.

Infectious Mononucleosis

Infectious mononucleosis is included here only because of its popular name, "the kissing disease." Neither a nonvenereal disease nor a sexual disorder, it is an acute infectious disease of the lymph glands which is characterized by sudden onset of fever, marked fatigue, chills, sweating, headache, sore throat, and loss of appetite.

Many authorities suspect that deep kissing with an infected person is the means of transmission of mononucleosis. One study found that 71 of 73 "mono" patients had engaged in deep kissing at the exact time the incubation period for mononucleosis would have commenced. Fever usually subsides after 5 days and other acute symptoms abate within 3 weeks, although some symptoms may persist for months.

Dermatoses

Dermatoses (skin diseases) of the genital region are fairly common. They have a wide variety of causes. Sometimes, for example, chemicals contained in soap that is not rinsed off after a bath or shower can collect in the sensitive areas of the genitalia and produce irritation or burns. Frequently the difficulty is compounded by the application of a medication that is too strong for the distressed area.

Tinea cruris, or "jock itch," is a fungus infection that afflicts the genital region. Reddish, scaly patches develop into large, highly inflamed zones with stressful itching and pain. The infection is strikingly similar to athlete's foot. Sweating, tight clothing, and inadequate drying of the genitalia after bathing provide a favorable environment for its development.

Scabies and *pediculosis* (crabs) are two of the dermatoses caused by parasites that can invade the genital area. Scabies is a highly contagious skin disorder in which a female mite burrows between the layers of skin and deposits her eggs. Little blister-like vesicles housing the mite and her eggs appear on the skin surface and soon develop into papules, pustules, and a rash that itches formidably, especially at night. Medication prescribed by a physician can usually rid the victim of scabies in a short time.

In *pediculosis pubis*, the pubic hair is infested with crab lice, the bites of which cause an itchy skin irritation. Scratching produces further irritation and a brownish discoloration of the skin may develop. The crab louse usually buries its head in the follicles of the pubic hair and attaches its body to the hair itself. These parasites, commonly passed from person to person through sexual contact, may also be picked up from a toilet seat or a bed.

Herpes genitalis is an acute skin disease affecting the external genitals. It is caused by a virus similar to those that produce cold sores or fever blisters on the lips and nose. Small blisters develop, burst, and then either form into small ulcers or dry and harden into a crust.

Psoriasis is a disease of the skin characterized by scaly red patches. It may attack the genital region as well as other parts of the body. *Pruritus,* an excruciating itching, especially at the anus, often accompanies psoriasis and other skin diseases. Medication usually provides relief for the itching and clears up the condition in a short time.

GENITAL INFLAMMATIONS

The suffix *-itis* added to the name of an organ indicates inflammation of that organ. Many disorders of the internal and external genitalia of both men and women fall into this category.

Vaginitis, a fairly common irritation, may be caused by bacteria, foreign objects, or by the use of strong chemicals. Douching with too high a concentration of chemicals, overmedication, tampons which are inserted and then forgotten, and incorrectly placed vaginal suppositories can all cause chemical burns and inflammation of the vaginal tract.

Excessive douching or the use of overly strong douches is frequently the basic evil, especially among the young and the newly married. Such douching destroys the protective organisms that naturally inhabit the vagina, reducing the acid condition and providing a suitable place for the development of hostile bacteria. Although most gynecologists agree that a healthy vagina needs no douching, studies have indicated that douching with water or with a mild vinegar or alkaline solution produces no harmful effects. Probably the best safeguard again vaginitis is good general physical health coupled with positive attitudes toward sex and personal hygiene.

Cystitis, inflammation of the bladder, may occur in a variety of ways. Symptoms include a severe burning sensation during urination, frequent urination, and sharp pain in the lower abdomen.

Irritation of a woman's bladder may occur as a result of frequent sexual intercourse due to the tendency of the bladder to become slightly displaced by the pressure of the penis and weight of the man's body. This condition frequently occurs during honeymoons when sexual intercourse is very frequent, and it is sometimes called "honeymoon cystitis."

It is advisable for a woman to empty her bladder before sexual intercourse and to use a lubricating jelly when there is an insufficient amount of vaginal secretion. Both these measures will decrease pressure on the abdominal organs through the vagina during coitus.

Sometimes cystitis is caused or aggravated by emotional factors, usually related to conflict over sexual matters. Whatever its cause, a physician should be consulted at the first sign of cystitis because early treatment helps to avoid complications. Daily cleansing of the external genitalia and of the urethral opening with surgical soap is an aid in treatment.

Epididymitis, a fairly common disorder among men, involves inflammation of the epididymis, the structure closely attached to each testicle. One in 5 cases of gonorrhea results in epididymitis. In mild cases there may be only slight swelling and tenderness, while in severe cases the entire testicular structure may be greatly swollen and painful. Mild cases respond readily to medical treatment, but some cases of chronic epididymitis persist for years and the condition can result in sterility.

Prostatitis, more common among older than younger men, is usually a chronic condition, although it can occur suddenly and become critical. There seems to be a clear relationship between infrequent sexual activity and the temporary enlargement of the prostate that accompanies chronic prostatitis. Prostatitis can also follow prolonged infection of other parts of the body, and it is estimated that from 30% to 40% of American men between the ages of 20 and 40 suffer from chronic prostatitis.

Symptoms include a thin mucous discharge from the urethra and pain in the lower back, testicles, perineum, posterior scrotum, and sometimes in the tip of the penis, especially at the time of ejaculation. Prostatitis can also lead to painful or inadequate erection, premature and sometimes bloody ejaculations, impotence, and sterility. Treatment by a urologist includes prostatic massage, antibiotics, and prolonged warm baths to clear up the infection and to bring about drainage of the congested gland.

PEYRONIE'S DISEASE

Although *Peyronie's disease* usually is found in men of middle or old age, it occasionally is seen in younger men. The disease is characterized by a deviation of the penis to the left or right, or upwards, often making erections painful and sexual intercourse impossible. It is caused by the development of a fibrous tissue in the space above and between the two large spongy bodies of the penis. X-ray treatment has reportedly improved or cured the disorder in more than 80% of patients treated.

CANCER

Cancer can strike any part of the sexual system. Its symptoms are diverse, and one should immediately consult a physician upon recognizing any suspicious signal, such as the seven outlined by the American Cancer Society:

Unusual bleeding or discharge
A lump or thickening in the breast or elsewhere
A sore that does not heal
Change in bowel or bladder habits
Persistent hoarseness or cough
Persistent indigestion or difficulty in swallowing
Change in the size or color of a wart or mole.

Some researchers maintain that smegma and other impurities collect more easily under the foreskin of uncircumcized men and that these impurities can predispose them to penile cancer or their sexual partners to cervical cancer. Other researchers dispute this theory and offer evidence that points to no higher incidence of either penile cancer or cervical cancer in uncircumcised men and their partners.

There seems to be some relationship between promiscuity in women and cervical cancer. It is not known whether this relationship is due to a woman's beginning sexual intercourse at an earlier age or to her engaging in intercourse more frequently and with a greater variety of partners. Research data from studies of nuns indicate, however, that chastity may be related to a low incidence of cervical cancer. The incidence of cancer of the uterus, ovaries, or breasts appears to be unrelated to chastity or to infrequent intercourse.

Whether or not the foreskin of a man has been removed by circumcision and regardless of how sexually active a woman is, sensible precautions against cancer should be taken by both sexes. Regular gynecological examinations, including a Pap smear test, could save the lives of thousands of women annually. The Pap smear test is a simple and painless procedure that involves taking a sample of cervical fluid by means of a cotton swab and examining the fluid for the presence of cancer cells. While there is no test analogous to the Pap smear test that will detect cancer in the male genital system, it is advisable for every man to have a thorough physical examination every year since many of the possible sites of cancer are routinely inspected in such an examination. For example, inspection of the prostate gland may reveal early signs of prostatic cancer.

SEXUAL DISORDERS

Sexual disorders are physical abnormalities of the genitalia which may be caused by hereditary factors, acquired during development in the uterus (*congenital* disorders) or at any time after birth (*postnatal* disorders). These conditions are much more rare than most venereal and nonvenereal diseases.

Priapism is a continuous and pathological erection of the penis. There is usually an erection of the corpora cavernosa without an accompanying erection of the glans of the penis or the small lower spongy body. The onset of priapism is sudden, painful, unaccompanied by sexual desire, and is usually caused by blood clots.

Hypospadia occurs once in every 500 male births and is a congenital defect in which the urethral opening is on the underside of the penis rather than at its tip. This condition is due to the failure of the genital fold to close completely during prenatal development and can be corrected by plastic surgery. Afflicted men in whom the condition is not corrected are usually capable of coitus but may have difficulty in impregnating a woman.

Phimosis is an anomaly in which the prepuce is abnormally long and tight and cannot be pulled back from over the glans of the penis. Fibrous growths sometimes attach the prepuce to the glans, making even the attempt to draw it back quite painful. Smegma may collect, leading to ulceration or inflammation of the penis. Surgery, usually in the form of circumcision, can correct this difficulty.

Polyps are benign tumors that may be found in any bodily cavity where there is mucous tissue. If they cause urinary disturbances or disturbances in sexual function, they can be removed by minor surgery.

Edema of the scrotum may result from inflammation, injury, allergic states, or insect bites and can cause the scrotum to swell to nearly the size of a basketball.

Undescended testes are found in about 1 boy in 50 at the age of puberty; its incidence dwindles to approximately 1 in 500 by adulthood. Testes that remain undescended after puberty will progressively degenerate if their placement is not corrected. Hormonal treatment often causes a successful descent of the testicles unless there is some physical blockage. In this case, surgery is indicated.

Monorchism is a condition in which there is only one testicle in the scrotum. The existing testicle produces sufficient quantities of both hormones and sperm for normal physiological and sexual functioning. Sometimes one testicle is much smaller than the other, causing one to suspect monorchism. This inequality is not monorchism, however, since two testicles are present, and the small testis in such cases is usually functional, at least to some degree.

Testicular failure may involve either the interstitial cells that produce male hormones, or the spermatic tubes where sperm develop, or both. In almost all instances, failure of the interstitial cells involves failure of the spermatic tubes, although the reverse is not necessarily true. *Hypogonadism* (insufficient hormonal secretion by the testicles) produces characteristics similar to those of a castrated man. Afflicted boys commonly develop excessive fat over the abdomen, around the mammary glands, above the pubis, and on the buttocks. Their external genitals are extraordinarily small and poorly developed, and their secondary sexual characteristics typically appear to be feminine.

Congenital anomalies of the vagina, uterus, and fallopian tubes are more common than many realize. The vagina, for example, may be closed or missing entirely. If it is missing, an artificial vagina that is functional for sexual intercourse can be surgically constructed. Double vaginas also occur, or the vagina may be divided into two parts by a septum, as the nose is. Similar anomalies are also found occasionally in the uterus and in the fallopian tubes, or either of these may be altogether missing. Such congenital anomalies are usually the result of the failure of the müllerian ducts (the embryonic forerunners of the female genitals) to fuse completely during prenatal development.

Chromosomal Anomalies

Several congenital sexual disorders are caused by *chromosomal anomalies*. The relationship between an abnormal *karyotype* (an arrangement of chromosomes) and certain disorders was first observed in 1938 and has since been studied in detail.

Best known of the chromosomal abnormalities are *Turner's syndrome* and *Klinefelter's syndrome*. These conditions are believed to arise from the faulty splitting of the 23 pairs of chromosomes during the formation of sperm and/or ova. The result is a germ cell (ovum or sperm) that contains an extra sex-determining (X or Y) chromosome or that is lacking one.

In *Turner's syndrome*, rather than the normal XX or XY karyotype, the total number of chromosomes in the fertilized egg is 45: 44 autosomes and only 1 X chromosome instead of the normal 2. The abnormality will produce a woman having the primary external sex structure of a female, although poorly developed and infantile in size, but having no ovaries. Besides the deficiencies in the primary and secondary sex characteristics, other typical indications of this disorder are a short stature, winglike folds of skin extending from the base of the skull to an area over the clavicle, and a broad, stocky chest. Deafness and mental deficiency are also fairly common.

In *Klinefelter's syndrome* there is an extra female (X) sex chromosome in the fertilized egg producing a man of incomplete virilization and distinctly feminine appearance. The testicles are small and incapable of producing mature sperm, and breast development is prominent. These men, furthermore, show a tendency toward mental impairment and a large number can be characterized as having inadequate personalities. Predictably, their sex drive is low.

A third form of chromosomal abnormality discovered in certain men, which has attracted considerable attention of late, involves extra Y (male) chromosomes. Some investigators have speculated that the disorder creates a man who is more prone than average to undisciplined, aggressive, criminal, or sociopathic behavior.

An *imperforate hymen* is a condition wherein the vagina is sealed off by a solid mass of hymenal tissue. The condition may go unnoticed until the onset of menstruation. Unless the hymen is punctured at the menarche, however, the menstrual fluid is retained in the vagina and the uterus must enlarge in order to contain the flow. Incision of the hymen corrects the condition easily and quickly. The hymenal tissue in this instance is inordinately thick and tough and must be surgically incised before penile penetration is possible.

Abnormal uterine bleeding is the most frequent gynecological complaint encountered by physicians. *Functional uterine bleeding* refers to hemorrhages not precipitated by detectable abnormalities. If ovulation does not occur, too little or no progesterone is secreted yet the secretion of estrogen continues. The result in some instances—although not all—is that the proliferation or growth phase of the menstrual cycle persists, and with it comes a thickening of the uterine lining.

In these circumstances there is no growth stimulation of the ovarian follicles because ovarian estrogen inhibits the release of the follicle-stimulating hormone from the pituitary gland. The uterine lining shows unnatural growth, and the follicles gradually convert into cystic structures. The irregular hormonal interplay frequently produces uterine bleeding which is abnormal both in frequency and amount.

Cervical erosion may result when any break in the cervical tissue, such as unhealed lacerations caused by childbirth, or any unusual exposure of the cervical mucous glands to the bacteria inhabiting the vaginal tract makes the cervix susceptible to infection. Infection of this area, which is usually chronic and low-grade, may lead to erosion and ulceration of the cervical tissue, correction of which may require a partial removal of the cervix.

Displacement of the uterus is said to exist when the womb becomes fixed in an abnormal position. The usual uterine position in a woman standing erect is approximately at right angles to the axis of the vagina, putting the uterus in an almost horizontal plane above the bladder. For various reasons, the ligaments supporting the uterus may become too taut or too loose, and the organ shifts to an unusual position, exhibiting a slight to great degree of deviation. The shift frequently causes painful menstruation, backaches, and pelvic congestion and makes sexual intercourse uncomfortable.

Endometriosis involves abnormal growth of the endometrium (lining of the uterus). Symptoms of the disorder may include sterility, painful and irregular menstruation, backaches, and painful sexual intercourse. The condition can occur as long as the ovaries produce hormones; it is most often found in women in their 30s. The tissue can commence growth in any of various parts of the afflicted woman's body—the cervix, abdominal walls, intestines, Bartholin's glands, vulva; even the navel may be affected. Treatment depends upon the severity of the symptoms. If required, surgery usually involves removal of the organs or areas invaded, together with the surrounding tissue.

Menstrual cramps, when of a physiological origin, are usually caused by a tilted or infantile uterus, inadequate dilation or blockage of the cervical os, endometrial disorders, or similar anomalies. However, psychological factors are much more likely to be the cause of menstrual cramps than physiological factors.

Hermaphroditism

Hermaphroditism is the condition in which an individual has the gonads of both sexes; that is, both ovarian and testicular tissue is present. Cases of true hermaphroditism are extremely rare; perhaps fewer than 200 valid incidences appear in the medical literature of the entire world. It would be possible, technically, for a hermaphrodite to impregnate as a male and also to conceive as a woman. Indeed, Brazilian doctors recently reported the case of a true hermaphrodite who had a developing fetus in the womb, and who also possessed testicles capable of producing sperm. Furthermore, the person claimed to be both the father and the mother of the child. Even if the report of pregnancy were true—which, undoubtedly it is not—the individual's dual parenthood seems most unlikely because the female hormones produced by the ovary would undoubtedly sterilize the testis, making the person incapable of fertilizing ova and rendering self-impregnation impossible.

Pseudohermaphroditism is a much more common disorder than true hermaphroditism. Some form of it appears in about 1 infant of every 1,000 born. The male pseudohermaphrodite has gonads that are testes, but his external genitalia are either ambiguous or feminine in appearance. The gonads of a female pseudohermaphrodite are ovaries, but her external genitalia (and often other of her bodily characteristics) appear, to a greater or lesser degree, to be those of a male.

Because pseudohermaphrodites usually have both male and female sex organs in rudimentary form, their genetic sex is difficult to determine. Because accurate identification is so difficult, it is not uncommon for a pseudohermaphrodite to be brought up as a member of the wrong sex. Childhood influences quite naturally predispose the individual to assume the interests, attitudes, and sexual behavior of one sex, however much his physical characteristics may be those of the opposite one—another indication of the superiority of psychological over physiological factors in sexual matters.

Congested ovaries and testicles occur following prolonged sexual stimulation without orgasmic relief. Since this is a common occurrence in women during an engagement period, the term "engagement ovaries" is frequently used. In men, the condition is referred to as "stone ache."

Congenital and acquired anomalies of the breast are found in both men and women. The most frequent of these disorders among men is *gynecomastia,* in which there is an abnormal increase in breast size due to hormonal imbalance. Excess tissue can be shrunk by endocrine medication or removed by simple surgery.

Women may also possess abnormally enlarged breasts, or they may possess more than two breasts or nipples. Extra breasts and nipples usually are located somewhere in the milk line, which starts under the arm and extends through the breasts and down both sides of the abdomen in a line to the lips of the vulva, terminating in the inner thighs. Plastic surgery can correct all of these abnormalities.

Our society is so breast-conscious that a woman who has inherited small breasts is apt to feel that she is abnormal. Many small-breasted women—especially those over 30—have become victims of the "mammary merchants" who pander to women's feelings of sexual inadequacy by offering various creams, salves, or special exercising equipment designed to increase the size of the breasts. In an effort to emulate the bulbous attributes of women who are pictured in the centerfold of "girlie" magazines, some women go to such lengths as having silicone injections or plastic surgery to increase the size of their breasts. Brassiere manufacturers trade on women's fears of inadequacy by advertising their products in terms that are erotically suggestive, and which promise to make every woman look as if her breasts were larger and firmer than nature made them.

The most unfortunate aspect of this obsession with breasts is that many women become so fearful of losing their breasts through surgery that they avoid having physical examinations for breast cancer, thus endangering their lives.

The desire to have large breasts stems, of course, from the erroneous view of many men that a woman with large breasts is more "sexy" than a woman whose breasts are smaller. Women who see men ogle large-breasted women thus conclude that small-breasted women are less desirable and, in some mysterious way, sexually inadequate. While there are many nerve endings in the breasts which afford sexual excitement and pleasure, the number of these endings is the same in both small and large breasts. One could therefore make the calculation that small breasts are more erogenous per square inch than larger ones!

In the last few years, there has been a healthy trend in younger men and women to discard much of the artifice that sometimes stands in the way of honest relationships. Cleanliness and naturalness are beginning to replace applications of cosmetics and forcing of body and hair into unnatural shapes. This trend seems to include a wholesome acceptance of the body and less emphasis on the female body as a commodity for exhibition. Younger men and women are therefore less apt to be caught up in the worship of the female breast as a symbol of ultimate sexuality. If the trend toward "bralessness" continues, in fact, the woman with small breasts will have a distinct advantage over the woman who must support her large breasts with a brassiere in order to be comfortable.

Normal, healthy breasts vary a great deal in size. Increasing acceptance of this diversity will help both men and women to distinguish normal breast conditions from those which are caused by disease or disorder. Small breasts do not require medical attention simply because of their size, but any growth, pain, or change in the feel, function, or appearance of the breast —whatever its size—should be investigated immediately by a physician.

FURTHER READING

Advances in Sex Research, edited by H. G. Biegel. New York: Harper & Row, 1963.

This book contains a wide range of findings and experiments in theoretical and clinical aspects of sexual problems. Chapters 21, 23, and 24 are concerned with sexual disorders.

The Reproductive System, by F. H. Netter. Summit, N. J.: CIBA Pharmaceutical Products, 1961.

Sections III, IV, and V are related to sexual diseases and disorders of men and Sections VII, VIII, IX, X, and XI are related to those problems in women.

Human Sexuality, 2d ed., by J. L. McCary. New York: D. Van Nostrand, 1973.

The last part of Chapter 20 contains material on nonve-nereal diseases and sexual disorders.

13 SEXUAL BEHAVIOR

We have seen throughout this book that human sexual behavior is determined by multi-faceted combinations of physiological, psychological, and social factors. The degree of sex drive in an individual and his expression of that drive are intricately influenced by each of these factors. The desire and ability for sexual expression therefore vary widely in intensity among both men and women. Individual variations in sex drive are common in people of the same sex and age and in the same person at different times in his life. This chapter will give some indication of the incidence of various forms of sexual behavior that are common in our society.

To some extent, sex drive is influenced by age. A young man in his teens ordinarily has a very strong sex drive and is capable of almost instant erection; four to eight orgasms a day are not unusual. He may be ready for another orgasm only seconds after his first one. He usually desires sexual release whether or not he has any emotional attachments, and whether or not he is occupied with other matters such as school or sports. If no sexual partner is available, he will achieve sexual release through masturbation and nocturnal emission.

As a man approaches his 30s, he remains highly interested in sex, but the urgency is less acute and he is satisfied with fewer orgasms. Erections still occur quickly and recede slowly, but by his late 30s it may be 30 minutes or more before he is capable of another orgasm after his first one. Sexual slackening continues through the 40s. By age 50, the average man is satisfied with two orgasms a week, and they are usually no closer together than 8 to 24 hours. At this age, the focus of sexual pleasure has usually shifted from an intense, genitally centered sensation to a more generalized, sensuously diffused experience.

There is far more individual variation among women than among men in the development of sexuality. Typically, women's sexual awakening is a slower process, not reaching its peak until the late 20s to early 40s. In her 30s, and frequently after childbirth, a woman begins to respond more intensely to sexual stimulation and to initiate the sex act more frequently than she did in the past. Vaginal lubrication—the equivalent to male erection so far as sexual response is concerned—occurs almost instantly for women in this age group, and many experience multiple orgasms.

Women in their 50s and 60s continue to seek out and respond to sexual situations, but there is a slight decline in their sex drive, and they are usually less preoccupied with sex than in their earlier years. Masturbation is quite commonly employed as a supplement to coitus or as the sole sexual outlet. Although a woman's sexual response moderates as she ages, she remains quite capable of multiple orgasms—even until her late years. A woman apparently has the same physical potential for orgasm at age 60 or even older as she had at age 20.

Human sexuality expresses itself most commonly in any of 5 ways: masturbation, nocturnal orgasm, heterosexual petting, homosexual relations, and heterosexual intercourse. (A sixth way, sexual contact with animals, is so rare that we shall not discuss it here.) Typically, the individual finds outlets for his sexual feelings through several different forms of sexual behavior. The level of a person's formal education and the degree of his religious commitment often influence both the amount and the forms of sexual expression which he chooses.

MASTURBATION

Any type of self-stimulation that produces erotic arousal may be considered *masturbation*, a practice which is common among both men and women in premarital, marital, and postmarital states. Boys and girls begin the practice at an early age. In addi-

tion to providing a means of self-discovery and sensory awareness, masturbation also provides the most sensible form of sexual
relief for those who do not have sexual partners.

About 95% of all men admit to having masturbated to orgasm at some time in their lives. More men with college training
have masturbated than men with high–school or grade–school
education. A little more than one-third of all boys experience
their first ejaculation through masturbation, and about three-
fourths of them learn how to masturbate by being told by others
or by reading about it.

On the average, adolescent boys masturbate about 2.5 times
a week, although many may masturbate from 4 to 7 or more
times a week. As a man ages, the incidence of masturbation progressively declines, although some men continue to masturbate
on a sporadic basis throughout adult life. About 70% of married
American male college graduates masturbate occasionally; this
activity makes up a little less than one-tenth of their total sexual
outlet. Religiously inactive Protestant men masturbate most frequently, and orthodox Jews and devout Roman Catholics masturbate least frequently.

Masturbation is second only to heterosexual petting among the
erotic activities of unmarried young women, and it is second
after coition among married women. It accounts for about one-
tenth of the total sexual outlet of married women; the percentage
of masturbation in the total sexual outlet of unmarried and previously married women varies widely, depending on the sub-
cultural group to which the woman belongs.

Of all the types of sexual activity among women, masturbation
is the most successful method of reaching orgasm—a climax is
reached 95% of the time in masturbation. Furthermore, women
reach orgasm more quickly through masturbation than through
any other sexual technique—three-fourths of all women reaching orgasm in under 4 minutes.

The majority of all women masturbate at one time or another
in their lives, whether or not they are aware of it. Many women
do not recognize that indirect, pleasurable stimulation of the
genitals, in behavior such as squeezing the thighs together or
riding horseback, can be considered a form of masturbation.

As is true with men, the higher the educational level, the
higher the incidence of masturbation in women. The incidence
ranges from 63% of college–educated women to 59% of high–school

–educated and 34% of grade–school–educated. The range of frequency of masturbation among women is from once or twice in a lifetime to 100 orgasms an hour. Of those women who masturbate to the point of orgasm, however, the frequency is usually once every 2 to 4 weeks, regardless of age or marital status.

In contrast to men, the incidence of masturbation to orgasm increases among women up to middle age and then remains fairly constant. Most women prefer to masturbate by genital manipulation, while a few others employ thigh pressure, muscular tension, or simply fantasy without physical stimulation. More than half the women who masturbate invariably use erotic fantasy to accompany their physical stimulation, but a few others only occasionally use fantasy.

Women who have previously masturbated to orgasm have been found to be far more likely to reach orgasm during coitus the first year of marriage than are women who have never masturbated to orgasm before marriage. Women who are devoutly religious are less likely to masturbate than are less religious women.

NOCTURNAL ORGASM

It has long been recognized that men experience *nocturnal orgasm* or "wet dreams." Women also have erotic dreams which frequently culminate in orgasm although, since they do not ejaculate, they cannot have nocturnal emissions.

Almost all men have experienced erotic dreams, and almost 85% have had dreams that culminated in orgasm. Erotic dreams occur most frequently among young men in their teens and 20s, but approximately half of all married men continue to have nocturnal emissions occasionally.

The incidence of nocturnal emission has been found to be considerably higher among young men in college than among those who do not attend college, probably because college men do more petting that is not followed by orgasm so that their sexual tensions are more often at a high pitch at bedtime. Almost all college–educated men have sexual dreams to orgasm at some time during their lives. The incidence of nocturnal emission, unlike other forms of sexual behavior, bears little relationship to religious affiliation or strength of religious conviction.

Nocturnal orgasm among women is much more common than

is usually supposed. More than two-thirds of all women have had dreams of sexual content, although only about half report having had dreams culminating in orgasm. Because a woman, unlike a man, reveals no physical evidence of nocturnal orgasm, the data on women's dreaming to orgasm have been questioned. There is no question in the minds of the women involved, however, that orgasm has occurred. The incidence of sexual dreams to orgasm reaches a peak among women in their 40s. There is no correlation between frequency of nocturnal dreams to orgasm and a woman's religious or educational background.

HETEROSEXUAL PETTING

Heterosexual petting refers to sexual contact between men and women that does not culminate in intercourse. This discussion of the significance of petting as a means of sexual expression will be limited to premarital petting.

By the age of 15, more than half of all boys have done some petting. The percentage increases to 84% by age 18, and to 89% by age 25. While almost all men become erotically aroused while petting, only about one-third become involved in petting to orgasm.

There is a distinct correlation between the frequency of petting and educational level. Men with the least formal education pet the least; men of the middle group are next; and college men pet most of all. More than a third of men who have petted have had 21 or more partners; about one-fourth have had 5 or fewer petting partners.

Individual experiences in petting vary markedly according to the man's educational level. Almost all males have engaged in simple kissing; 55% to 87% have engaged in deep kissing; 78% to 99% in manual manipulation of the woman's breasts; 36% to 93% in mouth-breast contact; 79% to 92% in manual manipulation of the woman's genitalia; and 9% to 18% of unmarried men (4% to 60% of married men) in oral stimulation of their partner's genitalia. (The two percentages in each instance refer to men at the two extremes of educational achievement.)

Almost all married women have had some sort of petting experience prior to marriage and 90% of the entire female population, whether or not they ever marry, engage in petting at one time or another. Women who have attained an advanced level of education engage in heavier forms of petting than do less well-educated women. The more sophisticated and liberal the method of petting, however, the fewer are the women at all education levels who have tried it.

Recent studies show that 60% to 90% of college women have engaged in heavy petting, usually defined as genital stimulation of one or both partners in an unclothed state. More than one-fourth of college women have had heavy-petting experiences with three or more partners, and over half have engaged in heavy petting with someone they did not love. One study found that almost 60% of the college women sampled had experienced heavy petting while still in high school.

Oral-genital contact, a form of petting that has been more slowly accepted than others, is now widely utilized as an erotic outlet by the majority in the higher socioeducational groups. Even in the 1940s, at the time of the early Kinsey studies, about two–thirds of the younger women at the upper educational levels who had experienced coitus more than 25 times had also experienced oral–genital stimulation prior to marriage; slightly fewer of these women had orally stimulated the genitals of their partners. These percentages have risen significantly since the Kinsey studies were conducted.

The number of partners with whom women engage in petting varies from only one to more than 20. Over one-third of all women experience premarital petting with more than 10 men.

Like most other forms of sexual behavior in women, petting is significantly related to religious background. The more pronounced the commitment to a religion, the more restricted the sexual behavior. Interestingly, however, religion ultimately has little influence, one way or the other, on frequency of petting to orgasm, even among the most religiously devout. Once religiously devout women achieve orgasm through petting, they engage in this sexual outlet as often as less devout women.

HOMOSEXUALITY

In our society, *homosexuality*, sexual gratification obtained through relations with a partner of the same sex, is usually deplored as a mode of sexual behavior. Sanctions against it are considerably more stringent for men than for women. In New York City in one 10-year period, for example, only one woman was convicted of "homosexual sodomy," while over 700 men were found guilty on the same charge.

Most forms of sexual expression which are publicly disapproved are more common than is usually supposed. Homosexuality is no exception. More than one-third of all men and nearly one-sixth of all women have had some experience with homosexual relations to the point of orgasm. (Further discussion of the incidence of homosexuality and of attitudes toward it is found in Chapter 14.)

Both homosexual men and women have their first *heterosexual* intercourse at an earlier age than most heterosexuals do. About 17% of lesbians (homosexual women) and 18% of homosexual men have had their first coitus before the age of 15, as compared with only 6% of heterosexual women and 9% of heterosexual men.

About 4% of all men in the United States are exclusively homosexual all their sexual lives; 8% are exclusively homosexual for at least 2 years between the ages of 16 and 55, and 37% have experienced at least some form of homosexual activity to the point of orgasm in their lifetime. Furthermore, one-tenth of all men have some homosexual experience after marriage. These figures are based on Kinsey's conclusions from his study in the 1940s, and have been confirmed by a recent study of 20,000 well-educated, liberal men of high socioeconomic status.

For all single men, there is a gradual increase before the age of 40 in the percentage of total sexual outlet that homosexuality affords. For married men, homosexuality represents less than 1% of the total outlet. For the previously married in the under-40 age group, there is also a gradual increase in total outlet, from 9% to 26%. Generally speaking, the more intense an individual's commitment to religion, the less likely he is to participate in homosexual activity at all.

Homosexual men do not ordinarily concern themselves with finding a steady or permanent partner until they reach about age 30. Prior to that, they are more interested in seeking the satisfactions of the moment rather than in establishing a lasting relationship. Although slightly more than one-half of homosexual men have only one or two sexual partners, almost one-fourth have over 10 partners.

Homosexuality is less common among women than among men. The occurrence of both exclusive and partial homosexuality among women is only two-thirds of that among men. By age 30, 6% of women with a grade-school education have experienced homosexual contact to the point of orgasm, as have 5% of women with a high-school education, 10% of college-educated women, and 14% of women with graduate-school training. Almost twice these numbers have had homosexual contacts which stopped short of orgasm.

Some studies have indicated that as many as half of all women have harbored "intense feelings" for another woman at some point during their sexual lives. Most authorities, however, agree with the more conservative conclusion that less than one-third of all women (compared with one-half of all men) have experienced some sort of homosexual feelings.

No more than 1% and 3% of all women between the ages of 20 and 35 are exclusively homosexual, while an additional 2% to 6% of women in this age bracket are homosexual with rare heterosexual contact. Only 13% of all women (compared with 37% of all men) have had homosexual contact to the point of orgasm. In homosexual relationships, twice as many men as women experience a sexual response short of orgasm, while three times as many men as woman experience orgasm. In addition to women who have actually engaged in homosexual activity, a substantial number of other women (22%) have considered doing so.

Most female homosexuals are *bisexual;* that is, they have sexual interest in both men and women. Either they have had heterosexual experiences in the past, they will have them in the future, or they will shift back and forth between homosexuality and heterosexuality. Only a third of all lesbians are exclusively homosexual.

In contrast to the more promiscuous male homosexual, half the women engaging in homosexual activity limit their experience to a single partner, another one-fifth have 2 partners, and only 4% have 10 or more partners (as compared with 22% of the men who have 10 or more partners). Furthermore, the duration of established lesbian partnerships is comparable to that of heterosexual relationships. About two-thirds of the lesbians in one study had remained 1 to 9 years in a single partnership, 17% for 10 years or more. By comparison, nearly half of the heterosexual women in the study had stayed for 1 to 9 years with one male partner, 40% for 10 years or more.

The sexual expression of greatest importance and most cherished by the lesbian, as is the case with many heterosexual women, is embracing and close total body contact. Genital activity and orgasm are frequently of secondary importance. Lesbians are more likely to reach orgasm than heterosexual women are, however, and are twice as likely to be multiorgasmic on each sexual occasion. This finding is a reflection of the fact that orgasm, multiple orgasm, and greater intensity of response in women are more likely through masturbation or manual manipulation than through sexual intercourse.

About a fifth of the female prison population are officially identified as being homosexual, although prison staff members estimate the percentage of women having lesbian affairs while in prison to be between 30% and 70%. Female inmates themselves estimate the incidence of lesbian affairs to be higher.

Only a fifth of all women who have had extensive homosexual experience express definite regret. Almost 90% declare that they would keep as a friend any woman with a history of lesbianism. Regardless of religious affiliation, the more devout adherents have less homosexual contact to the point of orgasm than the nondevout.

HETEROSEXUAL INTERCOURSE

Although other methods of sexual outlet are significant for both men and women, the average person is more interested in *heterosexual intercourse*, coitus with a member of the opposite sex, than in any other type of sexual expression. Heterosexual intercourse is found not only in marriage but in premarital, extramarital, and postmarital heterosexual relationships as well.

Premarital intercourse commonly refers to coition between two single persons, although the term is also used to describe the experience of the single partner in coition between a single person and a person who is married to someone else.

Kinsey's studies in the 1940s found that 98% of men with a grade-school education, 84% of men with a high-school education, and 67% of men with a college education had had sexual intercourse before marriage. More recent studies have found that the rate of premarital coitus for college men approximates the earlier Kinsey figures. For example, a 1970 study of 200 newlyweds, conducted in Pennsylvania, revealed that 75% of the couples had had coitus with each other before marriage.

Premarital Intercourse

Although the incidence of premarital sexual intercourse among college men has not changed appreciably, its psychological and sociological aspects have altered considerably. College men today tend to have intercourse with a woman whom they love or care for deeply rather than with a prostitute or casual pickup, as their fathers would have done. College men are now faced at a somewhat earlier age with the necessity for integrating their sexual attitudes and behavior, their emotional feelings, and their standards of appropriate conduct.

Research indicates that grade–school–educated men between the ages of 16 and 20 have had intercourse with 7 times greater frequency than college–educated men of the same age. Unmarried men at the lower educational levels also first experience intercourse 5 or 6 years earlier than the unmarried college–educated man does. Coital frequency continues to be much greater among the less educated than the better educated at all age levels. The grade–school educated man obtains 40% to 68% of his total premarital sexual outlet from coitus, in contrast to the high–school educated man, for whom the percentage is 26 to 54, and the college educated, for whom it is 4% to 21%.

The correlation between premarital intercourse with prostitutes and educational level follows the same trend. Of the grade-school educated in the Kinsey study, 74% of men had had coitus with prostitutes by the age of 25, in contrast to 54% of the high-school educated of the same age, and 28% of the college educated.

Recent studies have produced conflicting data on the percentages of college men having coitus with prostitutes, with figures ranging from 4% to 43%. Of the college men in one study who had visited a prostitute, half had done so in the company of a group of other young males. A sidelight of this study was that

29% of the men in the total college sample had participated in some form of "group sex" in which one woman (not necessarily a prostitute) and two or more men were involved.

The incidence of premarital sexual intercourse among men may range from the extremes of a single contact to 35 or more coitions a week (the latter pattern sometimes persisting for as long as 5 years or more). Many men, particularly those at the upper end of the social-educational scale, limit their premarital coition to one woman—often the woman they eventually marry. Other men, particularly at the lower end of the social-educational scale, may have sexual intercourse with as many as several hundred women.

Although a few single men have sexual intercourse with older women—single, married, or divorced—almost all the coital experiences of single men are with single women, usually of their own age or slightly younger. A scant 4% of college men have engaged in coitus for money or favors.

At all social-educational levels, religion has a direct relationship to the incidence and frequency of premarital sexual intercourse—the greater the religious involvement, the less premarital coital experience.

The majority of engaged couples (92.6% of the men and 90.6% of the women) have reported that they believe premarital coitus has a strengthening effect on their relationship.

At the time of the Kinsey studies, almost half of all women had experienced coitus before marriage and about two-thirds had experienced orgasm. Only 17%, however, had experienced orgasm as a result of coition, which lags far behind masturbation as the unmarried woman's primary source of sexual outlet. The high percentage of women in Kinsey's sample who engaged in premarital coitus surprised and disturbed many people. It should be pointed out, however, that about half the coitally active single women had sexual intercourse only with the men whom they eventually married. Furthermore, most of the women's premarital sexual experience took place only during the year or two preceding their marriage.

About half of the women who married between the ages of 20 and 25 had had premarital intercourse. However, between 40% and 66% of women who married between the ages of 26 and 30 had experienced coition. The frequency of premarital intercourse does not reach its peak in women until they are in their late 20s, after which it remains remarkably regular. Single women under the age of 20 who have premarital intercourse typically do so on the average of once every 5 or 10 weeks, while the frequency is once every 3 weeks among older single women. There is much individual variation among women, however: about 20% of women have premarital intercourse as often as 7 times a week, with 7% having it 14 times a week.

In the Kinsey study in the 1940s, young women with little education were found to begin coital activity at an earlier age than women with more education. Between the ages of 16 and 20, 38% of the grade-school educated, 32% of the high-school educated, and about 18% of the college educated had had premarital intercourse. Of all women who have premarital intercourse, about half have only one partner and only 13% have 6 or more partners. About one-third have from 2 to 5 partners. Since the attractive woman is more apt to be involved in romantic episodes with young men than the less attractive woman, she is also more likely to have premarital intercourse and to have a larger number of sex partners.

Recent investigations have indicated that premarital intercourse among college women is increasing. Between 1945 and 1965, it is estimated that fewer than one-third of college women of all ages and class standings were sexually active. Studies in the late 1960s and early 1970s show the rate now to be about 35% to 50%. The percentage varies, of course, from a high of 55% among women in certain liberal eastern colleges to lows of 19% in a southern university and 12% in a church affiliated college.

The contention that there has been a liberalization in both the sexual attitudes and the behavior of college women has been supported by other investigations, one of which compared women in the same urban university in 1958 and 1968. In 1958, 10% of the women had premarital coitus in the context of a dating relationship; in 1968 the percentage was 23%. The rate of coitus while going steady rose from 15% to 28%; during engagement, it rose from 31% to 39%.

Most women having premarital coitus in 1958 were engaged to their partners. In 1968, however, the greatest number were merely dating or going steady with their partners. The rate of coitus among college women in both decades was lowest among

Catholics and highest among Protestants, with Jews in between.

In the same 10-year span, the incidence of premarital intercourse increased significantly among women but not among men. The percentage of premarital coital experience among women on a Mormon campus rose from 10% in 1958 to 32% in 1968, while it remained at 37% among men. On a midwestern campus the rate of premarital coitus for women increased 16% (from 21% in 1958 to 37% in 1968); for men it was about 50% in both years.

Not only was there more premarital intercourse among the 1968 college women, but there was less guilt about it than among those questioned in 1958. Whether premarital intercourse had occurred in a dating relationship, while going steady, or while engaged, the number of women in 1968 who thought they had "gone too far" was roughly half that of the women in 1958.

Further evidence of an increase in sexual activity comes from a longitudinal study of women at a state university, where 7% were nonvirgins as freshmen in 1967 and 39% were nonvirgins by the time they were seniors, 3 years later. Furthermore, of freshman women entering the same university in 1970, 15% had already engaged in premarital sexual intercourse, more than double the 1967 figure.

It is interesting in this connection to contrast Kinsey's 1953 finding that 23% of white women subjects were nonvirgins at age 21 with the results of a survey made in 1971, which shows that 40% of the 20-year-olds were nonvirgins.

While a small percentage of women attending college and living away from home have coition in the college town, by far the greater number have it in their hometowns during visits and vacations. Almost half have some part of their coital experience in their partner's home, while 40% have some part in a hotel or similar accommodation, and 41% have a portion of their experiences in an automobile. (Moralists who pronounce the automobile the downfall of the modern-day virgin, however, will be interested to know that many of the older subjects in Kinsey's study reported having sex relations in a horse-drawn buggy!) The first coital experience for both men and women is typically with someone near their own age whom they have known for some time. It quite likely takes place in the home of the young woman's parents and is usually remembered without regret.

Premarital coital experience is directly related to a woman's religious involvement: women who are the least religiously devout engage most frequently in sexual intercourse; the moderately devout are the next most active, and the devout are least active.

Marital Intercourse

According to the legal and moral codes of our Anglo-American culture, coitus between husband and wife is the one totally approved type of sexual activity. Although intercourse is the sexual outlet most frequently utilized by married couples, the sexual relationships in at least one-third of all marriages have been found to be inadequate to some degree. Some researchers in sexual inadequacy have set the figure as high as 50%.

An unsatisfactory sexual relationship in marriage usually generates other problems, partially because so much is expected of sex. About 90% of husbands and 75% of wives enter their bedroom on their wedding night with attitudes of eager anticipation; the remaining husbands and wives do so with attitudes of disgust, aversion, or indifference toward sexual relations.

Men's sex drive is usually somewhat greater than that of women during the early years of marriage. As a group, husbands desire sexual intercourse (or at least report that they desire it) more frequently than their wives. In a recent study of middle-class married couples in their late 30s, the husbands reported an average *desired* intercourse of 9.28 times per month, compared to the wives' average desire of 7.78 times. The husbands reported that the *actual* frequency was 6.98 times per month (25% below preference), whereas the wives reported the *actual* frequency as being 7.78 times per month (the same as their preference). Husbands underestimated their wives' desire for coitus, whereas wives overestimated their husbands' desire. Only 6% of the respondents reported that the wife's desire for intercourse exceeded that of her husband, but in actual fact the coital desire of 15% of the wives exceeded that of their husbands.

The effects of the change in women's sexual attitudes and behavior over the past half century can be seen in the research findings through those years. In the 1920s, two out of every three married women reported that their sex drive was weaker than that of their husbands. In the 1940s, nearly two out of every three women studied reported satisfaction with the frequency of marital intercourse. Sixteen percent reported that it occurred too frequently, and 20%, too infrequently. A recent study showed that two out of every three wives considered the frequency of marital coitus to be "about right." Two percent said it was "too frequent," and 32% "too infrequent."

Only a very small number of married men fail to participate, at least occasionally, in marital coitus. But the sexual activity of married people is not confined to marital coitus. It actually provides only 85% of the total sexual outlet for married men, the remaining 15% being derived from masturbation, nocturnal emissions, petting, homosexual activity, extramarital coitus, and, in some rural areas, animal contact. About half of the sexual outlets of the entire male population are socially disapproved and, to a large extent, illegal and punishable by law.

The percentage of the total outlet provided by marital intercourse varies according to the educational level of the man. Men with a high-school education obtain about 80% of their total outlet in the early years of marriage from marital coitus; this percentage increases to 90% as the marriages continue. By contrast, marital coitus provides about 85% of the total outlet during the early part of the marriages of college-educated men, but the figure decreases with age, and by the time they reach the age of 55, only 62% of their total sexual outlet is provided by marital coitus. The assumption could be made that these college-educated men reevaluate the moral restraints placed on them during their early life and find them less constrictive and threatening than they formerly were. However, it should be emphasized that half the remaining 38% of their total sexual activity is not with another woman or man but consists of solitary masturbation or nocturnal emissions.

Differences exist between various subgroups in frequency of sexual intercourse. The early Jews went so far as to stipulate the frequency of intercourse expected of each man according to his occupation. Those with constant leisure could copulate nightly, camel drivers only once every 30 days.

The frequency of marital coitus for men decreases with age, from an average of 3.9 times per week during the teens to 2.9 at age 30, 1.8 at age 50, and 0.9 at age 60.

The average college-educated man will spend from 5 to 15 minutes—sometimes an hour or more—in precoital petting. Once coitus is under way, he will attempt, more often than a man of less education, to delay orgasm (although three-fourths of all men reach orgasm within 2 minutes). About 90% of college-educated men prefer to have intercourse in the nude, but only half as many of the grade-school-educated have ever had intercourse unless partially clothed. Since college-educated men are often capable of higher levels of abstraction, they can be considerably excited by external erotic stimulation. Consequently, they prefer to have intercourse in a lighted room where they can observe the nude body of their partner and the act of coition itself.

Among less educated people, the belief exists that men are much more highly sexed than women and that a woman's sexual gratification is less important than a man's. According to this belief, the woman's gratification comes from knowing that her partner has been satisfied. College-educated women and increasing numbers of others hold that women have as much right to sexual fulfillment as their partners do. These women are consequently more satisfied with their sex lives than less educated women are. In contrast to men with less education, highly educated men are sensitive to the sexual needs of their wives. Among men with some college education, 82% express concern for their partner's satisfaction, in contrast to a mere 14% of men with no college education.

Because marital coitus is the only sexual outlet—with the exception of nocturnal emissions—totally sanctioned by all religious groups, one would expect the frequency of marital coition to be greater among the religiously devout than among the religiously inactive. The frequency of marital intercourse, however, has been found to be lower among religiously active Protestants than among inactive Protestants. The inescapable conclusion is that the early puritanical religious training of devout Protestants carries over into marriage and continues to inhibit sexual expression, despite the couples' conscious acceptance of the "rightness" of marital coitus.

Practically all married women participate in sexual intercourse, although there is a gradual decline in frequency after the first 2 years of marriage. The frequency of intercourse declines more among women than among men with advancing years. Curiously, marital coition is the only form of sexual outlet among women that undergoes such a decline with advancing age.

Women who marry in their late teens have intercourse on an average of 2.8 times a week in the early years of marriage. This decreases to 2.2 times a week at age 30, 1.5 times a week at age 40, once a week at age 50, and once every 12 days at age 60. This decline in frequency is puzzling in light of research findings that women reach their peak of sexual desire between their late 20s and 40. It is probably the aging of men that causes the decrease in women's marital coital frequency, since men's sexual drive peaks between the late teens and the age of 25, and thereafter shows a steady decline.

The decline in frequency of marital intercourse after the first 2 years of marriage does not, of course, necessarily imply that interest in other forms of sexual activity declines. The incidence of masturbation and nocturnal dreams involving orgasm increases after marriage, remaining fairly steady at its maximum level until women become 60 years of age or even older. Between the ages of 21 and 25, 89% of a married woman's total sexual outlet is derived from marital coition. After age 25, there is a gradual but consistent decline, so that by the time a woman reaches age 70, only 72% of her total sexual outlet is provided by marital coitus.

During the first year of marriage, three-fourths of all women attain orgasm at least once during coitus. The percentage increases to 90% after 20 years of marriage. It should be noted that these figures apply only to orgasm during marital sexual intercourse; practically all women are capable of orgasm through oral-genital stimulation, manual stimulation, use of an electric vibrator, or other methods of erotic arousal.

Investigations have concluded that more than 15% of all women regularly respond with multiple orgasms; it is a capacity naturally existing in all women. The reason more women do not experience multiple orgasms can be traced to sexually ignorant or indifferent male partners, or to misconceptions held by the women concerning their sexual capacity and what is "normal" in sexual behavior.

There is little evidence that aging produces a decline in the sexual capacity of women until possibly quite late in life. Apparently, women struggle with some success through the early marriage years to throw off inhibitory shackles forged by the taboos of their early sex education. Once they reach their maximum sexual peak, they maintain this level. By this time, however, the husband's interest in sexual intercourse typically begins to slacken. The unfortunate result is often all-round frustration, which frequently leads the wife to seek other means of sexual gratification.

While the amount of education a woman has appears to be highly significant in many areas of sexual activity, it does not appear to be a factor in the frequency of marital coitus. The more education a woman has, however, the more likely she is to reach orgasm in marital intercourse. About three-fourths of all college-educated women reach orgasm through marital intercourse during the first year of marriage, but only about two-thirds of all grade-school-educated women do so. (High-school-educated women fall midway between the other two groups.) The incidence of orgasm in coition increases during the later years of marriage for all educational levels, but the incidence is consistently greater among women with higher education.

It should be mentioned in this regard that the need for cuddling and closeness is considerably more important to many women than the need for coitus itself. In fact, some wives lure their husbands into sexual intercourse just to satisfy this very real need to be held or cuddled. They are willing to barter coitus for close body contact, which tends to reduce their anxieties and to promote relaxation and feelings of security.

As previously noted, the incidence of masturbation, premarital petting, and premarital coitus are negatively influenced by a woman's religious devoutness. Once a woman has had these sexual experiences, however, the frequency of her sexual activity bears little or no relationship to her religious inclinations. The same pattern applies to marital coitus. More devout women are slower to develop a pattern of frequent coition, but once the frequency is established it is not affected by the degree of religious involvement. Devout Catholic women, however, are less likely to have orgasms during marital coitus than women of other religious groups. This tendency probably stems from a fear of pregnancy that would affect Catholic women more than others, because of their church's proscriptions against certain effective birth-control measures.

Extramarital Sexual Activity

Extramarital sexual behavior is synonymous with *adultery* to most people. In this discussion it will refer to nonmarital sexual intercourse between a man and woman, at least one of whom is married at the time to someone else.

For men, the frequency of extramarital coitus decreases with age, but for women, both the frequency of extramarital coitus and the percent of total outlet that it represents increase with age. Because of society's attitude toward extramarital affairs, the participants will usually go to rather extreme lengths to hide or deny their adultery. As a result, only the most careful, detailed, and sophisticated investigations can uncover even an approximation of the actual incidence and frequency of extramarital coition. Even psychotherapists find that their patients are reluctant to admit to adulterous conduct, despite the confidential nature of the therapeutic relationship.

Although changing ethical values are producing a shift today in attitudes toward both premarital and extramarital sexual activity, the negative judgments of religious and social groups are still powerful enough to make adultery a relationship that is sometimes destructive to marriage. One study of divorced couples whose marriages had included adulterous relationships found that over a third of them believed adultery to have been a prime factor in the disruption of their marriages.

A recent study of politically liberal, well-educated young men and women of high socioeconomic status revealed that men having extramarital coitus usually begin their affairs sooner after marriage than women do. The first affair occurs within 5 years of marriage for almost three-fourths of the men and for more than half of the women. Once women begin to have affairs, however, they have extramarital intercourse with about the same frequency as men.

Almost three-fourths of all married men admit to at least an occasional desire to have an extramarital affair, and a conservative estimate is that about half of them actually do have extramarital coitus at some point during their marriage.

Men of lower education have more extramarital coitus during the early years of marriage than men of other educational levels, although the less educated men become involved in extramarital intercourse less often as their marriages continue. Among college–educated men, however, the incidence of extramarital intercourse increases with advancing years.

Among white American married women, 7% have had extramarital intercourse by age 26, and 26% by the age of 40. Women experience orgasm in extramarital affairs with about the same frequency as in marital coition.

The notion is almost universal that men prefer sexual intercourse with somewhat younger partners. Research has shown, however, that men frequently prefer intercourse with middle-aged or older women. The reason appears to be that an older woman is likely to be more sexually responsive than a younger woman. Furthermore, she is more experienced sexually and has a better knowledge of sexual techniques. She has also thrown off many of the taboos and inhibitions that plague most younger women, making her a freer and more responsive partner.

Almost a third of all college-level women have had extramarital intercourse by the age of 40, whereas only about one-fourth of those in the same age group with only grade-school or high-school education have had similar experiences.

About half of all women who have extramarital coitus believe that their husbands know of it or suspect it. When these figures are added to the percentage of wives whose husbands have no suspicion whatever of their wives' affairs, it indicates that for about three-fourths of the adulterous wives no marital difficulty develops because of their activity.

Of those women who experience extramarital coitus, more than two-thirds also experienced premarital intercourse. A large percentage of those women who have not had extramarital coitus state that they do not expect to do so, but more than half of those who have had extramarital intercourse intend to renew their activity.

As one would expect, the religiously devout are least involved in extramarital intercourse at every age level. By age 30, for example, only 7% of religiously active Protestant women have had extramarital intercourse, as compared with 28% of religiously inactive Protestant women.

THE PROBLEM OF THE ILLEGITIMATE CHILD

All societies tend to perpetuate themselves. The manner in which they do so is always regulated by the society, with procreation generally approved only within the legal bonds of marriage. An *illegitimate* child—one born of parents who are not married to each other—has traditionally been viewed as an affront to marriage and the social order.

One can cite limited counter trends of late. The media may carry an announcement by some unmarried actress that she is pregnant. Sometimes the expectant father joins her in the announcement, while in other cases the woman declines to reveal his identity. Removed from the disapproval of the average citizen, these individuals have the money and the life-style which allow them to openly flout the norms of society. In some cases, in fact, the publicity boosts their box-office appeal.

This trend among the rich and famous to acknowledge illegitimate pregnancies publicly is perhaps a reflection of a movement among the young to reject traditional middle-class moral judgments. Members of the "hippie" movement display a similar lack of concern for the legitimacy of their children. Some communes extend this tendency to total disregard for the identity of either parent. Every child is considered the child of all commune members, all of whom share responsibility for the child. In some ways this is a commendable attitude, but the transitory nature of most communes may prevent such a child from ever establishing any permanent, close relationship with a significant adult.

While one can look at these unconventional attitudes of film stars or commune members with some envy and mixed admiration, the typical young unmarried woman who becomes pregnant is neither an actress nor a hippie. Instead, she is a woman whose pregnancy, if revealed, will result in considerable unhappiness for her and for her family.

In the United States, illegitimacy has historically been considered morally wrong, and both mother and child have been subjected to social condemnation and legal punishment. The popular opinion of the unwed mother, reflected in statements made in the pulpit and in the press, is that she is oversexed and underprincipled. Society applies its traditional double standard to illegitimacy, judging the mother more harshly than the father. (Surprisingly, women may be harsher in their condemnation than men. The unwed mother bears visible evidence that she has had "illicit sex." She is therefore a threat to many women who doubt their own sexual desirability or whose marriages are shaky.)

The unmarried father bears no physical evidence of having had premarital sex, and his violation of the voiced moral standards of the community therefore escapes much of society's censure. Even within a marriage, it is the woman who is blamed for an unwanted pregnancy. This attitude carries over into public thinking regarding illegitimacy and may account for the requirement in some states that an unmarried woman be sterilized after several nonmarital pregnancies. No such laws exist for the man who has fathered several illegitimate children.

In general, unmarried fathers constitute a fairly representative cross section of the American male population. Furthermore, despite generally held opinions, the typical unwed father is not necessarily an exploiter of the woman whom he impregnates, or does he lack concern about his responsibility to the child and its mother.

The unwed mother is not only condemned by society, but in some cases the man who impregnated her may also turn against her because of his guilt feelings about the illegitimate child. To reduce his feeling of guilt, the father rationalizes his part in the situation and decides that all illegitimate mothers are immoral. While he once may have felt tenderness toward the woman, he may attempt to relieve his conscience by statements such as "the kid's not mine"; "she'll go to bed with anything that wears pants"; "she got what she deserved because she didn't take precautions"; "she had plenty of fun, the same as I did"; "I spent lots of money on that bitch"; and so forth. Despite such attempts to rid himself of guilt, his feelings usually persist.

Legally, the unwed mother bears all financial responsibility for the baby's birth and subsequent care unless the father acknowledges paternity or unless paternity is established by the courts. The responsibility for attempting to establish the paternity of the child, however, lies with the mother; the law makes no effort to find the child's father.

Over 40 million American women alive today have had or will have premarital intercourse; of this number, 1 out of 5 has become or will become pregnant. Of these 8 million premaritally pregnant women, over 1.5 million will marry during their pregnancy. Of those who do not marry, about 400,000 will have a miscarriage and about 500,000 will give birth to illegitimate children. The remaining premarital pregnancies—about 5.5 million of them—will end in induced abortion.

It is estimated that 6% of all unmarried women in the United

States have been pregnant by age 15, and 25% by age 40. While it appears that there has been a marked increase in illegitimate births in the last few decades, the increase is actually in the number of *recorded* illegitimate births. Whereas in the past unwed mothers gave birth to their babies at home as secretly as possible, a large number now have them in hospitals or maternity homes where careful records are kept. To be sure, there is an increase in the *number* of illegitimate births in the United States, owing to the increased number of women of childbearing age, but the increase in *rate* of illegitimate births is small.

Increases in the rate of illegitimate births during the past several decades show some interesting trends. According to the U.S. Bureau of the Census, during the 20-year span from 1940 to 1959, the smallest increase in incidence of illegitimate births was among the 15- to 19-year-olds (89%). The largest increase was in the 25- to 29-year-old group (348%); the next highest occurred among women 30 to 34 years old (316%); followed by those 20 to 24 years old (234%); then those 35 to 39 years old (230%); and finally the 40- to 44-year-old group (with a 131% increase).

The change in incidence of illegitimate births within age groups from the 1955–59 period to 1968 shows quite a different pattern. Here the greatest increase was among the 15- to 19-year-olds (28%); the next greatest was in the 40- to 44-year-old group (27%); followed by the 35- to 39-year-old group (22%); then those aged 30 to 34 (9%); and, finally, the 20- to 24-year-old group and those 25 to 29 years old, all of whom showed practically no increase in illegitimacy (1%).

Much has been written about the high incidence of illegitimate births among nonwhites. While it is true that the illegitimacy rate among black and other non-Caucasian races has been several times higher than among whites in the past, the margin has narrowed in recent years. For example, the recorded illegitimacy rates for all races nearly tripled between 1940 and 1961. However, between 1961 and 1968, the recorded illegitimacy rate among nonwhite races declined by 14%, while that for whites increased by 3.2%. Furthermore, many researchers have shown that the problem of illegitimacy in this country is ascribable not to race but to poverty, being directly related to inferior education, the poor living conditions in our city ghettos, and insufficient income.

It is interesting to note that, historically, explanations of the causes of illegitimacy have tended to reflect the social ills or set of social problems prevalent at that particular time. Before 1930, for example, unwed mothers were presumed to be the victims of mental deficiency, immorality, and bad companions. Investigations made during the 1930s, on the other hand, found that these "wayward girls" were more often than not victims of broken homes, poverty, and disorganized neighborhoods. The conclusions drawn from research done in the 1940s and early 1950s, in contrast, underscored the emotional problems of unwed mothers. Today, as we have stated, the causes are believed to be related to poverty and living conditions.

Studies into illegitimacy have attempted to uncover personality or sociological similarities in the unwed mothers. Ignorance of birth-control methods and the financial inability to obtain either legal or illegal abortions seem to be the overriding factors. The majority of unwed mothers have less than a high school education and come from families with substandard incomes. They are less likely to know about or to use contraceptives than better educated and more affluent women are.

But even women who have received adequate instruction in birth-control methods may become pregnant. Sex may be used deliberately in hopes of forcing a marriage, for example, or the young woman may be rebelling against her parents. More frequently, she has such marked feelings of inadequacy and insecurity that she tries to buy love with sex. Also, in an effort to maintain her self-image of being virginal and spontaneous, she avoids any method of birth control, with pregnancy an all too frequent result.

Nonetheless, studies consistently show not only that those women who have more accurate information about sexual matters have fewer experiences of premarital sexual intercourse, but that those knowledgeable women who do involve themselves in premarital coitus are far less likely to become pregnant than are their less informed counterparts.

When an unmarried woman discovers that she is pregnant, she has three alternatives: marriage, abortion, or illegitimate childbirth. If she marries, the man may not be one she would otherwise have chosen, so that chances for a successful marriage are slim. Even if she and the baby's father love and respect one another, they both will probably have to forego their education, resulting in a lower standard of living than they may have anticipated. The strain thus imposed on their relationship lessens the chances for a happy marriage.

If she choses to have an abortion, there are ethical, psychological, religious, social, and economic considerations which she must face. Although a recent Supreme Court ruling has declared abortion legal in all 50 states, many people—including some members of the medical profession—have serious reservations about the practice of abortion. The unwed mother herself and many of the people with whom she will have to deal during this time may share these reservations and may be affected by them.

If she elects to remain unmarried and have the baby, the unwed mother must decide whether to keep the child, give it to relatives to rear, or place it for adoption through an agency, an attorney, a doctor, or the black market. If she decides to keep it, her life immediately becomes predictable. She will probably have to drop out of school; she will find it difficult to find a steady job that pays enough to support her and her baby; and both she and the child will be stigmatized by society. Had she been able to prevent her pregnancy, she would have been able to continue her education, improve her vocational skills, find a job, marry someone she wanted to marry, and have a child when she and her husband were ready for it. The mother, perhaps even more than the child, pays—and pays—for sexual activity that results in an illegitimate child.

The illegitimate child, alternately branded the "natural child," the "love child," or the bastard child, suffers his share of social abuse. Even in cases where the child is legally adopted at birth, prejudice and ignorance may prompt relatives and friends of the adoptive parents to watch the child for evidence of inherited "immorality." When the child remains with his natural mother, his birth certificate in many states contains the information that his birth was illegitimate. While he has inheritance rights to his mother's property in most states, he may not inherit from her relatives. In 44 states, the illegitimate child does not have the right to inherit from his father. In only two states, Arizona and North Dakota, are *all* children accorded equal rights.

State laws undoubtedly reflect society's prejudices against

the illegitimate child. Even more important than improving legislation, however, is softening the public's attitude toward illegitimacy. The home, the church, and the school should make every effort to remove the stigma of unworthiness from an illegitimate child and the judgment of moral unfitness from his parents. Our society professes to believe that sexual behavior should be strictly confined to the marriage bed, yet the actual behavior of much of our population includes a broad range of sexual experiences outside of marriage. Our guilt about the distance between what we say and what we do causes us to point a finger of shame at those whose behavior is not so different from our own.

One of the most important facts which emerges from research into human sexuality is that there is a clear distance between what many people believe to be usual in sexual experience and the sexual behavior that is actually practiced by most people. Many of our social norms still reflect the ignorance and prejudice of those whose only criterion for normality is their own sexual expression. Both society as a whole and the individuals in it would be well served if the confusion and guilt which surround human sexuality could be dispelled by the facts. Human sexual expression, in all of its complexity and diversity, could then become a more accepted part of our lives.

FURTHER READING

The New Sexuality, edited by H. A. Otto. Palo Alto: Science and Behavior Books, 1971.

> Almost every chapter of this excellent book contributes to the understanding of human sexual behavior.

The Sexual Wilderness, by V. Packard. New York: David McKay, 1968.

> Now in paperback, this book presents the findings of sex surveys on attitude and behavior conducted on college campuses across the United States.

Unmarried Mothers, by C. E. Vincent. Glencoe, Ill.: Free Press, 1961.

This book is available in both hardbound and paperback editions. It presents demographic data, research findings, theory, and clinical observations on all aspects of problems related to births outside of marriage.

Extra-Marital Relationships, by G. Neubeck. Englewood Cliffs, N. J.: Prentice-Hall, 1969.

This paperback book gives the best available overview of the causes and results of extramarital sexual relationships.

Sexual Life after Sixty, by I. Rubin. New York: New American Library, 1967.

This paperback book gives a most complete evaluation of present and potential sexual behavior of men and women who are in the advanced years of life.

Sexual Behavior in the Human Male, by A. C. Kinsey, W. B. Pomeroy, and C. E. Martin. Philadelphia: W. B. Saunders, 1948.

The entire book is pertinent to the study of sexual behavior in American men.

Sexual Behavior in the Human Female, by A. C. Kinsey, W. B. Pomeroy, C. E. Martin, and P. H. Gebhard. Philadelphia: W. B. Saunders, 1953.

The entire book is pertinent to the study of sexual behavior in American women.

Human Sexuality, 2d ed., by J. L. McCary. New York: D. Van Nostrand, 1973.

Chapters 15, 17, 21, and 22 are directly related to the study of sexual behavior.

14 SEXUAL VARIANCE

One of the major issues in the field of sexology today—and, indeed, in the whole realm of mental health—is the question of what is "normal" sexual behavior and what is "abnormal."

Too many people are ready to label as aberrant or perverted any sexual activity that deviates from their own sexual practices. Yet in the course of human history, sexual behavior and ethics have varied widely within and among different cultures. What is usual in one culture may be unusual and branded abnormal in another, although unusual sexual behavior is not perversion simply because it is out of the ordinary for a given culture.

Many terms are used by the public and by professionals to describe sexual behavior that, in their view, differs from the normal; *sexual abnormality, deviation, aberration, perversion,* and *variance* are among them. As the subject is studied more objectively, it becomes increasingly apparent that true sexual abnormality is very difficult to define and pinpoint. The term *variance* is therefore gaining increasingly broad acceptance as the fairest word to use—the one least emotionally charged or connotative of disapproval.

It is possible for an individual to label himself "perverted" simply because he lacks basic knowledge of what normal sexual behavior really is. He consequently believes that his fantasies and behavior, or the frequency of either, deviate markedly from the norm. When individuals do engage in truly abnormal sexual behavior on a continuing, compulsive basis, however, the behavior is typically unrelated to sexual needs. Rather, it is a symbolic, ongoing attempt to solve deep-seated personal problems.

Sociologists and other behavioral scientists have recently begun to view sexual variance as a social process rather than as a social disorder. Society seems to be progressing toward a more liberal definition of what constitutes normal sexual activity. Generally speaking, most authorities in the field believe that if the sexual behavior is not harmful to the participants, if it is carried out by consenting adults who are willing to assume all responsibility for their acts, if it is free of any sort of coercion, and if it is out of sight and sound of unwilling observers, the behavior should be considered acceptable, whether or not others would care to participate in similar acts. These criteria serve as a valid basis on which to judge what is and is not variant sexual behavior.

Men have a greater tendency to engage in variant sexual behavior than women do, possibly because boys develop a strong sex drive earlier in life than girls do. Boys are therefore exposed to a greater number of sexual experiences that could possibly lead to sexual variance.

Sexual variance may be said to fall into three categories: (1) variance in the method of sexual functioning; (2) variance in the choice of the sexual partner, either person or object; and (3) variance in the degree of desire and strength of the sexual drive.

VARIANCE IN METHODS OF SEXUAL FUNCTIONING

Sadism

Sadism is a sexual abnormality in which the disturbed person gains sexual gratification, or at least an increase in sexual pleasure, by inflicting either physical or psychological pain upon his partner in the sexual relationship. The aggressive act has no purpose other than that the pain it causes is the source of sexual gratification.

The causes of sadism are as varied as the means of expressing it. The disturbed person may have been taught, consciously or unconsciously, to have disgust for anything sexual. Because normal sexuality is unacceptable to him, his acts of cruelty are a punishment of his partner for engaging in something so shameful. Another source of sadism is feelings of inferiority; the sadistic acts reassure the sadist that he is more powerful than his partner, thereby reducing his fear.

Whipping, biting, pinching, and slapping are typical of the acts of physical pain inflicted by the sadist. Normal sexual expression, of course, frequently includes biting, pinching, and scratching during moments of heightened passion. These acts are not motivated by cruelty or the desire to inflict pain, and do not reflect sadism. It is when such actions are of a violent, hostile nature and are the goal of the sexual act itself that they constitute sadism. If sadism is expressed verbally, it is in the form of sarcastic remarks, belittling, threatening, teasing, or bullying.

Masochism

Masochism is the mirror image of sadism. The disturbed person receives sexual pleasure or gratification from being hurt, physically or mentally, by his sexual partner.

Masochism, like sadism, develops from an attitude of shame and disgust toward normal heterosexual relationships. The masochist uses the pain and punishment inflicted on him to wash away the guilt he associates with his sexual desires. In other cases, he feels that he dominates his partner through his ability to endure punishment, which to his way of thinking proves his strength and superiority, and also serves to make him the center of attention. Often, the sexual partner is identified with a parent-figure who dominated him as a child. For example, the masochist may remember experiencing sexual excitement in childhood while being beaten, a sensation centered in the erogenous zones of the skin about the buttocks and the muscles below the skin. In all events, it appears that the masochist is so fearful of rejection that he is willing to be subjected to almost any humiliation or punishment that will please his partner and win for him, as he sees it, affection and acceptance. This aberration may also take the form of mental masochism wherein the individual seeks out mental rather than physical suffering.

Sadomasochistic behavior has been observed to be an essential part of the mating relationship of many lower primates and other animals. And, indeed, in certain primitive societies forms of sexual violence, such as deep scratch and bite wounds, are commonplace. However, when an individual in our culture deliberately conjures up fantasies of ill-treatment that are sexually exciting, or when he actively seeks physical or psychological pain—as through chaining, beating, switching, kicking, or verbal abuse—as means of enhancing his sexual powers and pleasures, there is cause for concern and psychological treatment is definitely indicated.

Exhibitionism

Exhibitionism is a variance in which sexual gratification is derived from exhibiting the genitals to unwitting (and typically unwilling) prey. It is considered abnormal because sexual satisfaction is gained in a vicarious manner rather than through a straightforward sexual experience. A relatively common sexual problem, exhibitionism is involved in 35% of all arrests for sexual violations. Far more men than women are exhibitionists, although just how many women do actually exhibit themselves is impossible to determine. The public has a more tolerant attitude toward the exposed bodies of women than it does toward those of men, and women found exposing themselves would probably not be reported by the beholders.

The cause of this behavior is, classically, the exhibitionist's feeling of insignificance or inadequacy; he hopes to gain the notice he craves through exhibition. The usual male exhibitionist is a quiet, timid, submissive individual who lacks normal aggressiveness and who is beset with feelings of inadequacy and insecurity. He is usually described as being "nice" but immature. Characteristically he was reared in a family atmosphere of overstrict and puritanical attitudes toward sex, and his formative years were dominated by a powerful, engulfing mother.

Since the exhibitionist obviously hopes his actions will have a profound shock effect on the viewer, the woman who responds hysterically to his behavior merely feeds his disturbance. If one is confronted by an exhibitionist, the most sensible approach is to ignore the act calmly and possibly to suggest that he seek psychological help.

One should not confuse the normal desire to show one's nude body or genitals to his sexual partner with exhibitionism. In the latter instance, the goal is simply exposing the genitals, while in the former, the exposure is merely one means of increasing the pleasure of sexual foreplay.

Pseudoexhibitionism is often confused with true exhibitionism. The pseudoexhibitionist is under stress because heterosexual relations are not available; he thus exhibits himself only as a poor substitute for the sexual intercourse that he prefers.

It should be remembered that the exhibitionist is more of a nuisance than a menace. He rarely becomes involved in more serious crimes, and when he does, his criminality is classically of a nonsexual nature. The exhibitionist seldom exposes himself while he is close to his victim. He chooses, rather, to remain at a safe distance—usually 6 to 60 feet away.

Nudism is regarded by some as an aberration because they erroneously equate it with exhibitionism. Social nudism, however, is not a sexual deviation. As a matter of fact, the overall atmosphere in most nudist camps is, because of rigidly enforced rules of behavior, more suggestive of asexuality than of sexual permissiveness. The average nudist is also the average citizen, although he may have freed himself of certain taboos with which the rest of us remain shackled, and he does not regard the naked body as sexually exciting outside of a specifically sexual context.

Voyeurism

Voyeurism is a disturbance in which the viewer of sexual acts and erotic material derives unusual sexual pleasure and gratification simply from looking. The voyeur (commonly called a "Peeping Tom") usually does his viewing secretly. In his efforts to observe the sexual activity or nude bodies of others, he peers through windows, or he may go to such lengths as to bore peepholes through walls and doors of toilets, dressing rooms, and guest rooms. Only a small number of women are known to be voyeurs. According to FBI reports, nine men to one woman are arrested on charges of "peeping."

Like other sexually variant behavior, voyeurism is believed to develop as a defense mechanism against what the individual feels is a threat to his self-evaluation. By engaging in surreptitious examination of sexual details, rather than in more overt sexual behavior, he guards against any personal failure in coitus, while at the same time he enjoys a feeling of superiority over those whom he secretly observes.

As in the case of exhibitionism, many of the milder incidents of voyeurism may in fact be classified as *pseudovoyeurism*, since they are merely substitutes for preferred but unattainable coitus. Furthermore, the desire to view the naked body of one's sexual partner is certainly normal; so also is the pleasure a couple experience in viewing themselves by way of mirrors in the act of coitus itself. Viewing becomes abnormal only when it is consistently preferred to petting or sexual intercourse.

Transvestism

Transvestism, or *cross-dressing,* refers to excitement or gratification, either emotional or sexual, derived from dressing in the clothes of the opposite sex.

The practice usually begins in early childhood and is often evoked by parental rejection of the child's sex. An unattractive woman who feels rejected may retaliate by dressing in men's clothing. Whatever the cause, most transvestites engage only in normal and acceptable sexual activities, their strange dressing habits on "special occasions" being their only deviation. Most of these people are able to make a satisfactory adjustment to sex and marriage, especially when they receive understanding and cooperation from their marriage partner.

Authorities agree that the majority of transvestites are not homosexual. The typical male transvestite is married and has children. In one study of male transvestites, only 25% admitted to ever having homosexual experience. (This figure is especially interesting since 37% of the men in the general population admit to having had homosexual experience to the point of orgasm at least once in their lives.) Transvestism, furthermore, is typically a secret pursuit involving only one person; homosexuality obviously must involve two people. The homosexual must reveal himself as a homosexual in order to attract a partner, while the transvestite has no such need to reveal his transvestism.

There is considerable difficulty in estimating accurately the number of transvestites since perhaps 90% of transvestites keep their cross-dressing habits a secret. It is believed, however, that transvestism exists in possibly less than 1% of the population.

The pattern of cross-dressing varies among transvestites. In one instance, the man may wear women's apparel only periodically. In another, the man has a fetishlike fondness for a particular article of women's clothing—e.g., panties or a brassiere—which he habitually wears under his own masculine clothing. In yet another, the yearning to wear women's finery may be so deeply ingrained that the transvestite discards men's clothing entirely to embark upon a lifelong masquerade as a woman.

There is nothing in the present-day understanding of genetics to support the contention that transvestism results from an inborn predisposition. Attempts to alter the variant behavior include psychotherapy, with a particular emphasis on aversive conditioning techniques.

Transsexualism

Transsexualism, also called *sex-role inversion,* is a phenomenon in which an individual's sexual anatomy and his sex-role (or gender) identity are incompatible. The problem in transsexualism is far more profound than that in transvestism. With rare exceptions, the transsexual is genetically a male. He possesses normal male genitals, internally and externally; and he is capable of impregnating a woman. In no instance is the difference between the *sex* assigned by nature and the *gender identity* acquired through social conditioning more dramatically demonstrated than it is in the transsexual. The man knows that he is a male, yet he rejects his maleness totally. Not content with dressing as a female, as the transvestite is, he wishes to go all the way and live the life of a woman—emotionally, physically, sexually. The male sex organs become such hated objects that attempts at self-castration or suicide are not uncommon among transsexuals.

The transsexual wishes to be loved as a woman by a "straight" man. He does not wish to be loved by a homosexual, whose love-sex object is another man. He is firmly convinced that some cruel caprice of nature has imposed upon him the body of a male while at the same time endowing him with the emotionality and mentality of a woman.

The causative factors of transsexualism appear to be much like those of transvestism and homosexuality for which authorities postulate such divergent theories as neuroendocrine predisposition and environmental factors—especially parent-child interaction. As is the case with other sexual variances, much more research into the neurological, sociological, and psychological factors is needed before any definitive understanding can be attained.

The rejection of the sex assigned them by nature accounts for the dogged determination of many transsexuals to undergo a sex-change operation, in which the genitals are reconstructed through plastic surgery to resemble those of the opposite sex. Despite the inherent legal and social difficulties attending such a procedure, there are perhaps 1500 people throughout the world who have undergone sex-reassignment operations. A guess is that about 400 of them live in the United States although, for obvious reasons, the identity of very few is known.

Many doctors shrink from what is to them a mutilation of the human body and a consequent sexual neutrality. But all forms of psychotherapy have been singularly unsuccessful in helping these people who, in company with the transvestite and homosexual, are notoriously resistant to change. Since the transsexual's mind cannot be made to adjust to his body, the only sensible and humane course to follow is to make the body adjust to the mind.

In order to receive sex-conversion surgery, the male transsexual must have lived as a member of the opposite sex for a considerable time—at least 6 months—and he must have undergone female hormonal treatment. It is significant that persons approaching such operations—which involve, in a man, the removal of testicles and penis, leaving sufficient penile and scrotal skin to form an artificial vagina—very rarely get "cold feet" and back out. Their determination to shed the appendages of their hated genetic sex is that strong.

Although sex-conversion surgery has been performed on a few females, the procedure is much more complicated and less esthetically and functionally successful than it is in the case of male transsexuals.

Oralism and Analism

Sexual oralism refers to pleasure obtained from the application of lips, tongue, and mouth to the sexual organs of one's partner. It is considered deviant, however, only when it is used to the exclusion of all other methods of sexual outlet. Fellatio (oral stimulation of the penis) and cunnilingus (oral stimulation of the vulva) have gained reasonably wide acceptance as methods of sexual foreplay and outlet, especially in the higher educational groups. Many people will not readily admit to these practices, however, for fear of being denounced as abnormal.

Sexual analism refers to the use of the anus for copulation. *Sodomy* is another term for this act, although the legal interpretation of sodomy may encompass a much wider range of sexual variance. Sexual analism is seldom practiced in heterosexual contacts except for occasional experimentation, but up to 50% of male homosexuals in the United States use this technique as a preferred method of sexual intercourse.

When anal intercourse is preferred over vaginal coitus (except as a matter of simple experimentation), the explanation typically offered by psychotherapists is that it represents an extension of a childhood association between excretion and coitus. There are those who regard sex as something "dirty" and feel the need to satisfy their sex drive in a way that is, to them, highly symbolic of this "dirtiness." Sodomy is not widely practiced, however; only about 3% of husbands engage in it with their wives.

VARIANCE IN THE CHOICE OF A SEXUAL PARTNER

Homosexuality

Homosexuality implies that an individual is sexually attracted to a member of the same sex, or has sexual relations with him or her. This mode of sexual expression has existed since the dawn of civilization. The ancient Greeks not only regarded homosexual love as natural but also as more exalted and tender than heterosexual love. Among the citizen class, heterosexual love often represented the fulfillment of practical needs—an ordered household, tax refuge, and the means of producing legitimate progeny. Homosexual love, on the other hand, was considered more properly entwined with the philosophical, intellectual, and spiritual pursuits so prized by the Greeks.

Homosexuality was practiced openly and widely by the Romans. Public attitude toward homosexuality today, however, is quite different from what it was in the distant past. Many people who are exclusively heterosexual consider homosexuality to be among the worst of perversions.

Kinsey and his co-workers established that there are degrees of sexuality, and they devised a seven-point scale to categorize the heterosexual-homosexual balance. At one extreme is exclusive heterosexuality in which no homosexuality is involved. This is followed by predominant heterosexuality with only incidental homosexuality; then follows predominant heterosexuality with more than incidental homosexuality. At midpoint, there is sexual functioning at equal heterosexual and homosexual levels. Still further along the continuum is predominant homosexuality with more than incidental heterosexuality; then predominant homosexuality with only incidental heterosexuality; and, finally, exclusive homosexuality with no heterosexual leanings at all.

According to Kinsey's research findings, 60% of boys and 33% of girls have engaged in at least one act of overtly homosexual sex play by the age of 15. Research also shows that the average male homosexual has his first homosexual experience some time before his fourteenth birthday; the average lesbian, at about 19 or 20 years of age.

Homosexual Behavior   Homosexual expression falls into three patterns: *active,* wherein the individual plays the male role regardless of his own sex; *passive,* in which the participant, whether man or woman, plays the female role; and *mixed,* in which the individual assumes an active role one time and a passive role the next. The mixed role is the pattern most frequently followed by homosexuals.

Principal homosexual practices include masturbation; sodomy; fellatio; cunnilingus; and interfemoral coitus, in which the genitals of one partner are rubbed against the thighs of the other. These activities may or may not also involve sadism, masochism, fetishism, and other behavior indicative of emotional problems. In view of these practices, the terms "passive" and "active" are not accurately descriptive of most homosexuals or most homosexual acts. A homosexual male may be active with one partner and passive with another, although he typically does not play the active and passive role with the same partner. Evelyn Hooker, one of the best known researchers in the area of homosexuality, considers the terms "insertor" and "insertee" to be more definitive than "active" and "passive."

It is interesting to note that homosexual practices vary from one culture to another. The results of most investigations carried out in the United States and England suggest, for example, that oral intercourse is preferred over anal coitus by most Anglo-American male homosexuals. In Mexico, however, the majority of male homosexuals prefer and practice anal intercourse. Furthermore, most of the Mexicans who have engaged in oral-genital intercourse more than occasionally have been found to have done so with men from the United States.

Contrary to popular belief, there are no physical characteristics common to all homosexuals. Far too often, passive or frail men and aggressive or robust women are unfairly stigmatized as homosexuals. It is not unusual, on the other hand, to find men and women who are quite masculine and feminine, respectively, in their appearance and behavior and nonetheless lead homosexual lives. Only about 15% of the men—and about 5% of the women—who have extensive homosexual experience can be identified by their appearance as being homosexual.

Some Causes of Homosexuality   Theories concerning the dynamics of homosexuality are various, emphasis typically falling on the roles of hereditary tendencies, environmental influences, or sex hormonal imbalance.

There is convincing evidence that homosexuality is the outgrowth of environmental pressures and other conditioning factors. The individual may seek homosexual outlets, for instance, as the result of an accidental but pleasurable homosexual incident in childhood, or because of having been segregated with others of the same sex for long periods of time (e.g., in a boarding school or correctional institution).

Pathogenic patterns in the family life of homosexual men have been noted. Often, the boy's mother is unhappy in her marriage. She turns to her son, developing a close and intimate relationship with him that is tinged with romance and seductiveness but that stops short of physical contact. The relationship engenders guilt in the son because of his own incestuous desires toward his mother, causing him eventually to avoid all women. A serious involvement with another woman would be a gross disloyalty to his mother, he feels, or, worse, would be tantamount to incest.

Many other psychological pressures may act together or separately to veer an individual toward homosexuality. In the case of a man, the father may have been a weak, aloof, and ineffectual force in his son's life, leaving the boy to develop an excessive attachment to the mother that he never outgrows.

A more common father-son interaction that can culminate in the son's becoming homosexual, however, is one in which the father is harsh, overly aggressive, and too much of a "tough guy" to allow his son to enter into a close relationship with him. The boy does not identify with his father and does not learn the masculine role in life. This sort of father frequently attempts to teach his son to be a real "he-man." But he prevents the very thing he wants for his son by not establishing a relationship rooted in the tenderness, acceptance, understanding, and love that are necessary to a healthy association between father and son. Thus, the son may become frightened of the "masculine" role epitomized by his father, or be otherwise unable to accept it, and he may go in the opposite direction. That is to say, he identifies with the feminine role, with its implications of warmth and understanding, as a defense against the unfortunate relationship he has with his father.

Homosexuality is not generated solely in the home, however. Other sociological forces can be equally powerful, particularly upon vulnerable adolescents. For example, a young man's relationships with his women peers may have been so unsatisfactory and threatening that he seeks instead the companionship of his own sex in order to avoid a repetition of his failures. Similarly, a sensitive young woman who has been callously rejected by a man she loves may decide never again to run the risk of another rejection, and therefore may turn to other women for warmth and acceptance. Some behavioral scientists conjecture that homosexuality is always associated with an unconscious fear of heterosexuality.

Another theory advanced regarding the cause of homosexuality concerns an imbalance of sex hormones. The urine of a normal man or normal woman contains hormones of both sexes; however, one dominates the other. It is suggested that if the dominance is reversed, homosexuality will result. This theory has alternately gained and lost support over the years. While it is not usually considered significant in the etiology of homosexuality, the sex research team of Masters and Johnson has recently renewed interest in the biological correlates of homosexuality. When the testosterone and sperm-count levels of a group of 18- to 35-year-old male homosexuals were compared, the levels in bisexuals did not differ from those in heterosexuals. But in those subjects who were predominantly or exclusively homosexual, there were reduced levels of testosterone and impaired sperm production.

Researchers have been unable so far to determine whether this endocrine dysfunctioning is testicular, pituitary, or hypothalamic in origin. They also warn that the abnormality has yet to be found in a majority of homosexuals. Even if it were to exist, however, it might be primarily the result of the homosexual's psychosocial orientation rather than the cause of it.

A recent and comprehensive compilation of research into the psychodynamics of homosexuality reaffirmed that early childhood experiences are the major influence in the individual's ultimate sexual adaptation or maladaptation. Very little trauma may be required to interfere with the course of normal psychosexual development, especially in boys, who are extremely vulnerable to any real or imagined threat to their masculinity. One should not view child-parent conflict as the only possible cause of homosexuality. Greater significance must be accorded to peer relationships in childhood.

Many authorities believe that those homosexuals who can be turned from their variance by psychotherapy are not truly homosexual but are, rather, *pseudohomosexuals*—people who look to members of their own sex for love, affection, and sexual expression because, although they have an emotional preference for members of the opposite sex, they are distinctly afraid of them. Other authorities are firm in their conviction that true homosexuality exists, but can often be corrected if the person has a desire to change. Still other authorities believe that psychotherapeutic efforts should be directed simply toward helping the individual to accept his homosexuality and adapt to it. Many homosexuals avoid psychotherapy when they are having interpersonal or emotional problems because they believe that a therapist will focus on their sexual orientation rather than on their personal relationships. This unfortunate state of affairs causes needless suffering for many homosexuals. A homosexual should be able to expect—and receive—counseling in all areas of his life, and his sexual orientation should not be considered a problem for therapeutic intervention unless the homosexual himself sees it as such.

Attitudes Toward Homosexuality   The attitude of the average American toward homosexuality differs from that of many other cultures. In the typical American community, male homosexuality is severely denounced, often to the point of violence, while female homosexuality receives only token disapproval, if any at all.

Within the American culture, male homosexuality is more of a threat to men than female homosexuality is to women. It is widely recognized among psychotherapists that men who have an underlying fear of their own homosexual tendencies are frequently vociferously abusive in their attacks against homosexuality. Those who do not feel threatened by any homosexual leanings within themselves are more understanding and relaxed in their dealings with homosexuals.

An authority on homosexuality has summarized the basic requirements for a child's normal heterosexual development. First, the same-sex parent must be neither so punishing nor so weak that it is impossible for the child to identify with him. Second, the opposite-sex parent must not be so seductive, or so punishing, or so emotionally erratic that it becomes impossible for the child to trust members of the opposite sex. Third, the parents must not reject the child's biological sex and attempt to teach him cross-sex role behavior.

It is an unfortunate experience for a youngster between the ages of 7 and 16 to be seduced by a homosexual, but the effects are seldom permanent. Boys who have had this experience are no more liable to become homosexuals than boys who have not been seduced, and the evidence is that they later marry and lead quite normal lives.

It should be remembered that homosexuals—or people with almost any other sexual variance—can be as religious, moralistic, loyal to country or cause, inhibited, bigoted, or censorious of other types of sexual variance as anyone else can. Also, they manifest no greater number of serious personality problems than one would expect to find in the normal population. In fact, when skilled clinicians compared the life histories and the results of batteries of psychological tests of a carefully matched homosexual and heterosexual sampling, no distinction between the two groups could be found, refuting the concept that homosexuality is an illness. Fortunately, Western societies are finally making an effort to evaluate homosexuality with compassion rather than with condemnation.

Promiscuity

Promiscuity is generally defined as the participation in sexual intercourse with many people on a more or less casual basis. Promiscuity is to an extent condoned—or at least tolerated—for men, but it is strenuously condemned for women.

Studies involving personality and family backgrounds of promiscuous women indicate that they have generally made an uneven and perhaps incomplete progression to physical, emotional, intellectual, and social maturity. The investigations show that these women, before they left home, participated minimally in such organized group experiences as sports and other extracurricular activities. They have difficulty accepting responsibility for their own behavior and characteristically they blame parents, husbands, and friends for their own failures and shortcomings. Their promiscuity is not caused by a strong sex drive; rather, it results from their attempt to use sex to cope with other emotional problems.

To a large extent, men follow the same behavioral patterns in their promiscuity (which has been called "Don Juanism," after the legendary Spanish libertine) as woman do. In the case histories of almost all of the men studied, promiscuous behavior proved to be the result of feelings of inadequacy, emotional conflicts, and other personality problems. There is no evidence that the sex drive of these men is stronger than that of average men.

Adultery

Adultery is an act of sexual intercourse between a married person and someone other than the legal spouse. Where legislation against adultery exists, prosecution is rare and the penalties assessed are usually relatively light. In American society the traditional double-standard approach to sex has altered over the past few decades, so that both partners are now expected to restrict their sexual activities to the marriage. Earlier, husbands were accorded more sexual latitude. The seriousness with which this violation of marital vows is held can be judged from the fact that in many states adultery is the only legal grounds for divorce.

Whether the husband or the wife is the offending party seems to determine how serious a threat adultery is to the marriage —a remnant, perhaps, of the double standard. A single transgression by the wife may very well do irreparable damage to the marital relationship, while a similar transgression by the husband is often forgiven if he has not become involved in a lengthy affair, which would suggest his having formed a love relationship with the other woman. The explanation for these two divergent attitudes probably lies in the notion that a married man supposedly can have sexual relations with a woman other than his wife for physical pleasure only, conferring on the relationship no emotional commitment, whereas it is assumed (erroneously in some cases, as we have noted) that a woman must be in love with a man before she wants a sexual relationship with him.

In the Kinsey study, about half of the adulterous wives believed their husbands knew about their affairs; in most of these instances the husbands took no retaliatory action nor posed any difficulty for the wives. In fact, more often than many would think, these husbands had encouraged their wives to have extramarital affairs. Some wished to provide themselves with an excuse for their own adulterous behavior, but, more commonly, the encouragement stemmed from a desire to allow the wives the opportunity for additional sexual satisfaction. Certainly this latter reasoning reflects a shift in attitude on the part of American husbands and offers interesting grounds for speculation on the future of sexual mores in our culture. Even with these changes in attitude, however, adulterous relationships often put a great strain on the marriage and frequently cause greater unhappiness than the experiences are worth.

Mate-Swapping

Mate-swapping (also called *swinging*) is the sexual exchange of partners among two or more married couples. The old term *wife-swapping* is now generally rejected by those who participate in such exchanges, as it implies an inequality between the sexes wherein the wife is the property of the husband, to be traded off to another man.

The custom is an acceptable and normal one in certain of the world's cultures. In some Eskimo tribes, for example, offering one's wife to a guest is considered a matter of courtesy and hospitality. In the American culture, however, mate-swapping is generally viewed negatively and the participants are felt to be strange, at least, if not downright neurotic or depraved. That the phenomenon is not as rare as most people believe can be judged by the estimate that in 1970 approximately one million Americans regularly engaged in mate-swapping. Only recently have behavioral scientists begun to study mate-swapping with proper objectivity and an appropriate scientific approach.

Because people (men especially) tend to become bored by routine sex with one partner, some social scientists think that an acceptable outlet for the need for novelty must be found. Prostitution was once thought to fulfill the need for novelty without threat to the marriage, because the risk of romantic involvement with a prostitute was slim. Later, pornography was regarded as serving the same purpose. More recently, according to these behaviorists, mate-swapping has been adopted by some as a means of providing sexual variety. Swingers maintain that the practice is not damaging to marital relationships, since the woman's sexual needs are taken into account as well as her husband's. And, indeed, with the development of essentially failure-proof contraceptive methods, women can now indulge their sexual desires with more freedom and pleasure than ever before.

Mate-swappers, to the surprise of many, frown on an extramarital affair unless all of the marriage partners involved are fully aware of it. They believe that the real danger to marriage in extramarital sex lies in the risk of romantic involvement with another person and the dishonesty inherent in a secret affair. Swappers maintain that they engage in swinging to improve and support their marriage.

Swingers are a relatively mobile group of higher-than-average education. They are primarily Caucasian, affluent, and upper–middle class. Despite the fact that they do not regularly attend church, they consider themselves neither atheistic nor agnostic. In the samplings studied, the proportion of Jews, Catholics, and Protestants matched that of the general population. There is apparently no difference between swingers and nonswingers in strength of either childhood or present religious interest. Mate-swappers, surprisingly, are more politically conservative than nonswingers are, although (not surprisingly) their sexual attitudes and behavior are more liberal. As examples, they do not condone the double standard and are accepting of such sexual behavior as oral-genital contact and homosexuality.

In contrast to nonswingers, mate-swappers prefer marriage partners who have had premarital sexual experience. In addition to their extramarital sexual activity, swingers have more sexual intercourse within the marriage than nonswingers do. In one study, mate-swappers scored significantly higher on a sex information test than nonswingers, but both groups reported the same history of unsatisfactory discussions of sexual matters with their parents. Also, there appears to be no difference between the two groups in attitudes toward pornography or in frequency of contact with it. Female swingers are orgasmically more responsive than nonswinging women. In most cases, the husband is the one who first suggests mate-swapping. But once the couple has started swinging, the wife is usually eager to continue. Conclusions drawn from what little research has been done into the psychodynamics of mate-swapping suggest that swingers are not sexual perverts nor are they mentally or emotionally disturbed.

Group sex sometimes involves many people. Men and women

may participate in equal or unequal numbers of whom none, some, or all may be married. Heterosexual or homosexual relations, or both, may occur at the same time within the same group. The significant aspect of group sex is that the experience is shared by all of the participants, physically or visually.

Prostitution

Prostitution, the participation in sexual activities for monetary rewards, has existed in one form or another throughout recorded history. It has been called, with much justification, the world's oldest profession. Through the ages it has been condemned, cursed, and attacked by people of nearly all societies and from all walks of life. Yet prostitution is with us today, and it is safe to predict that it will remain with us in the future, even though it is illegal almost everywhere in the United States and is frequently prosecuted.

As the sexual freedom of women becomes more equal to that of men and as the sexual relationship within marriage improves, indications are that prostitution will become less and less important.

Kinsey and his associates found that 69% of white males had had some experience with prostitutes. However, over the past several decades there apparently has been a steady decrease in the number of professional prostitutes in America, and in the frequency with which men visit them. For example, the 1948 Kinsey study revealed that about 20% of its college-educated sample had had their first coital experience with a prostitute. But in the 1967 companion study, this figure had fallen to an estimated 2% to 7%.

Men visit prostitutes for many reasons: they want variety in their sex life; they are too shy, too embarrassed, or too physically handicapped to find heterosexual outlets elsewhere; they need to gratify their variant sex urges, such as sadomasochistic or fetishistic tendencies, and can pay to have them satisfied; they wish to have sexual activity without the troublesome obligations so often associated with less anonymous sexual intercourse; or perhaps their wives are pregnant, or a child has been born and they feel in competition with it for the wife's affection. In associating with prostitutes, however, men often forget that, since prostitution is illegal, they run the risk of blackmail, arrest, and scandal, to say nothing of the dangers of contracting VD or of being robbed. Many prostitutes enter the profession because of easy money, although most are disappointed in this respect, as they become victimized by pimps, corrupt city officials, or black-mailers. Some enter out of a sense of adventure, others to find romance and a husband. (Far more often than many realize, the client develops a strong attachment to a prostitute and offers to marry her.)

Some women become prostitutes because of a neurotic need to punish and degrade themselves, or as an act of rebellion against parents and society. Many prostitutes are simply mentally deficient, emotionally disturbed, lazy, or otherwise unable to engage in regular employment. A great many women enter the profession on a temporary basis. Once their financial difficulties are in better control, they return to their work as salesgirl, teacher, secretary, or housewife.

Many people believe that women are often forced into prostitution through "white slavery" channels. However, only about 4% of prostitutes have actually been forced into the profession.

One study has revealed that the attitude of the prostitute toward her clients is similar to that of anyone else providing a service to customers: she likes some, dislikes others, and feels indifferent toward still others. Over 66% of those surveyed expressed no regrets over having entered the profession.

The male prostitute generally serves a male clientele, although from time to time brothels have been established for the pleasure of women. The award-winning film *Midnight Cowboy* gives an excellent characterization of a young man attempting to earn money specifically from his sexual services to women. (A man's failure in this profession is no doubt attributable to his physio-logical inability to function beyond the point of sexual satiation, whereas a woman can function endlessly despite the absence of any erotic desire.) The "gigolo" is often thought of as a male prostitute, but he is usually employed more as a companion or escort than for sexual services.

Some male prostitutes ("hustlers") are homosexual. Most, however, are young men who think of themselves as being quite masculine in appearance and orientation. They allow themselves to be "picked up" by men, usually older ones, in order to make some easy money. The hustler allows his male client to perform fellatio on him, for which privilege he receives money; there is rarely more to the relationship. A homosexual seeking a male prostitute wants a "straight" partner. A hustler therefore attempts to magnify his masculine image by wearing such attire as a leather jacket, boots, and skin-tight bluejeans.

Pedophilia

Pedophilia is a form of sexual deviation in which adults derive erotic pleasure from relationships of one form or another with children. Pedophilic practices include exposure of the genitals to the child, and manipulation and possible penetration of the child. Of all sex offenders, about 30% are classified as pedophiles, most of them being men. This group is usually less aggressive and forceful than rapists, although public outrage against them is often stronger.

Many child molesters are mentally dull, psychotic, alcoholic, and asocial. Most are between the ages of 30 to 40 years. Older offenders typically seek out very young children, while younger offenders usually concentrate their attention on adolescent girls.

The child molester is among the world's most feared and despised men. He is typically branded as a "sex fiend," "sex maniac," "dirty old man," or "pervert." Yet excessive physical violence occurs in probably no more than 3% of all cases of sexual molestation; and only about 15% of all adult-child sexual contacts involve any kind of coercion, including threats.

It is interesting that these offenders have a Victorian attitude toward sex in that they typically believe in the double standard, assess women as being either "good" or "bad," insist that their brides be virgins, and so forth. It is both curious and disquieting that imprisoned sex offenders in general exhibit strong religious convictions. They see themselves as very devout, practice religious rituals faithfully, respect the ministry, read the Bible regularly, and take part in long and self-centered prayers that they believe can alter their deviancies. Almost all sex offenders admit to having received religious training in childhood, yet very few report that their sex education came from their fathers or mothers.

Typically, the child molester is not a stranger lurking in the shadows as many parents think. Studies consistently show that from 50% to 80% of all child molestation is committed by family friends, relatives, or acquantances. Adults typically react with horror when a child is sexually molested, and any lingering effects the child has from the experience are probably caused by parents' or teachers' hysterical reaction to the incident.

This deviation usually develops as an attempt on the part of the pedophile to cope with a fear of failure in normal interpersonal and heterosexual relationships, especially with a sexually experienced woman; or the attempt to satisfy a narcissistic love of himself as a child. Efforts to rehabilitate pedophiles through psychotherapy have shown promising results, although some of them do revert to their deviant behavior after treatment. A prison sentence, however, does little if anything to alter the subsequent behavior of sexual deviates, although society is, of course, protected from them during their term of imprisonment.

Not all men charged as sex offenders against children are disturbed or sick; some have simply been trapped. Our society's emphasis on looking "sexy" causes some 12- to 15-year-old girls, especially those who have been poorly guided by their parents in the matter of healthy self-evaluation, to feel inadequate. These young girls use cosmetics and sophisticated clothing and conduct in an effort to give the appearance of being older than they really are. Unable to judge such a girl's true age, a man frequently becomes sexually involved with her and is caught in the legal trap of a statutory rape charge.

Rape

Rape is sexual intercourse forced on an unconsenting person, nearly always a woman. Legal penalties for rape are quite severe, most states assessing life imprisonment (or the death penalty, before the recent Supreme Court ruling that declared such a sentence to be unconstitutional) as the maximum sentence. The rape victim is usually between the ages of 18 and 25, although the person attacked is occasionally a very young child or an old woman.

Typically, the rapist is about 26, is from a low-income, culturally deprived background, and is mentally retarded or of dull-normal intelligence. He is likely to have had emotionally unstable parents and a weak, often alcoholic, father; the majority of rapists, however, come from broken homes. The rapist is usually emotionally immature, received little supervision from his parents in his youth, and is frequently physically unattractive.

By legal definition, rape does not require full penile penetration of the vagina; the slightest attempt at penetration is sufficient to constitute rape. Neither must ejaculation have occurred to satisfy this definition. Furthermore, tricking a woman into coitus—by pretending to be her husband while she is under hypnosis, for example—constitutes rape even though she gives her full consent.

Statutory rape involves a girl under the age of lawful consent —usually 18 years. The legal definition of this felony revolves around the concept that a minor is incapable of giving her partner permission to engage in coition with her. Many girls in these cases have lied about their ages and purposely enticed the accused into coitus. They are nonetheless, because of their tender years, considered legally incapable of assessing and comprehending the nature of their actions. Most men convicted on charges of rape are accused on statutory grounds. There is an occasional case in which a woman is charged with raping a young man; the charge is almost always statutory rape because the man involved is underage.

Incest

Incest is sexual intercourse between two persons, married or not, who are too closely related by blood or affinity to be legally married. Laws relating to incest bear little uniformity from state to state and are often highly confusing.

Incest cases do not come before the courts often. Of all convicted sex offenders, only 6% or 7% were charged with incest. While the number of reported cases of incest in the United States is only about 2 per million population each year, the act of incest nonetheless probably occurs more frequently than statistics reveal or the average citizen realizes. Since it is an intra-familial experience, outsiders will often not know of it; and the shame and guilt felt by the family members cause them to hide and deny it. The offense is more likely to occur in families of low socioeconomic levels than in others.

The person who commits incest against children usually comes from an unhappy home background, shows a preoccupation with sex, and drinks heavily. He is often unemployed, which gives him ample opportunity to be at home with his children. The incest offender against adults is typically conservative, moralistic, restrained, religiously devout, traditional, and uneducated. In about 60% of the known cases of adult father-daughter incest, the daughter was a voluntary participant; in only about 8% of the cases did she resist.

The most common form of incest is probably brother-sister, especially in poor families where children of both sexes must share a bedroom; the next most common is father-daughter incest. Mother-son incest appears to be rare; its incidence may be somewhat higher than is suspected, however, because neither party is likely to report it.

Bestiality

Bestiality is sexual gratification obtained by engaging in sexual relations with animals. Kinsey and his investigators reported that 17% of men reared on farms have reached orgasm through sexual relations with animals, and many others probably have had some sort of sexual contact with animals. It is thought that in some rural societies where there is an insufficient number of cooperative women, this behavior has no more significance than masturbation as a sexual release.

If the pattern of behavior becomes fixed, however, bestiality might be considered a mechanism to avoid feared failure with the opposite sex. In other cases the individual shows his hostility or contempt toward women by identifying them with animals, or by choosing animals in preference to them.

Fetishism

Fetishism is a psychosexual abnormality in which an individual's sexual impulses become fixated on a sexual symbol that substitutes for the basic love-object. Usually the articles are fondled, gazed upon, or made part of masturbatory activities. Among the most commonly used symbols are underclothing, shoes (especially high-heel shoes), and gloves. Articles made of rubber have very strong appeal to the fetishist. Or the object of the fetishist's fixation may be a bodily part of the opposite sex, such as hair, hands, thighs, feet, ears, or eyes. The fetishist is almost always male, and in acquiring his sex symbols he often commits burglary or even assault.

Fetishism is actually an intensification of the normal tendencies existing in all males. Men are more erotically responsive to visual stimuli than women are, and they find certain objects more sexually exciting than others—sweaters, hair, breasts, buttocks, or legs. Men often jokingly refer to themselves as being "breast men," or "leg men," or "fanny men." It is therefore understandable that the symbol of the basic love object can become the love object itself in certain personality structures.

Fetishists are typically aggressive and antisocial, and are beset with fears of impotency. Fetishism is a form of sexual regression; the individual obtains sexual gratification from a particular object or bodily part because of its unique relationship to some childhood conditioning.

VARIANCE IN THE STRENGTH OF SEXUAL DRIVE

Nymphomania refers to the behavior of a sexually deviant woman whose abnormally voracious sexual hunger overshadows all her other activities. It is sometimes, although rarely, the outgrowth of certain physiological anomalies; more often, the disorder has a psychological basis.

Characteristically, true nymphomania involves an uncontrollable sexual desire that must be fulfilled when aroused, no matter what the consequences. The sexual craving is unquenchable regardless of the number of orgasms and the pleasure received from them. Nymphomania is compulsive sexual behavior in the true sense of the word, impelling the victim to irrational and self-defeating activities with all the stresses and problems that any compulsion causes. Typically, the nymphomaniac is consumed with feelings of self-contempt because of society's attitude toward excessive sexual behavior in any form.

It must be stressed, however, that few words in our language are as misapplied as "nymphomania." It is bandied about by the man-on-the-street; it is a popular theme in Grade-B films, and a frequent topic of discussion in fraternity houses; and everyone from the minister to the mailman claims to know at least a half-dozen such women. Yet, as a sexual disorder, nymphomania is quite rare.

Most men are sexually fulfilled after one orgasm and care very little about continuing sexual activity afterwards. Sexually mature women, however, are not usually satisfied with one climax only. Men who do not understand this normal sexual need of many women are likely to believe they are involved with a sensual freak who refuses to recognize the end of a good thing when she arrives there. Not understanding female sexuality, such men often stigmatize a perfectly normal woman as being a nymphomaniac simply because she happens to have a healthy sexual appetite.

There is yet another type of man who, through ignorance or cruelty, accuses his wife of nymphomania because her sexual desire exceeds his own. If such a man has feelings of inferiority and uncertainty about his own masculinity, he is likely to be so threatened by such a woman that he must find some way to fight her. Hence he calls her a nymphomaniac; by branding her as "abnormal," he preserves his self-image of "normalcy" by implication.

Psychological explanations for genuine nymphomania are that the woman may be attempting to compensate for sexual deprivation in adolescence and early adulthood, or that she is perhaps seeking a means for release of excessive emotional tensions. She may have fears of frigidity or latent homosexuality, which she seeks to disprove through her nymphomania, or she may be using the opposite sex as an unconscious means of revenge against her father. Probably the most frequent cause is an irrational need to be loved and accepted, involving a carry-over of early-childhood emphasis on the value of the physical body as a tool to gain attention, recognition, and acceptance. A therapeutic program through which the patient can reevaluate herself is about the only successful method of treating nymphomania.

Satyriasis is an exaggerated desire for sexual gratification on the part of a man. Causative factors in this condition parallel those in nymphomania. Additional factors may include an unconscious fear of castration or a faltering self-image regarding masculinity and adequacy.

The public does not show as much concern over men who are "oversexed" as it does over similarly "afflicted" women. As might be expected, this disparity in attitudes has its roots in the traditional sexual role designated to females. Women's deviation from their assigned erotically passive role is therefore likely to be more noticeable. The incidence of true satyriasis and nymphomania is about the same—both are very rare disorders—and each can usually be successfully treated with psychotherapy.

OBSCENITY AND PORNOGRAPHY

Obscenity consists of utterances, gestures, sketches, and the like that have sexual content and are judged repugnant according to the mores of our society. Most obscene behavior—such as crude writing on the walls, telephone calls (usually anonymous), or public remarks—is sexually assaulting in nature. The subject of sex is no doubt chosen because of its almost certain shock effect, or because the behavior is indicative of actual fantasy.

By generating fright or shock in his victim, the person making an obscene telephone call, like the exhibitionist, is attempting to deny (at least unconsciously) a deep-seated, morbid fear of sexual inadequacy. The anonymity of the telephone protects him from being evaluated as he evaluates himself—as an uninspiring, physically laughable creature. Usually a poorly integrated, immature person who is severely deficient in self-esteem and meaningful interpersonal relationships, the offender attempts to satisfy his narcissistic needs through the responses of others.

The term *pornography* is derived from the Greek words meaning "harlot" and "writing," and is assumed to have originally referred to the advertisements made by prostitutes. It is by current definition written or pictorial material purposefully designed to cause sexual stimulation.

Both pornography and obscenity are illegal in all states, but there are widely varying interpretations of the offenses and their penalties.

Just what constitutes pornography? No matter how many laws are passed, lechery, like beauty, remains in the eye of the beholder. A massive Rubens nude will evoke admiration for its artistic merit in one person, some degree of sexual arousal in another, and moral indignation in a third. The same nude might evoke in a fourth only thoughts of the local reducing salon. Is

the Bible pornographic? Is Shakespeare? Chaucer? St. Augustine?
John Donne? Benjamin Franklin? All have, amazingly, been subjected to censorship, which is an indispensable tool in the business of purification.

The attitude of American men and women toward pornography is varied indeed. Many consider it informative or entertain-
ing; others believe that it leads to rape or moral breakdown, or
that it improves the sexual relationships of married couples, or
that it leads to innovation in a couple's coital techniques, or that
it eventually becomes only boring, or that it causes men to lose
respect for women, or that it serves to satisfy normal curiosity.
Many people report that their own experiences of the effects of
erotica have been beneficial. Among those who feel that pornography has detrimental effects, the tendency is to see those
bad effects as harming others—but not one's self or personal
acquaintances.

Does Pornography Harm Children?   Young adults, it is generally agreed, are particularly vulnerable to the arousal of
strong sexual desires as a result of reading erotic material. But
the contention that pornography has a degenerative effect upon
them—or even upon children—is highly debatable. Certainly
there is no research or clinical data to support the argument. In
the most recent refutation, the President's Commission on Obscenity and Pornography—a 19-man team of experts conducting
a 2-year study—stated among its preliminary conclusions in
August 1970: "There is no evidence to suggest that exposure of
youngsters to pornography has a detrimental impact upon moral
character, sexual orientation, or attitudes."

Sex-Related Criminality and Pornography   The consensus of
such professionals as psychiatrists, psychologists, sex educators,
social workers, and marriage counselors is that sexual materials
cause neither adults nor adolescents any harm. Yet the argument
persists that pornography stimulates people to commit criminal
sex acts.

As in the case of the harm that pornography is alleged to cause
children, there is no scientific evidence supporting the linkage
between pornography and sexual criminality. The preliminary
report of the Presidential Commission mentioned earlier concluded that erotic materials do not contribute to the development

of character defects, nor operate as a significant factor in antisocial behavior or in crime. The commission found no evidence
that exposure to pornography operates as a cause of misconduct
in either youths or adults. A careful examination of imprisoned
sex offenders shows that they grew up in strict families in an
atmosphere of sexual repression, suggesting that the repression,
not stimulation by pornography, led them to sex crimes.

For a man to respond strongly to pornography, two conditions
are important: youthfulness and imagination. As a group, sex
offenders are not youthful, and, being poorly educated, their
imaginativeness and ability to project, to "put themselves in some-
body else's shoes," are limited. Their response to pornography is
accordingly blunted. A typical reaction of a sex offender might
be: "Why get worked up about a picture? You can't do nothing
with a picture."

Pornography and Sexual Activity The President's Commission concluded from its investigation, according to its preliminary report, that during the 24 hours following the viewing of
highly erotic material there may be some sexual arousal and, in
some cases, increased sexual activity. But, the Commission observed, basic attitudes and sexual patterns do not change because
of such sexual stimulation. Furthermore, following erotic exposure, people show greater tolerance toward others' sexual behavior than they did before, although their own standards do not
change.

No one denies that the young are more vulnerable to what
they read than are those who are older, more sophisticated, and
more critical. However, by extrapolating from Mayor Jimmy
Walker's observation that no girl was ever ruined by a book, one
can safely say that pornography has a negative effect only on
the mind that was disordered to begin with. As the Kinsey researchers summed it up, "Pornography collections follow the pre-
existing interest of the collector. Men make the collections, collections do not make the men."

Who Are the Patrons of Pornography? Approximately 85% of
adult men and 70% of adult women in America have been exposed
at some time during their lives to material of explicitly sexual
content in either visual or textual form.

A variety of factors appears to relate to the incidence of individual exposure to erotica. Men are more likely to be exposed to it than women, young adults more likely than older ones, and people with more education more likely than the less well educated. The more socially and politically active have greater exposure than those who are less active. Those who attend religious services often are less likely to have contact with erotic material than those whose attendance is less regular.

Several recent studies of high–school– and college–age youths confirm that minors today have considerable exposure to erotica, much of it in preadolescent and adolescent years. More than half of the boys were so exposed by the age of 15, and the girls, a year or two later. By the time they reach the age of 18, roughly 80% of boys and 70% of girls have seen pictures of coitus or have read descriptions of it.

Persons younger than 21 rarely purchase pornography, and very little is obtained through the mail. By far the most common source of erotica is friends, the exposure usually occurring in a social situation in which the material is freely passed around. There is some evidence that the less socially active young person is less likely to see erotica than his more social friends.

Exposure to erotica in adolescence, then, is widespread, and occurs primarily in a group of peers of the same sex (or several members of both sexes). These experiences seem to have more social overtones than sexual ones.

Patrons of so-called "adult" bookstores and cinemas are predominantly white, middle-class, middle-aged, married males. The men who go to see pornographic films typically are dressed in business suits or neat casual attire; they usually attend the film alone, perhaps on an impulse while out shopping. Almost no one under 21 is observed in these establishments, even when it is legal for them to be there.

Individual Judgments of Pornography   Research investigations into the factors leading an individual to judge pictures or books as pornographic indicate that persons of lower socioeconomic status tend to rate nudity as obscene, even if no genitalia are shown. They are more likely than subjects of higher socioeconomic and educational strata to regard any nude photo as being sexually exciting. Black and white photos are judged more obscene than color photos; pictures of poor photographic quality more obscene than those of higher quality; unattractive models more obscene than attractive ones, regardless of the pose; and erotic scenes in an indoor setting more obscene than those in an outdoor setting.

No one denies that genuine pornography and obscenity exist. However, apart from the fact that they present sex often unrealistically, and sometimes as something ugly and inhuman, the chief objection must lie in their literary, theatrical, or pictorial worthlessness, rather than in their power to corrupt.

Any legal curbs on pornography and obscenity imply the imposition of censorship—an eventuality that any thinking person would wish to avoid. As early as 1644, John Milton—a Puritan among Puritans—addressed Parliament in opposition to censorship, which he regarded as the handmaiden of tyranny. He argued that reading everything one wishes is the means of attaining knowledge of the good and evil and the ugly and beautiful that flourish indiscriminately in the world. Corrupting forces, he said, are everywhere present, and they can only be met by building up an inner discipline and *the ability of rational choice*. Censorship serves no such purpose, especially since its course, as history reveals, has led inevitably to the imposition on the masses of the prejudices, tyrannies, and, usually, the stupidity of the few.

No one admires or wishes to encourage pornography (except, of course, the writers or purveyors thereof). But the alternative to it is censorship—which would mean that the biblical *Song of Solomon* could be in as much danger as an east coast publication called *Screw*.

FURTHER READING

Sexuality and Homosexuality, by A. Karlen. New York: W. W. Norton, 1971.

> A valuable contribution to the understanding of homosexuality, this book presents the most detailed analysis of the problem that is available today.

Sex Offenders, by P. H. Gebhard, J. H. Gagnon, W. B. Pomeroy, and C. V. Christenson. New York: Harper & Row, 1965.

> This book contains the results of the research conducted by

the Kinsey group into the sexual histories and social backgrounds of 1500 convicted sex offenders. Also studied were control groups of a "normal" population and a prison population convicted of various crimes not sexual in nature.

A Report of the Commission on Obscenity and Pornography, by the Commission on Obscenity and Pornography. New York: Bantam Books, 1970.

Included in this report are the findings of research studies pertaining to the incidence and effects on behavior of viewing pornographic materials.

The Encyclopedia of Sexual Behavior, Vol. I and Vol. II, by A. Ellis and A. Abarbanel. New York: Hawthorn Books, 1961.

Articles that are directly related to this chapter include: "Extramarital Sex Relations" (pp. 384-391), "Homosexuality" (pp. 485-493), "Sexual Perversions" (pp. 802-811), "The Psychology of Pornography" (pp. 848-859), "Prostitution" (pp. 869-882), and "Transvestism and Sex-role Inversion" (pp. 1012-1022).

Human Sexuality, 2d ed., by J. L. McCary. New York: D. Van Nostrand, 1973.

Chapter 19 contains the symptoms, causes, and types of sexual variances and the research findings pertinent to these problems. Chapter 22 discusses the legal aspects of sexual variance.

GLOSSARY

abortion Premature expulsion from the uterus of the product of conception—a fertilized ovum, embryo, or nonviable fetus.

abstinence A refraining from the use of or indulgence in certain foods, stimulants, or sexual intercourse.

adolescence The period of life between puberty (appearance of secondary sex characteristics) and adulthood (cessation of major body growth).

adultery Sexual intercourse between a married person and an individual other than his or her legal spouse.

amnion A thin membrane forming the closed sac or "bag of waters" that surrounds the unborn young within the uterus and contains amniotic fluid in which the fetus is immersed.

anaphrodisiac A drug or medicine that allays sexual desire.

androgen A steroid hormone producing masculine sex characteristics and having an influence on body and bone growth and on the sex drive.

anomaly An irregularity or defect.

aphrodisiac Anything, such as a drug or a perfume, that stimulates sexual desire.

areola The ring of darkened tissue surrounding the nipple of the breast.

Bartholin's glands Two tiny glands in the female, located at either side of the entrance to the vagina.

bestiality A sexual variance in which a person engages in sexual relations with an animal.

birth control Deliberate limitation of the number of children born through such means as contraceptives, abstinence, the rhythm method, *coitus interruptus,* and the like.

bisexual Literally, having sex organs of both sexes, as in hermaphrodites; having a sexual interest in both sexes.

caesarean birth (or **caesarean section**)   Delivery of a child through a surgical incision in the abdominal and uterine walls.

castration   Removal of the gonads (sex glands)—the testicles in the male, the ovaries in the female.

celibacy   The state of being unmarried; abstention from sexual activity.

cervix   Neck; in the female, the narrow portion of the uterus, or womb, that forms its lower end and opens into the vagina.

chancre   The sore or ulcer that is the first symptom of syphilis.

chancroid   A highly contagious disease characterized by ulcerations at the points of physical contact and typically spread through sexual intercourse.

change of life   *See* **climacteric; menopause.**

chastity   Abstention from sexual intercourse.

chromosome   One of several small rod-shaped bodies found in the nucleus of all body cells, which contain the genes, or hereditary factors.

circumcision   Surgical removal of the foreskin or prepuce of the male penis.

climacteric   The syndrome of physical and psychologic changes that occur at the termination of menstrual function (i.e., reproductive capability) in the female and reduction in sex-steroid production in both sexes; menopause; change of life.

clitoris (adj. **clitoral**)   A small, highly sensitive nipple of flesh in the female, located just above the urethral opening in the upper triangle of the vulva.

coitus   Sexual intercourse between male and female, in which the male penis is inserted into the female vagina; copulation.

coitus interruptus (or **premature withdrawal**)   The practice of withdrawing the penis from the vagina just before ejaculation.

conception   The beginning of a new life, when an ovum (egg) is penetrated by a sperm, resulting in the development of an embryo; impregnation.

condom   A contraceptive used by men consisting of a rubber or gut sheath that is drawn over the erect penis before coitus.

congenital   Existing at birth, but not necessarily inherited.

contraception   The use of devices or drugs to prevent conception in sexual intercourse.

copulation   Sexual intercourse; coitus.

corpus luteum   A yellow mass in the ovary, formed from a ruptured graafian follicle, that secretes the hormone progesterone.

Cowper's glands   Two glands in the male, one on each side of the urethra near the prostate, which secrete a mucoid material as part of the seminal fluid.

crabs   *See* **pediculosis pubis.**

cunnilingus   The act of using the tongue or mouth in erotic play with the external female genitalia (vulva).

cystitis   Inflammation of the bladder usually characterized by a burning sensation during urination.

detumescence Subsidence of swelling; subsidence of erection in the genitals following orgasm.

diaphragm A rubber contraceptive used by women that is hemispherical in shape and fits like a cap over the neck of the uterus (cervix).

dilation Stretching or enlarging an organ or part of the body, especially an opening.

douche A stream of water or other liquid solution directed into the female vagina for sanitary, medical, or contraceptive reasons.

dyspareunia Coitus that is difficult or painful, especially for a woman.

ejaculation The expulsion of male semen, usually at the climax (orgasm) of the sexual act.

embryo The unborn young in its early stage of development—in humans from one week following conception to the end of the second month.

endocrine gland A gland that secretes its product (hormone) directly into the bloodstream.

endometriosis The aberrant presence of endometrial tissue (uterine lining) in other parts of the female pelvic cavity, such as in the fallopian tubes or in the ovaries, bladder, or intestines.

epididymis The network of tiny tubes in the male that connects the testicles with the sperm duct.

erection The stiffening and enlargement of the penis (or clitoris), usually as a result of sexual excitement.

erogenous zone A sexually sensitive area of the body, such as the mouth, lips, breasts, nipples, buttocks, genitals, or anus.

erotic Pertaining to sexual love or sensation; sexually stimulating.

estrogen A steroid hormone producing female sex characteristics and affecting the functioning of the menstrual cycle.

eugenics A science that seeks to improve future generations through the control of hereditary factors.

excitement phase The initial stage in the human sexual response cycle that follows effective sexual stimulation.

exhibitionism A sexual variance in which the individual—usually male—suffers from a compulsion to expose his genitals publicly.

fallopian tube The oviduct, or egg-conducting, tube that extends from each ovary to the uterus in the female.

fellatio The act of taking the penis into the mouth for erotic purposes.

fertility The state of being capable of producing young; the opposite of *sterility*.

fertilization The union of egg (ovum) and sperm (spermatazoon), which results in conception.

fetishism A sexual variance in which sexual gratification is achieved by means of an object, such as an article of clothing, that bears sexual symbolism for the individual.

fetus   In humans, the unborn young from the third month after conception until birth.

follicle   The small sac or vesicle near the surface of the ovary in the female that contains a developing egg cell (ovum).

foreplay   The preliminary stages of sexual intercourse, in which the partners usually stimulate each other by kissing, touching, and caressing.

foreskin   The skin covering the tip of the male penis or the female clitoris; prepuce.

fornication   Sexual intercourse between two unmarried persons (as distinguished from *adultery,* which involves a person who is married to someone other than his or her coital partner).

fraternal twins   Two offspring developed from two separate ova (eggs), usually fertilized at the same time.

frenulum   A delicate, tissue-thin fold of skin that connects the foreskin with the under surface of the glans penis; frenum.

frenum   *See* **frenulum.**

frigidity   A common term for a form of female sexual dysfunctioning, implying coldness, indifference, or insensitivity on the part of a woman to sexual intercourse or sexual stimulation; inability to experience sexual pleasure or gratification.

gene   The basic carrier of hereditary traits, contained in the chromosomes.

genital organs   (or **genitals** or **genitalia**)   The sex or reproductive organs.

germ cell   The sperm (spermatozoon) or egg (ovum).

gonad   A sex gland; a testicle (male) or ovary (female).

gonorrhea   A venereal disease, transmitted chiefly through coitus, that is a contagious catarrhal inflammation of the genital mucous membrane.

graafian follicle   A small sac or pocket in the female ovary in which the egg (ovum) matures and from which it is discharged at ovulation.

granuloma inguinale   A disease most often affecting the genitals that is characterized by widespread ulceration and scarring of the skin and underlying tissues.

gynecologist   A physician specializing in the treatment of the problems of female sexual and reproductive organs.

hermaphrodite   An individual possessing both male and female sex glands (ovary and testicle) or sex-gland tissue of both sexes. *See also* **pseudohermaphrodite.**

heterosexuality   Sexual attraction to, or sexual activity with, members of the opposite sex; opposite of *homosexuality.*

homologous   Corresponding in position, structure, or origin to another anatomical entity.

homosexuality   Sexual attraction to, or sexual activity with, members of one's own sex; the opposite of *heterosexuality.*

hormone A chemical substance produced by an endocrine gland that has a specific effect on the activities of other organs in the body.

hymen The membranous fold that partly covers the external opening of the vagina in most virgin females; the maidenhead.

hypothalamus A small portion of the brain that controls such vital bodily processes as visceral activities, temperature, and sleep.

hysterectomy Surgical removal of the female uterus, either through the abdominal wall or through the vagina.

identical twins Two offspring developed from one fertilized ovum (egg).

impotence Disturbance of sexual function in the male that precludes satisfactory coitus; more specifically, inability to achieve or maintain an erection sufficient for purposes of sexual intercourse.

incest Sexual relations between close relatives, such as father and daughter, mother and son, or brother and sister.

infectious mononucleosis A virus-produced disease affecting the lymph glands.

intercourse, anal A form of sexual intercourse in which the penis is inserted into the partner's anus; sometimes termed *sodomy.*

intercourse, oral A form of sexual intercourse in which the mouth is used to receive the penis (*fellatio*) or the mouth and lips are used to stimulate the vulva, especially the clitoris (*cunnilingus*).

intercourse, sexual Sexual union of a male and a female, in which the penis is inserted into the vagina; coitus.

interstitial cells Specialized cells in the testicles that produce the male sex hormones.

intrauterine device (IUD) A small plastic or metal device that, when fitted into the uterus, prevents pregnancy. Also termed *intrauterine contraceptive device (IUCD).*

jock itch *See* **tinea cruris.**

labia majora (sing. **labium majus**) The outer and larger pair of lips of the female external genitals (vulva).

labia minora (sing. **labium minus**) The inner and smaller pair of lips of the female external genitals (vulva).

lactation The manufacture and secretion of milk by the mammary glands in a mother's breasts.

lesbian A female homosexual.

lymphogranuloma venereum A virus-produced disease that affects the lymph glands in the genital region.

maidenhead The hymen.

masochism A sexual variance in which an individual derives sexual gratification from having pain inflicted on him.

masturbation Self-stimulation of the genitals through manipulation; autoeroticism.

menarche   The onset of menstruation in the human female, occurring in late puberty and ushering in the period of adolescence.

menopause   The period of cessation of menstruation in the human female, occurring usually between the ages of 45 and 55; climacteric; change of life.

menstruation   The discharge of blood from the uterus through the vagina that normally recurs at approximately four-week intervals in the female between puberty and menopause.

miscarriage   Spontaneous expulsion of a fetus from the onset of the fourth to the end of the sixth month of pregnancy.

monilia (or **moniliasis**)   A yeast-like infective organism (fungus) causing itching and inflammation of the female vagina.

mononucleosis   *See* **infectious mononucleosis.**

mons veneris (or **mons pubis**)   A triangular mound of fat at the symphysis pubis of the female, just above the vulval area.

multipara (adj. **multiparous**)   A woman who has given birth to two or more children.

myotonia   Increased muscular tension.

narcissism   Excessive self-love; sexual excitement through admiration of one's own body.

nocturnal emission   An involuntary male orgasm and ejaculation of semen during sleep; a "wet dream."

nullipara (adj. **nulliparous**)   A woman who has never borne a viable child.

nymphomania   Excessive sexual desire in a woman.

obscene   Disgusting, repulsive, filthy, shocking—that which is abhorrent according to accepted standards of morality.

obstetrician   A physician specializing in the care of women during pregnancy, labor, and the period immediately following delivery.

orgasm   The peak or climax of sexual excitement in sexual activity.

orgasmic phase   The third stage in the human sexual response cycle during which the orgasm occurs.

orgasmic platform   The area comprising the outer third of the vagina and the labia minora, which displays marked vasocongestion in the plateau phase of the female sexual response cycle (term used by Masters and Johnson).

ovary   The female sex gland, in which the ova are formed.

ovulation   The release of a mature, unimpregnated ovum from one of the graafian follicles of an ovary.

ovum (pl. **ova**)   An egg; the female reproductive cell, corresponding to the male spermatozoon, that after fertilization develops into a new member of the same species.

paresis   A chronic syphilitic inflammation of the brain and its enveloping membranes, characterized by progressive mental deterioration and a general paralysis that is sometimes fatal.

parthenogenesis Reproduction by the development of an egg without its being fertilized by a spermatozoon.

parturition Labor; the process of giving birth.

pediculosis pubis An itchy skin irritation in the genital area caused by the minute bites of the crab louse.

pedophilia A sexual variance in which an adult engages in or desires sexual activity with a child.

penis The male organ of copulation and urination.

penis captivus A condition in humans in which it is alleged that the shaft of the fully introduced penis is tightly encircled by the vagina during coitus and cannot be withdrawn. Most authorities say this condition occurs only in animals, notably the dog.

perineum (adj. **perineal**) The area between the thighs, extending from the posterior wall of the vagina to the anus in the female and from the scrotum to the anus in the male.

petting Sexual contact that excludes coitus.

Peyronie's disease A condition, usually in men of middle age or older, in which the penis develops a fibrous ridge along its top or sides, causing curvature.

phallus The male penis, usually the erect penis.

pituitary Known as the "master gland" and located in the head, it is responsible for the proper functioning of all the other glands, especially the sex glands, the thyroid, and the adrenals.

placenta The cakelike organ that connects the fetus to the uterus by means of the umbilical cord, and through which the fetus is fed and waste products are eliminated; the afterbirth.

plateau phase The fully stimulated stage in the human sexual response cycle that immediately precedes orgasm.

pornography The presentation of sexually arousing material in literature, art, motion pictures, or other means of communication and expression.

postpartum Occurring after childbirth or after delivery.

potent Having the male capability to perform sexual intercourse; capable of erection.

precoital fluid Alkaline fluid secreted by the Cowper's glands that lubricates the urethra for easy passage of semen.

premature ejaculation Ejaculation prior to, just at, or immediately after intromission; *ejaculatio praecox*. Ejaculation occurs before the woman can climax in at least 50% of the acts of intercourse.

prenatal Existing or occurring before birth.

prepuce Foreskin.

priapism Persistent abnormal erection of the penis in males, usually without sexual desire.

progesterone The female hormone (known as the pregnancy hormone) that is produced in the yellow body or corpus luteum, and whose function is to prepare the uterus for the reception and development of a fertilized ovum.

prolactin A hormone secreted by the pituitary gland that stimulates the production of milk by the mammary glands in the breasts (lactation).

promiscuous   Engaging in sexual intercourse with many persons; engaging in casual sexual relations.

prophylactic   A drug or device used for the prevention of disease, often specifically venereal disease.

prostatic fluid   A highly alkaline, thin, milky fluid produced by the prostate gland that constitutes a major portion of the male's semen or ejaculatory fluid.

prostatic gland   The gland in the male that surrounds the urethra and the neck of the bladder.

prostitute   A person who engages in sexual relationships for payment.

pseudocyesis   False pregnancy.

pseudohermaphrodite   An individual who has both male and female external sex organs, usually in rudimentary form, but who has the sex glands (ovary or testicle) of only one sex, and is thus fundamentally male or female. *See also* **hermaphrodite**.

puberty (or **pubescence**)   The stage of life at which a child turns into a young man or young woman: i.e., the reproductive organs become functionally operative and secondary sex characteristics develop.

rape   Forcible sexual intercourse with a person who does not give consent or who offers resistance.

refractory period   A man's temporary state of psychophysiologic resistance to sexual stimulation immediately following an orgasmic experience (term used by Masters and Johnson).

resolution phase   The last stage in the human sexual response cycle during which the sexual system retrogresses to its normal non-excited state.

retrograde ejaculation   Backward ejaculation in the male into the posterior urethra and bladder, instead of into the anterior urethra and out through the meatus of the penis.

rhythm method   A method of birth control that relies on the so-called "safe period" or infertile days in the female menstrual cycle.

sadism   A sexual variance in which there is the achievement of sexual gratification by inflicting physical or psychological pain upon the sexual partner.

satyriasis   Excessive sexual desire in a man.

scrotum   The pouch suspended from the groin that contains the male testicles and their accessory organs.

secondary sex characteristics   The physical characteristics—other than the external sex organs—that distinguish male from female.

seduction   Luring a female (sometimes a male) into sexual intercourse without the use of force.

semen   The secretion of the male reproductive organs that is ejaculated from the penis at orgasm and contains, in the fertile man, sperm cells.

seminal emission (or **seminal fluid**) A fluid composed of sperm and secretions from the epididymis, seminal vesicles, prostate gland, and Cowper's glands that is ejaculated by the male through the penis upon his reaching orgasm.

seminal vesicles Two pouches in the male, one on each side of the prostate, behind the bladder, that are attached to and open into the sperm ducts.

seminiferous tubules The tiny tubes or canals in each male testicle that produce the sperm.

sex drive Desire for sexual expression.

sex flush The superficial vasocongestive skin response to increasing sexual tensions that begins in the plateau phase (term used by Masters and Johnson).

sex gland A gonad; the testicle in the male and the ovary in the female.

sex hormone A substance secreted by the sex glands directly into the bloodstream, e.g., androgens (male) and estrogens (female).

sexual inadequacy Any degree of sexual response that is not sufficient for the isolated demand of the moment or for a protracted period of time; frequent or total inability to experience orgasm.

sexual intercourse *See* **intercourse, sexual.**

sexual outlet Any of the various ways by which sexual tension is released through orgasm.

smegma A thick, cheesy, ill-smelling accumulation of secretions under the foreskin of the penis or around the clitoris.

sodomy A form of sexual variance variously defined by law to include sexual intercourse with animals and mouth-genital or anal-genital contact between humans.

sperm (or **spermatozoon**) The mature male reproductive cell (or cells), capable of fertilizing the female egg and causing impregnation.

spermatogenesis The process of sperm formation.

spermicide An agent that destroys sperm.

spirochete A corkscrew-shaped microorganism; one type of spirochete causes syphilis.

sterility The inability to produce offspring.

sterilization Any procedure (usually surgical) by which an individual is made incapable of reproduction.

syphilis Probably the most serious venereal disease, it is usually acquired by sexual intercourse with a person in the infectious stage of the disease and is caused by invasion of the spirochete *Treponema pallidum.*

testicle The testis; the male sex gland.

testis (pl. **testes**) The male sex gland or gonad, which produces spermatozoa.

testosterone   The male testicular hormone that induces and maintains the male secondary sex characteristics.

thrombosis   The clogging of a blood vessel as the result of the formation of a blood clot within the vessel itself.

tinea cruris   A fungus infection causing irritation to the skin in the genital region.

transsexualism   A compulsion or obsession to become a member of the opposite sex through surgical changes.

tranvestism   A sexual variance characterized by a compulsive desire to wear the garments of the opposite sex; cross-dressing.

trichomoniasis   An infection of the female vagina caused by infestation of the microorganism *Trichomonas* and characterized by inflammation, usually resulting in a vaginal discharge and itching and burning.

tubal ligation   A surgical procedure for sterilizing a female in which the fallopian tubes are cut and tied.

tumescence   The process of swelling or the condition of being swollen.

umbilical cord   The flexible structure connecting the fetus and the placenta; navel cord.

urethra   The duct through which the urine passes from the bladder and is excreted outside the body.

urologist   A physician specializing in the treatment of the diseases and disorders of the urinary tract of both sexes, as well as of the genital tract of the male.

uterus   The hollow, pear-shaped organ in females within which the fetus develops; the womb.

vagina   The canal in the female, extending from the vulva to the cervix, that receives the penis during coitus and through which an infant passes at birth.

vaginal lubrication   A clear fluid (like sweat) that appears on the walls of the vaginal barrel within a few seconds after the onset of sexual stimulation.

vaginismus   Strong muscular contractions within the vagina, preventing intromission of the penis when intercourse is attempted.

vaginitis   Inflammation of the female vagina, usually as a result of infection.

vas deferens (or **ductus deferens**)   The sperm duct(s) in the male, leading from the epididymis to the seminal vesicles and the urethra.

vasectomy   A surgical procedure for sterilizing the male involving removal of the vas deferens, or a portion of it.

venereal disease   A contagious disease communicated mainly by sexual intercourse, such as syphilis or gonorrhea.

virgin birth   *See* **parthenogenesis.**

virginity   The physical condition of a girl or woman before first intercourse.

voyeurism A sexual variance in which a person achieves sexual gratification by observing others in the nude.

vulva The external sex organs of the female, including the mons veneris, the labia majora, the labia minora, the clitoris, and the vestibule.

wet dream   *See* **nocturnal emission.**

womb The uterus in the female.

X chromosome A sex-determining chromosome present in all of a female's ova and in one-half of a male's sperm; the fertilization of an ovum by a sperm having an X chromosome will result in the conception of a female (XX).

Y chromosome A sex-determining chromosome present in one-half of a male's sperm; the fertilization of an ovum by a sperm having a Y chromosome will result in the conception of a male (XY).

zygote The single cell resulting from the union of two germ cells (sperm and egg) at conception; the fertilized egg (ovum).

INDEX

214; and sexual functioning, 159; of sex offenders, 249, 252
Reproductive organs and systems. *See* Genitalia
Respiration, in sexual response, 149, 153
Revolution, sexual, 100
Rhythm method. *See* "Safe" period
"Rubbers." *See* Condom

Sadism, 230
"Safe" period (birth-control), 39, 95; impregnation during, 95; rhythm method, 95; temperature method, 95
Salpingectomy, 75, 178
Salpingitis, 178
Saltpeter, 135
Salt solution (abortion), 85
Satyriasis, 254, 255
Scabies, 190
Scrotum, 26, 32, 143; in puberty, 26; in sexual response, 143, 152; in vasectomy, 78
Secondary sexual characteristics, 27, 29, 30
Seduction, 105, 106, 110; parental, 239
Self-stimulation. *See* Masturbation
Semen, consistency of, 33; content of, 33; loss and replacement, 33
Seminal fluid, 33, 147
Seminal vesicles, 33; in sexual response, 147
Sexual, abnormalities. *See* Variance, sexual; adjustment in marriage. *See* Marital adjustment; arousal, 188 *ff.*; attitudes. *See* Attitudes, sexual; behavior, abnormal. *See* Variance, sexual; behavior, cortical control of, 23; behavior, learning factor in, 15, 16, 17; boredom, 126, 245; change, surgical, 236; drive, declining, 202, 203; drive, differences in, 19, 52, 202, 211; drive, female, 50, 52, 90, 215; drive, male, 52, 215; drive, peaks, male-female, 218; drive, after sterilization, 79; drive, sublimation of, 100; drive. *See also* Aphrodisiacs; dysfunction, 156 *ff.*; education. *See* Education, sex; "excess," 122; excitation causing ovulation, 39; fantasies, 128, 205; "fascism," 9, 10, 18; "fiend," 249;

flush, female, 143, 145, 148, 152; flush, male, 143; foreplay, 117, 123 *ff.*; glands. *See* Ovaries; Testes; hormones, 23; inadequacy, 156 *ff.*; inexperience, overcoming, 118; intercourse. *See* Intercourse, sexual; maturation, 23, 47 *ff.*; maturity, 11, 12; offenders. *See* Offenders, sex; and older people. *See* Aging process and sexuality; oral-genital. *See* Oral-genital contact; reassignment surgery, 236; resolution period, coital, 151 *ff.*; response cycle, 128 *ff.*; revolution, 100; role inversion. *See* Transsexualism; satiation, 122; secondary characteristics, 27, 29, 195; stimuli, 118 *ff. See also* Aphrodisiacs; techniques, 118 *ff.*
Sexuality, development of, 121 *ff.*
"Signatures, doctrine of," 131
Skin disorders. *See* Dermatoses
Smegma, 36, 43, 166, 193
Smell acuity, and sexuality, 49, 119
Sodomy, 237, 238
Spanish fly, 133
Sperm, 4, 7, 26, 32, 33, 75; banks, 79; count per ejaculation, 57; count, reduced, 57; disorders involving, 57; early theories *re*, 7; in fertilization, 57; frozen, 79; manufacture of, 32, 33; "wastage," 7; X and Y, differences between, 55
Spermatozoa. *See* Sperm
"Squeezing" technique (ejaculatory control), 164
Statutory rape, 251
Sterility, disorders causing, 178
Sterilization, 74, 75 *ff.*; methods of, in men, 78 *ff.*; methods of, in women, 75 *ff.*
Stimulants. *See* Aphrodisiacs
"Stone ache," 199
Sweating process, vaginal. *See* Vagina, lubrication
Swinging. *See* Mate-swapping
Syphilis, 173, 179 *ff.*; congenital, 182; eradication attempts, 174

Techniques, sexual, 118 *ff.*
Telegony, 69
Temperature method (birth control), 95
Testes (Testicles), 29, 32; animal, as